D0074841

WITHDRAWN

ON-SITE INSPECTION
IN THEORY
AND PRACTICE

ON-SITE INSPECTION IN THEORY AND PRACTICE

A Primer on Modern Arms Control Regimes

GEORGE L. RUECKERT

PRAEGER

Westport, Connecticut
London

Library of Congress Cataloging-in-Publication Data

Rueckert, George L.
    On-site inspection in theory and practice : a primer on modern
arms control regimes / George L. Rueckert.
        p.   cm.
    Includes bibliographical references and index.
    ISBN 0–275–96047–1 (alk. paper)
    1. Arms control—Verification.   2. Disarmament—Inspection.
I. Title.
UA12.5.R84   1998
327.1'743—dc21   97–23346

British Library Cataloguing in Publication Data is available.

Library of Congress Catalog Card Number: 97–23346
ISBN: 0–275–96047–1

First published in 1998

Praeger Publishers, 88 Post Road West, Westport, CT 06881
An imprint of Greenwood Publishing Group, Inc.

Printed in the United States of America

The paper used in this book complies with the
Permanent Paper Standard issued by the National
Information Standards Organization (Z39.48–1984).

10 9 8 7 6 5 4 3 2 1

For my father
and
in memory of my mother

Contents

Part I

The Evolution of On-Site Inspection

Part II

Fundamentals of On-Site Inspection Regimes

Part III

Types of On-Site Inspection

Part IV

Implementing On-Site Inspection

Appendixes

Figures and Tables

FIGURES

TABLES

Acknowledgments

I would like to express my deep gratitude and appreciation to all who have assisted me in preparing this study. I am particularly grateful to the United States Institute of Peace, which funded the study and to Dr. Carol Edler Baumann, director, and the others at the Institute of World Affairs of the University of Wisconsin-Milwaukee who administered the grant. The views expressed in the study, of course, are mine only and do not necessarily represent the views of those organizations.

In developing material for this study, I interviewed a large number of people involved in various aspects of on-site inspection negotiation and implementation on a nonattribution basis. I would like to thank all of them for their generosity in making available their time and expertise. In addition, I would like to thank Dr. Edward Ifft, Colonel Paul Nelson, and Dr. Joseph P. Harahan from the U.S. On-Site Inspection Agency and arms control experts Louis Nosenzo, Dr. Victor Alessi, Alan Cameron, and Alan Labowitz of the DynMeridian Corporation, Alexandria, Virginia for their kind assistance in reading all or part of the text and providing their substantive and editorial comments. Mr. John Hardenberg also provided valuable help in developing graphic materials. While I benefitted greatly from the kind assistance of these and other individuals, I alone am responsible for any errors of fact, substance, and interpretation that may occur in the text.

Acronyms and Abbreviations

ABACC	Agency for Accounting and Control of Nuclear Materials (Argentina and Brazil)
ACDA	Arms Control and Disarmament Agency
ACI&C	(DoD) Office of Arms Control Implementation and Compliance
ACIS	Arms Control Intelligence Staff
ACIU	Arms Control Implementation Unit
AEDS	Atomic Explosion Detection System
AFB	Air Force Base
ALCM	Air-Launched Cruise Missile
ATTU	Atlantic to the Urals (CFE Region of Application)
BCC	Bilateral Consultative Commission
BIC	Bilateral Implementation Commission (of START II)
BVC	Baghdad Monitoring and Verification Center
BWC	Biological Weapons Convention
CCCW	Convention on Certain Conventional Weapons
CD	Conference on Disarmament
CDE	(Stockholm Conference on) Confidence (and Security-Building Measures and) Disarmament in Europe
CFE	Conventional Armed Forces in Europe (Treaty)
CFE IA	Concluding Act of the Negotiation on Personnel Strength of CFE
CIS	Commonwealth of Independent States
CMTS	Comprehensive Monitoring and Tracking System
CORRTEX	Continuous Reflectometry for Radius Versus Time Experiment
CRG	Compliance Review Group
CSBM	Confidence- and Security-Building Measure
CSCE	Conference on Security and Cooperation in Europe
CTBT	Comprehensive Test Ban Treaty

CTR	Cooperative Threat Reduction
CW	Chemical Weapons/Warfare
CWC	Chemical Weapons Convention
DCC	Data Collection Center
DOD	U.S. Department of Defense
DTIRP	Defense Treaty Inspection Readiness Program
EIF	Entry into Force (of a Treaty or Agreement)
EURATOM	European Atomic Energy Agency
EXCOM	(DOD) Executive Committee (for OSIA Oversight)
FBI	Federal Bureau of Investigation
FSU	Former Soviet Union
GEMI	Global Exchange of Military Information Program
IAEA	International Atomic Energy Agency
IAU	(UNSCOM) Information Assessment Unit
IC	Intelligence Community
ICBM	Intercontinental Ballistic Missile
INF	Treaty on Intermediate-Range and Shorter-Range Nuclear Forces
IMS	(CTBT) International Monitoring System
INFCIRC	(U.N.) Information Circular
IWG	Implementation Working Group
JCIC	(START) Joint Compliance and Inspection Commission
JCG	(CFE) Joint Consultative Group
JCS	Joint Chiefs of Staff
LTBT	Limited Test Ban Treaty
MC&A	Materials Control and Accountability
MIRV	Multiple Independently-Targetable Re-entry Vehicle
MOU	Memorandum of Understanding
MBFR	Mutual and Balanced Force Reductions (Talks)
NACI	(Belorussian) National Agency for Control and Inspection
NATO	North Atlantic Treaty Organization
NIS	New(ly) Independent States (of the former Soviet Union)
NPT	Non-Proliferation (of Nuclear Weapons) Treaty
NRRC	Nuclear Risk Reduction Center
NSC	National Security Council
NSDD	National Security Decision Directive
NTM	National Technical Means (of Verification)
ONA	Office of the National Authority (for the CWC)
OOV	(CFE) Object of Verification
OPCW	Organization for the Prohibition of Chemical Weapons
OSCC	Open Skies Consultative Commission
OSCE	Organization for Security and Cooperation in Europe
OSCE/FSC	Organization for Security and Cooperation in Europe/ Forum for Security Cooperation

OSI	On-Site Inspection
OSIA	On-Site Inspection Agency
OST	Outer Space Treaty
PNET	Peaceful Nuclear Explosions Treaty
POE	Point of Entry
PPCM	Perimeter and Portal Continuous Monitoring
PREPCOM	(CWC) Preparatory Committee
R&D	Research and Development
SALT	Strategic Arms Limitation Talks/Treaty
SAT	Site Assessment Team
SAV	(START) Visit with Right of Special Access
SCC	Standing Consultative Commission
SLBM	Sea-Launched Ballistic Missile
SLV	Space Launch Vehicle
SNDV	Strategic Nuclear Delivery Vehicle
SSI	Suspect Site Inspection
SSSF	(CWC) Single Small-Scale Facility
START	Strategic Arms Reduction Treaty
SVC	Special Verification Commission (of INF Treaty)
TLI	Treaty-Limited Item
TLE	Treaty-Limited Equipment
TTBT	Threshold Test-Ban Treaty
UN	United Nations
UNSC	United Nations Security Council
UNSCOM	United Nations Special Commission on Iraq
USD(P)	Under Secretary of Defense for Policy
USD(A&T)	Under Secretary of Defense (Acquisition and Technology)
VCC	Verification Coordinating Committee (of NATO)
VEREX	Ad Hoc Group of BWC Verification Experts
VMBP	Votkinsk Machine Building Plant (Portal Site)
WMD	Weapons of Mass Destruction
WP	Warsaw Pact
ZVBW	Zentrum fuer Verifikationsaufgaben der Bundeswehr

Introduction

Military power always has been, and remains today, the core of each country's national security policy. However, since at least the mid-1980s, arms control has assumed an increasingly important supporting role. During the waning days of the Cold War, the U.S. and U.S.S.R. began to use arms control agreements seriously as a means of breaking the periodic cycles of military arms build-ups that were proving unsustainably expensive to both sides. By the end of 1987, the two superpowers had agreed to the total elimination of two classes of ground based intermediate-range missiles, had begun to make major progress on deep reductions in their strategic offensive arms, and had laid the basis for improved verification provisions for nuclear testing accords designed to slow development of nuclear weapons of ever larger yield.

During and following the break-up of the Warsaw Pact in 1989, the reunification of Germany in 1990, and the dissolution of the Soviet Union in early 1992, arms control agreements were the principal instrument used to deal with the new military realities reflected in the transition from Cold War bilateralism to emerging multilateralism. In Europe, the agreements were used to codify deep cuts and to create new parity in conventional weapons systems and military personnel. Globally, they became a central element in dealing with the emerging threat of a more rapid proliferation of weapons of mass destruction—nuclear, chemical, and biological weapons. New agreements achieved in the 1990s established global bans on chemical weapons, nuclear testing at any level, and on landmines and led to improved biological weapons verification measures. Increasingly arms control verification measures, particularly on-site inspections, also have been applied to regional peacekeeping agreements, such as those in Iraq following the Persian Gulf war, in Korea in connection with its nuclear weapons program, and in Bosnia under the Dayton Agreements. Other arms control agreements, such as the Open Skies Treaty and the Vienna Documents have added new confidence-building inspections.

On the whole, the arms control agreements achieved in the past decade have established unprecedented levels of military cooperation, openness, and transparency, added importantly to military predictability and stability, and provided new verification tools to deal with the national security priorities of the century's end. By the mid-1990s, arms control had become a significant enough element of U.S. and multinational threat-control policies to be referred to by some policy makers as "preventive defense" and "defense by other means." [1] It was being viewed as a primary tool for addressing the new proliferation challenges posed by the more multipolar world, the rapid advances in weapons technology and information flow, and the unraveling of export controls and other constraints erected during the Cold War.

The increased reliance on arms control agreements in recent years began with the ascendancy of Mikhail Gorbachev as First Party Chairman in the U.S.S.R. during the mid-1980s and accelerated as the Soviet Union and its empire dissolved at the decade's turn. It was made possible by the readiness of the Soviet Union, faced with a rapidly deteriorating economy and other serious problems, to agree to much more comprehensive and intrusive verification provisions. These included, for the first time, intrusive on-site inspections of sensitive military facilities located on Soviet Union territory and on that of its allies. The change in the Soviet position on on-site inspection (OSI) opened the way for rapid agreement by the two superpowers and the international community on arms control verification regimes of unprecedented intrusiveness.

Prior to the conclusion of the seminal Treaty on Intermediate-Range Nuclear Force (the INF Treaty) in December 1987, most, although not all, arms control agreements were verified unilaterally by the signatories using national technical means (NTM) of verification. For the superpowers, in particular, these consisted of an impressive array of technical capabilities, including reconnaissance satellite systems with photographic, infrared, radar and electronic sensors; ground- and sea-based radars; seismographs; communications collection stations; and underwater acoustic systems. Such sophisticated technologies, however, were not available to most of the rest of the world.

To these verification capabilities, the INF Treaty added a new element: a comprehensive highly intrusive on-site inspection regime based on far-ranging cooperative measures. This regime was composed of extensive data exchanges, notifications, and five types of on-site inspections designed to accomplish multiple purposes, such as the confirmation of military data, the elimination of weapons, and the absence of illegal activity at declared sites. The INF Treaty also permitted, for the first time, the continuous stationing of on-site inspectors (monitors) at a missile production facility in each country.

The advantages of using on-site inspection were readily apparent, particularly to those countries without NTM. Almost all subsequent arms control agreements have contained verification regimes containing some elements of OSI. The more extensive regimes have all been modelled to some degree on the seminal INF Treaty, although the specific on-site inspection provisions of each agreement have varied somewhat in accordance with the specific objectives of each treaty.

The next arms control agreements to be concluded after the INF Treaty—the new verification protocols to the 1974 Threshold Test Ban Treaty (TTBT) and the 1976 Peaceful Nuclear Explosions Treaty (PNET), which were signed in June 1990—contain provisions for on-site inspections and monitoring by hydrodynamic yield measurements at the test site and seismic monitoring on the territory of the testing party. The verification structure of the July 1991 Strategic Arms Reduction Treaty (START) and the follow-up START II Treaty—which achieve deep reductions in strategic offensive forces—is strikingly similar to, but far more extensive and complex than, that in the INF Treaty. This is so since START covers a broader range of weapons systems and must confirm residual limits on, rather than the total elimination of, those systems. The START verification regime provides for twelve different kinds of on-site inspection as well as continuous monitoring of strategic mobile missile production facilities.

The Conventional Forces in Europe (CFE) Treaty, which entered into force in November 1992, codifies the elimination of the conventional forces imbalances between Eastern and Western Europe. It thus removes the threat of surprise attack in that region—once the most heavily armed area in the world. Its verification regime contains OSI provisions designed to verify reductions of large amounts of conventional military equipment within the region from the Atlantic to the Urals. The Chemical Weapons Convention (CWC), which was signed in January 1993 and bans chemical weapons, contains the most intrusive OSI provisions concluded to date. In addition to more routine inspections, it permits "anytime, anywhere" challenge inspections of suspect facilities.

The Comprehensive Test Ban Treaty (CTBT) combines provisions for a broad-ranging technical monitoring system with a regime of on-site inspections at any location where a seismic event is detected. Current efforts to strengthen the verification structure of the 1972 Biological Weapons Convention (BWC) also are aimed at adding on-site inspection provisions, which eventually could include an on-site inspection regime of even greater intrusiveness than that of the CWC. In addition, in the wake of bitter experience in Iraq and North Korea, the on-site inspection provisions in verification structure for the Nuclear Nonproliferation Treaty (NPT)—the safeguards regime of the International Atomic Energy Agency (IAEA)—have been further strengthened.

Arms control agreements with OSI provisions also have been used to deal with regional peacekeeping efforts. For example, the implementing agreements of the General Framework Agreement for Bosnia and Herzegovina (the Dayton Accords) contain provisions for inspections of military forces and activities. Negotiators of emerging arms control agreements, such as the global bans on landmines and on fissile materials for use in nuclear weapons and other nuclear explosions, also have discussed possible OSI measures to assist verification.

To be sure, there is an inevitable lag, often of years, between the conclusion of arms control agreements and their implementation. A number of the on-site inspection regimes agreed to at the negotiating table in recent years have not yet been fully implemented (CWC) or implemented at all (CTBT) as of this writing, and considerable dedicated effort and the expenditure of large resources will be necessary to ensure their effective application. But it is undeniable that the enhanced OSI regimes negotiated and implemented during the past decade have been the major factor enabling the increased use of arms control regimes to deal with national security issues since the later 1980s. Their continued application to new requirements and situations will assure that arms control agreements remain attractive tools for dealing with the evolving strategic and conventional arms reduction issues, proliferation threats, and regional peacekeeping concerns leading into the next century.

This study is an effort to improve understanding of how on-site inspection regimes are structured in the major arms control agreements and how they operate in practice. The principal focus of this assessment is on understanding the structure and functioning of the comprehensive "modern" on-site inspection regimes initiated by the INF Treaty and included, with appropriate variations, in most subsequent arms control agreements.

There is a wealth of government and academic information already available on the structure and implementation of these verification regimes, each of which has been minutely dissected and analyzed, not least in connection with the ratification process in the United States and other countries. By and large, however, such analysis has been largely treaty specific. It has tended to focus on the individual, often unique, aspects of each treaty's on-site inspection regime—on that specific treaty's structure and provisions, how it will be implemented and what its costs and benefits are likely to be. This approach has been rich and rewarding, contributing enormously to our understanding of the functioning of each treaty and to the current and future directions of on-site inspection regimes in general. At the same time, however, the tendency to analyze each on-site inspection regime as a separate entity has resulted in a huge amount of detailed information on OSI that is often difficult for the expert, let alone the laymen, to fully sort out, understand, and digest.

In this study, I strive to simplify understanding of the modern on-site regimes by taking a broader, more generic look at their construction and operation. The work looks at core concepts and focuses, in particular, on fundamental elements. While recognizing that each arms control agreement has differing goals and contains unique on-site inspection provisions to achieve those aims, the study illustrates that modern on-site inspection regimes have many common elements. In short, they are variations on a theme. In sorting out the underlying fundamentals, I have considered, in addition to treaty provisions, the common national and multinational structures that have been set up in recent years to implement those provisions. By clarifying basic elements, I hope to aid understanding of how modern arms control agreements are constructed, operate in practice, and contribute to national and multinational security goals.

To keep the study to a manageable size, I have not attempted to cover all possible OSI regimes, nor even all of those currently in effect. Rather, I have concentrated my analysis on the major arms control agreements containing on-site inspection provisions, particularly on those concluded in the late 1980s and 1990s. While doing so, I recognize that OSI is by no means a new or novel concept developed in those decades, but has its roots in earlier proposals and applications. I also recognize that OSI can, and has been, used for many and varied purposes other than verification of major arms control agreements. OSI proposals were included in many postwar comprehensive disarmament proposals and limited OSI provisions are contained in a number of earlier arms control agreements. During the Cold War, on-site inspections were used by the United States and some other countries to verify the end-use of controlled technologies. On-site inspections also have been used to monitor regional disarmament and peace keeping agreements, such as those by the United Nations in Angola and Cambodia and by the Organization for Security and Cooperation in Europe in Bosnia. A number of arms control treaties, such as the Open Skies Treaty and the Vienna Documents, use types of OSI as confidence-building measures. In addition, the U.S. On-Site Inspection Agency has been called upon periodically to perform subsidiary activities requiring the use of U.S. arms control inspectors. These have involved on-site assistance to humanitarian relief efforts in the former Soviet Union; on-site help in the removal of weapons grade nuclear materials from a former Soviet Republic; and the on-site auditing of U.S. assistance provided to countries of the former Soviet Union under the Nunn-Lugar legislation to aid destruction of nuclear and chemical weapons. The details of these early on-site inspection proposals and models or of subsidiary types of on-site inspection, while important, are beyond the purview of this study.

In preparing this study, I have relied heavily on basic treaty documents, interviews with personnel involved in on-site inspection activities, and on my own personal experience in the negotiation and implementation of on-site inspection regimes. As all students of arms control are aware, the language of arms control agreements tends, of necessity, to be highly legalistic and specialized. Individual provisions of arms control treaties often contain multiple cross references, which complicate ready understanding of their meaning. In addition, treaties are living documents. Their on-site inspection provisions are subject to continuing interpretation and modification in the implementation and compliance bodies set up by the various treaties to deal with inspection-related problems. At the risk of losing some of this nuance, I have focused on basic concepts and used layman's language, avoiding overly technical explanations and terminology. For reference purposes, I also have added a list of acronyms and two appendixes that provide basic information on the treaties cited in the text and on the implementation and compliance bodies set up by those agreements.

Finally, semantically the terms "on-site inspection" and "on-site monitoring" are used in several different ways in arms control literature. Sometimes they are used interchangeably to mean the same thing. At other times they are given specialized meanings. Some authors, for example, use the term "monitoring" to mean the full range of national information gathering techniques used by individual governments.[2] In this study, I use "on-site inspection" to describe the activity undertaken by arms control inspectors in accordance with treaty provisions that involve a relatively brief, time-limited stay of inspectors and inspection equipment on the soil of the inspected party. Such inspections typically permit intrusive inspections of the interior of the inspectable site. "On-site monitoring," on the other hand, is used to describe types of on-site inspection that involve a protracted or "continuous" presence of the monitoring team and/or of technical monitoring equipment at a specific location on the soil of the inspected party. A monitor's inspection activity may be limited to the periphery of an inspectable site, rather than involve intrusive inspection of the interior of the facility.

NOTES

1. Then Secretary of Defense William Perry is quoted as referring to arms control as "preventive defense" in John D. Holum, *Remarks to the Congressional Research Service Seminar on the Future of Arms Control* (Washington D.C.: U.S. Arms Control and Disarmament Agency, Office of Public Affairs, January 9, 1997), p. 2. See also John D. Holum, *Threat Control through Arms Control* (Washington D.C.: U.S. Arms Control and Disarmament Agency, Office of Public Affairs, January 1997).

2. Sidney Graybeal and Patricia McFate, for example, use monitoring to describe "essentially a function of intelligence collection and analysis using all information available concerning a particular activity; it includes the legitimate functions of diplomats, military attaches and scientists, and the analysis of commercially available journals and periodicals." Sidney Graybeal and Patricia McFate, *Verification to the Year 2000* (Ottawa, Canada: The Arms Control and Disarmament Division, External Affairs and International Trade, 1991), p. 3.

Part I

The Evolution of On-Site Inspection

Chapter 1

The Early Evolution of
On-Site Inspection

Serious discussions of on-site inspection as a mechanism to verify compliance with the provisions of arms control agreements developed only in the period after World War II. Prior to that time, arms control agreements, such as the Rush-Bagot Treaty of 1817 between the United States and Great Britain regulating the number of warships on the Great Lakes and the naval and chemical weapons treaties negotiated in the period between the two world wars, contained virtually no verification provisions. They were, in essence, "gentlemen's agreements" to refrain from prohibited activities. Compliance problems that arose in connection with such agreements were handled as broader foreign policy issues.

A major peace treaty—the 1919 Treaty of Versailles terminating World War I—did contain a number of verification provisions, including on-site inspections, designed primarily to ensure the payment of reparations and restrict the regrowth of German military power. Among the treaty's provisions were measures to demilitarize the Rhineland and to impose a number of military reduction and production restrictions. To verify compliance with these provisions, the treaty set up three inter-allied control commissions—one each for land, air and naval services—to carry out on-site inspection activities. These relatively small (less than 1,500 personnel in total) multinational commissions were made up of military officers and noncommissioned officers drawn from combat and intelligence units. They were headquartered in Berlin, but inspectors were authorized to exercise their rights to travel in any part of Germany. During the period between 1920 and 1927, these commissions scheduled and carried out frequent on-site inspections of Germany's armed forces. They monitored and reported on the treaty-mandated destruction and demobilization of German weapons, personnel, fortifications, and facilities and the treaty provisions prohibiting the manufacture, testing and development of modern military weapons.[1] The demilitarization provisions of the Versailles Treaty, however, were not backed by the political will to enforce them, enabling the Nazis to rearm, and undermining international public trust in weak arms control measures for many decades after World War II.

THE IMMEDIATE POST WORLD WAR II PERIOD

Following World War II and, particularly, as Cold War tensions increased, arms control proposals, nonetheless, became a frequent element of many U.S. and multinational initiatives. Several major factors influenced this development. Principal among them was the postwar emergence of a bipolar world dominated by the United States and the Soviet Union with opposed political and social systems. The resulting military and political competition and the hostile confrontation that soon arose between the blocs controlled by these two superpowers provided impetus for frequent initiatives to control armaments. These were further stimulated by the rapid development of nuclear arsenals by both sides and the horrifying implications of their possible further military use.

Reflecting the high state of distrust between the competing blocs and the interwar experience, many postwar arms control initiatives of both sides contained demands for stricter verification provisions. On the Western side, in particular, these often contained calls for various types of on-site inspection. On-site inspection proposals were a logical verification measure, since prior to the development of such modern monitoring technologies as satellite and radar systems, they were the only reliable means of confirming compliance. On-site inspection offered the possibility of trusted inspectors "taking a close look" at a situation to determine whether commitments were being kept, especially where it was deemed essential to check inside military structures or to monitor vital military transit points or facilities. From the beginning, on-site inspection also was considered a useful way to increase overall transparency, especially of Soviet and Eastern Bloc military activities, to test intentions and to build confidence.

The disarmament and arms control proposals in the period immediately following World War II tended to be sweeping in nature and often contained commensurately broad verification provisions. For example, the Baruch Plan proposed by the United States in the United Nations in June 1946, which aimed at establishing international control of atomic energy, called for the creation of an international atomic development authority to provide direct oversight and control of atomic energy through ownership of all fissionable materials production and distribution. A key element of this plan was the establishment of continuous monitoring and unlimited OSI of all atomic energy-related facilities. The Baruch Plan also called for unspecified penalties for illegal activities, without the right of veto in the Security Council.[2]

Parallel discussions in the United Nations of early conventional force reductions also contained on-site inspection proposals as part of the verification structure. The conventional arms reduction proposals in the U.N. Commission on Conventional Armaments in 1947 called for all U.N. members to provide detailed data on their military manpower, weapons levels, and deployments within the framework of an international military census. This data was to be verified through spot checks and physical counts undertaken by an international inspectorate. Various other U.S.-initiated arms control proposals in the immediate postwar period also called for inspections, including both aerial and on-site inspections of key transportation nodes, power lines, and declared nuclear installations.[3] These early U.S. disarmament proposals were heavily influenced by its desire to establish its leadership role in the Western Alliance during a period of steadily increasing confrontation with the Soviet Union, culminating in the Korean War.

The U.N. disarmament debates surrounding these early proposals quickly established major differences between the United States and the Soviet Union on mandatory on-site inspections. The United States favored such initiatives while the Soviets consistently opposed them. These differences persisted in various degrees until the accession to power of Mikhail Gorbachev in the mid-1980s. They were grounded in the opposite nature of the two societies—one open, the other closed. The Soviet Union, which already had open access to a huge amount of Western public and governmental information was less concerned about strict verification provisions. On the other hand, the United States, faced with a secretive, repressive, and closed Soviet society, continuously sought greater access to Soviet military data, intentions, and information.[4] Reflecting these considerations, the Soviet Union, especially under the leadership of Josef Stalin and his early successors, was not prepared to acquiesce to on-site inspection by outside observers of militarily sensitive areas under its control— although Soviet positions were not entirely opposed to OSI in certain limited circumstances. The Soviets based their rejection of early Western OSI proposals on several arguments. They insisted that agreement on inspection and control regimes should follow, not precede, actual weapons reductions. In addition, they argued that the proposals were only thinly veiled efforts at espionage and infringements of national sovereignty.

Such Soviet intransigence was quickly exploited by U.S. negotiators. U.S. proposals for intrusive on-site inspection regimes frequently were tabled with the expectation that they would be rejected. This helped to isolate the Soviets internationally, focused attention on their arms control inflexibility, and put them on the defensive in international fora, such as the United Nations. U.S. OSI proposals also served to undercut Soviet disarmament initiatives and enabled the United States and its allies to maintain the high ground in the East-West political competition. Moreover, the United States used its flexibility on verification issues to strengthen its position within the Western Alliance, increase alliance solidarity in key countries, and promote important U.S. domestic political objectives, such as strengthening public opposition to the nuclear freeze movement and to unilateral disarmament proposals.

OSI AFTER STALIN'S DEATH

After Stalin's death in 1953, the Soviets began to show somewhat greater flexibility on OSI. They probably hoped in part that this would help them to regain some of the political ground lost by their former stonewalling. But their increasing flexibility also reflected a growing appreciation that it was in the Soviet, as well as U.S., national interest to support initiatives aimed at controlling nuclear proliferation and that the price for this would have to be acceptance of some intrusive inspection provisions. During this period, they accepted the concept of limited OSI in principle. But they continued to insist that any OSI on their territory be so tightly controlled as to be virtually useless and to reject any OSI posing a potential risk to their vital security or technical developments. The Soviets initially rejected President Dwight D. Eisenhower's 1953 Atoms for Peace proposal, which called for the transfer of some U.S. and Soviet fissionable material to a new international agency. However, by 1957 they had shifted their position and were prepared to agree to the establishment of the International Atomic Energy Agency and to its safeguards regime, which provided for on-site monitoring and inspection.

Earlier, in a May 1955 disarmament proposal, the Soviets also proposed establishing a control organ to set up ground control posts at key locations in connection with staged reductions and the eventual prohibition of nuclear weapons. That proposal called for later rights of unimpeded inspection of all objects of control and would have allowed—for the first time—foreign inspectors on Soviet soil. But when asked to clarify their proposal, it became clear that only one or two carefully controlled outside inspectors would be allowed on Soviet territory under conditions that amounted to virtual self-inspection by the Soviets.

Shortly after this Soviet proposal, President Eisenhower offered his 1955 "Open Skies" proposal, which called on both sides to list their military installations and to permit inspection of both listed and undeclared facilities from the air. He also proposed ground inspections of limited facilities with no sensitive operations. The Soviets rejected the proposal but, in ensuing discussions, indicated they were willing to discuss OSI in peripheral geographic areas, although not on Soviet territory itself. In 1959, they gave substance to this position by agreeing to the 1959 Antarctic Treaty, which established the first comprehensive post-war on-site inspection regime, albeit of non-military installations in an isolated and remote geographic area.

The Antarctic Treaty

The multinational Antarctic Treaty was signed December 1, 1958, and entered into force on June 23, 1961. It pioneered a number of on-site inspection concepts, including routine inspections; "anytime, anywhere" inspections; and aerial overflights. The treaty reflected superpower concurrence with the views of the other countries then active in Antarctica that the continent should be used solely for peaceful purposes.[5] It prohibits the establishment of military bases and fortifications, the carrying out of military maneuvers, and the testing of any type of weapon in Antarctica. In addition, the treaty bans nuclear detonations and the disposal of nuclear waste there. To verify compliance, the treaty gives all signatories the right to conduct on-site inspections anywhere on the Antarctic continent.

During negotiation of the treaty, New Zealand was the first country to propose the use of "observers" to confirm compliance. The United States supported and expanded this proposal to include unlimited, unilateral on-site inspections. Although it initially opposed the concept, the Soviet Union eventually agreed to an inspection system that included an unlimited number of on-site inspections by an undefined number of national observers.[6]

The concept of "anytime, anywhere" inspections is encapsulated in Article VII of the treaty, which permits a State Party to "designate observers to carry out any inspection" and gives these observers "complete freedom of access at any time to any or all areas of Antarctica." These include all stations, installations and equipment and all ships or aircraft at points of discharging or embarking cargos or personnel in Antarctica. In addition to on-site inspection, Article VII provides that aerial observation may be carried out at any time over any or all areas of Antarctica, thus creating the first "open skies" regime. It also establishes other on-site inspection precedents by requiring that inspection personnel must be nationals of the inspecting state, be specifically "designated," and have their names "communicated to every other Contracting Party," with like notice given of the termination of their appointment.

It is noteworthy that the initial implementation of this early on-site inspection regime was delayed for over two years after the treaty entered into force due to fears that the on-site inspection process might become confrontational. To test the waters, the first on-site inspection was conducted in November 1963 by New Zealand, rather than the United States, and involved inspections only of U.S., not Soviet, installations. Indeed, the first U.S. on-site inspection in Antarctica was judged to be of sufficient political sensitivity to require the personal authorization of President Kennedy in September 1963.[7] In January 1964, the first on-site inspection of a Soviet facility anywhere occurred when U.S. observers inspected the Soviet *Mirnyy* research facility. Since then, on-site inspections in Antarctica have been held on a routine, though relatively infrequent, basis. As of this writing, these inspections have never revealed a violation of treaty provisions by any party.

In the United States, planning and approval of Antarctic inspections is coordinated through an Antarctic Policy Group chaired by the State Department and containing representatives from all U.S. government Departments and Agencies involved with Antarctica. The State Department, recommends the timing of inspections and the facilities to be inspected. In practice, due to the severity of weather, inspections occur almost invariably during the Antarctic summer months (December-March). Advance notice of inspections is not required by the treaty, but for logistical reasons, the sites to be inspected are usually notified at least a day in advance. A typical U.S. Antarctic inspection team consists of five to seven observers, including a team leader, one or more translators, and inspectors from interested U.S. government agencies. For the inspections, U.S. inspectors use helicopters or ski-equipped fixed wing aircraft, except for sites close to a U.S. base where motor transport is used. A typical Antarctic inspection can last two to four weeks and visit a dozen or so facilities.

THE SHIFT TO NATIONAL TECHNICAL MEANS

In the early 1960s, important breakthroughs in satellite and sensor technologies enabled both superpowers to obtain high resolution monitoring from space and significantly improve monitoring of communications. These technical advances increased confidence in their ability to confirm compliance by use of their own national technical means (NTM) of verification. In addition, the arms control agenda, in general, began to swing away from highly generalized disarmament proposals and focus on specific agreements of a more limited scope. Accordingly, from the early 1960s until the later 1970s, less emphasis was placed on on-site inspections as a verification tool in arms control discussions, with the important exception of the negotiations on a Nuclear Proliferation Treaty designed to slow the global spread of nuclear weapons.

Treaties Restricting Nuclear Testing

The shift to primary reliance on NTM for verification became most evident in the Limited Test Ban Treaty (LTBT), concluded in 1963, and in the subsequent agreements in the 1960s and 1970s restricting other aspects of nuclear testing. The LTBT prohibits the United States, Great Britain and the Soviet Union—the only nuclear powers at the time—from testing nuclear weapons in the atmosphere, outer space, or underwater. The United States initially included OSI in its LTBT verification proposals but later dropped OSI as a requirement when Soviet Chairman Nikita Khrushchev proposed in April 1963 that all nuclear tests be banned, except those conducted underground. U.S. acceptance of this proposal came in the aftermath of the Cuban missile scare and amidst growing domestic concerns about the effects of radioactive fallout from atmospheric tests. However, the negotiating shift on OSI also reflected a widely held U.S. conviction that new developments in land- and space-based sensors and reconnaissance satellites permitted adequate verification without OSI. To be on the safe side, the United States also adopted a number of safeguards against any Soviet violations, including decisions to continue the U.S. underground test program and ensure the continuing viability of the U.S. nuclear laboratory facilities, programs, and resources.[8]

The verification provisions of several follow-up nuclear testing treaties also relied on NTM. The 1967 Outer Space Treaty (OST), concluded four years after the LTBT, prohibits placing nuclear weapons or other weapons of mass destruction in outer space, in orbit around the earth, or on the moon or any other celestial body and bans nuclear testing on the moon.[9] The Seabed Treaty concluded in 1971 reinforced the LTBT by, among other things, prohibiting nuclear tests on the ocean bottom. Two additional treaties concluded in the mid-1970s—the 1974 Threshold Test Ban Treaty and the 1976 Peaceful Nuclear Explosions Treaty, as originally signed—also relied on NTM for verification. However, by the time these treaties reached the U.S. Senate for ratification, the pendulum was swinging back, and, amidst concerns about possible Soviet cheating on nuclear test levels,[10] their negotiated verification provisions were no longer considered adequate for verifying compliance.

The SALT Talks

In 1969 the U.S. and U.S.S.R. began the Strategic Arms Limitation Talks (SALT) to establish limits on the size and capability of strategic forces. The SALT I Interim Agreement, the related 1972 Anti-Ballistic Missile (ABM) Treaty, and SALT II relied on the use of NTM for verification. The United States raised OSI proposals during the negotiations, not least for domestic political reasons,[11] that called for continuous on-site inspections of airfields, missile launching sites, and critical production sites for strategic delivery systems. The SALT and ABM agreements, as concluded, had no OSI provisions, but they did contain significant new verification elements that later would become integral parts of subsequent OSI regimes. For example, they explicitly recognized the legitimacy of NTM, contained provisions to refrain from actions designed to interfere with each other's legitimate NTM, and established the first formal treaty mechanisms for dealing with compliance concerns.

The SALT I Interim Agreement on Strategic Offensive Arms specifies that for the purpose of providing assurance of compliance with the provisions "each Party shall use national technical means of verification at its disposal in a manner consistent with generally recognized principles of international law." [12] For such verification, the United States relied primarily on photo-reconnaissance satellites and the Interim Agreement contained a ban on interference with such NTM, including deliberate concealment measures that impede verification. The ABM Treaty also established a U.S.-Soviet Standing Consultative Commission (SCC) to consider compliance questions, discuss ambiguous situations, and develop procedures for implementing the agreements. The SCC's mandate subsequently was continued and broadened under START II.

From the LTBT to SALT II, American presidents generally supported a flexible approach to verification, with the general principle that the agreed regime must be of sufficient rigor for the United States to detect Soviet cheating of any consequence in time to take appropriate countermeasures. This operational principal was characterized by President Richard Nixon during the SALT I discussions as "adequate verification"—terminology that was used during ratification of that agreement.[13] The phrase subsequently was also used by the Ford and Carter administrations in connection with arms control proposals. President Kennedy used different terminology but a similar standard for verification during the LTBT debate.[14] During this period, administration officials did not contend that they could detect every instance of Soviet cheating, but rather that they could detect any cheating that mattered. Risks of lesser undetectable cheating were deemed acceptable as the price for achieving the greater benefits of the agreement and because of a generally recognized assumption that the United States would respond vigorously should cheating of military significance be detected. Later, President Ronald Reagan rejected "adequate" verification as insufficiently rigorous and set new standards, discussed later, for U.S. acceptance of verification regimes.

The Biological Weapons Convention

In addition to the nuclear agreements, another treaty covering weapons of mass destruction—the Biological Weapons Convention (BWC)—signed in 1972 relied solely on NTM for verification. The BWC prohibits the development, production, stockpiling, acquisition, and retention of biological agents or toxins of types and in quantities that have no justification for prophylactic, protective, or other peaceful purposes. It also bans the weapons, equipment, or means of delivery to use such agents or toxins for hostile purposes or in armed conflict. All such materials were to be destroyed within nine months after entry into force (EIF) of the convention, which occurred on March 26, 1975. Biological weapons are defined in the treaty as disease-causing micro-organisms (e.g. bacteria, viruses, rickettsia, and fungi) and toxins (poisonous chemicals synthesized by living organisms) that could be used against humans or livestock to cause massive casualties or economic damage as a means of warfare or terrorism.

The BWC, as originally concluded, contains no verification provisions, although it does permit signatories to refer suspected noncompliance to the United Nations Security Council for action. The lack of verification provisions was a tacit admission that its provisions could not, in fact, be verified without a highly complex and intrusive verification regime incapable of achievement at the time of its negotiation. Indeed, given the formidable tasks of verifying biological weapons research and production, which can take place unobtrusively under cover of legitimate research activities, not even the most sophisticated NTM then available—that of the United States—was adequate to reliably detect violations of the BWC. Later, in the late 1980s and 1990s, efforts were made to provide some semblance of verification by adding a number of confidence-building measures, such as data exchanges and on-site visits to military and civilian biological research facilities. But experts have continued to point out that highly intrusive and costly on-site inspection regimes are needed to ensure truly effective verification of compliance with the agreement.

Exceptions to Reliance on NTM

Despite a general reliance on NTM as the primary means of verification in the 1960s and 1970s, there remained a few arms control areas where the United States, in particular, continued to insist on inclusion of on-site inspection provisions as an essential element of the verification regime. These involved nuclear non-proliferation, where the United States continued to insist on an international safeguards regime with on-site inspection provisions and certain areas of nuclear weapons testing where cheating could provide a potential adversary with a technological, and thus military, edge.

The Nuclear Nonproliferation Treaty

By the mid-1960s, the increasing use of nuclear energy to produce electricity raised concerns that fissionable materials—particularly plutonium—could become abundantly available, increasing the political and military temptation among non-nuclear states to produce nuclear weapons.

The conclusion of the LTBT, abandonment by the Soviet Union of its hostility to the safeguards regime of the International Atomic Energy Agency, and some easing of East-West tensions in the mid-1960s opened the way for superpower agreement on the Nuclear Nonproliferation Treaty (NPT). The NPT was designed to control the spread of nuclear weapons beyond the then five nuclear powers—the United States, Soviet Union, France, Great Britain and China. It was signed on July 1, 1968, by the U.S., U.S.S.R., U.K. and about sixty other governments and became the centerpiece of international effort to control the spread of nuclear weapons.

The NPT establishes two categories of member states: (1) the nuclear weapons states defined as the five nuclear powers, and (2) all other states, defined as non-nuclear weapons states. The nuclear weapons states agree (Article I) not to transfer to any state nuclear weapons or nuclear explosive devices or control over them and not to assist, encourage, or induce any non-nuclear weapons state to acquire or manufacture them. The non-nuclear weapons states agree (Article II) not to receive nuclear weapons or explosive devices, control over them, nor any assistance in their manufacture.

The only verification provision in the NPT is found in Article III.1, which requires each non-nuclear weapons state party to enter into a separate agreement with IAEA to apply that agency's safeguards to all nuclear material in the state's peaceful nuclear activities, wherever they are carried out. The IAEA safeguards system has extensive data reporting requirements that permit auditing of nuclear materials and facilities, establish requirements for containment of such materials within certain areas, and permit continuous surveillance of diversion pathways by technical monitoring equipment. In addition, inspectors from the IAEA can undertake on-site inspections at all peaceful nuclear facilities to determine whether nuclear material is being diverted for any reason. These inspections are designed to make attempts at proliferation more likely to be discovered and permit timely corrective action should proliferation occur. More than 100 such comprehensive agreements, based upon the model in Information Circular (INFCIRC)/153, are in force.

To accommodate the already existing safeguard regime that had been set up by the European Atomic Energy Agency (EURATOM)—an organization established by the Treaty of Rome to apply safeguards to all states of the European Union—an agreement was concluded to provide for the joint conduct of inspections at facilities in non-nuclear states within the European Union by both IAEA and EURATOM inspectors, while preserving the basic principle of an independent IAEA inspection if necessary. A similar arrangement subsequently was set up between the Brazilian-Argentine Agency for Accounting and Control of Nuclear Materials (ABACC) and IAEA to conduct joint inspections in Argentina and Brazil, which have agreed to mutual inspection of all of their nuclear facilities.

Less comprehensive safeguards agreements are negotiated and concluded individually by the IAEA with other states based on INFCIRC/66, which involves application of safeguards only to specific facilities or material.[15] While most non-nuclear weapon states are covered by comprehensive safeguard agreements, a few, most importantly Israel, India and Pakistan, are covered by the less comprehensive INFCIRC/66 agreements, leaving significant nuclear activities in these states uncovered by peaceful use obligations or safeguards.

Many on-site inspection concepts developed by the IAEA safeguards systems were later incorporated into other arms control inspection regimes. These include highly detailed data exchanges, restricting treaty-related items to specific locations, the use of joint inspection teams, and the origins of some continuous monitoring concepts. As noted later in this study, the IAEA organizational structure also served as the model for later multinational inspection agencies.

Reassessment of the TTBT/PNET Verification Regime

As late as 1957—the conclusion of the Threshold Test Ban Treaty (TTBT)—U.S. negotiators were still prepared to rely on NTM for verification. The TTBT, which set an upper threshold of 150 kilotons on all nuclear weapons tests, left it to each party to use its own seismic network to measure the magnitude of weapons test explosions carried out by the other party and estimate the yield of each test. To assist these measurements, the treaty provided for an exchange of scientific and technical data about each test site, including provision of the geographic coordinates of test site boundaries and of key data on the geology of the testing area, such as density, water table depth, seismic velocity, and porosity. However, there were no provisions in the treaty that permitted an independent confirmation of the accuracy of the data provided by each side.

When the Peaceful Nuclear Explosions Treaty (PNET) was concluded two years later, it contained a significant compromise between the superpowers that included the use of OSI along with NTM for verification. The PNET governs all nuclear explosions carried out at locations other than those that had been specified as nuclear weapons test sites under the TTBT. While the United States was prepared to ban all peaceful nuclear explosions, the Soviets, who were still considering possible use of nuclear explosions for excavation purposes, insisted on a right to continue tests within the limits set by the TTBT. The PNET restricted the yield of any single explosions to 150 kilotons and that of any group of explosions to 150 kilotons each and a total of 1,500 kilotons. To help verify that none of the individual explosions used in group explosions exceeded the 150 kiloton TTBT threshold, the treaty requires each party to provide the purpose, location, and type of geological medium in which any explosion would be conducted. It also allowed American "personnel"—the Soviets objected to use of the term "inspectors"—to make necessary on-site measurements under specified conditions. To ensure that the measuring equipment to be used for this purpose could not be used for espionage, the treaty stipulated that prior to the on-site visit two identical sets of equipment would be presented to the inspected party. One of these sets would be selected at random for examination by the inspected party and the other for use in making the measurements. Similar procedures were later incorporated into other OSI regimes. During the ratification process, neither the verification provisions of the TTBT nor PNET were found to be acceptable by the U.S. Congress. The provisions of the agreements continued to be observed by both parties, but neither treaty was ratified until major changes were made in their verification structures in the late 1980s.

Early Comprehensive Test Ban Discussions

In early discussions of a Comprehensive Test Ban Treaty (CTBT) in the 1970s, the United States insisted upon, and the Soviets were prepared to agree to, OSI under limited conditions. During these negotiations, the United States originally insisted on mandatory on-site inspections to verify compliance but eventually indicated its readiness to accept challenge inspections with a right of refusal by the inspected Party.[16] However, there was a surreal aspect to these initial negotiations, since there never was a realistic chance in the 1970s that a

CTBT would be accepted by the U.S. Congress. The talks eventually foundered as that decade ended in a general deterioration of East-West relations brought on by the Soviet intervention in Afghanistan and increased Soviet aggressiveness in other Third World countries.

NOTES

1. For a more complete description of the on-site inspection activities carried out under the Treaty of Versailles see J. Harahan, "Comparative history of arms control from World War I, World War II and the Cold War," *Militaire Spectator* No. 7 (July 1994). pp. 285–294.

2. Comprehensive discussions of the development of on-site inspection in the post–World War II period are to be found in Edward Ifft, "The Use of On-Site Inspection in the Avoidance and Settlement of Arms Control Disputes," in *Avoidance and Settlement of Arms Control Disputes*, ed. Julie Dahlitz (New York: United Nations, 1994). pp. 9–22; and in Timothy J. Pounds, "Proposals for On-Site Inspection over the Years: from the Baruch Plan to the Reagan Initiatives," in *Arms Control Verification and the New Role of On-Site Inspection*, ed. Louis Dunn and Amy Gordon (Lexington, MA: Lexington Books, 1990). pp. 69–89. Pounds notes that from the beginning the effectiveness of OSI was a matter of debate. The Acheson-Lilienthal report, which preceded the Baruch Plan proposal, stated "We have concluded unanimously that there is no prospect of security against atomic warfare in a system of international agreement controlled only by a system which relies on inspection." Thus the Baruch Plan called also for international ownership of, management of, and control over fissionable material.

3. Pounds, "Proposals for On-Site Inspection," pp. 73–75.

4. For an overview of Soviet attitudes toward verification, see U.S. House of Representatives, Committee on Foreign Affairs, *Verifying Arms Control Agreements: The Soviet View*, report prepared for Subcommittee on Arms Control, International Security and Science, House Committee on Foreign Affairs (Washington, D.C.: U.S. Government Printing Office, May 1987.

5. At the time the Antarctic Treaty was negotiated, twelve countries were active in Antarctica: Argentina, Australia, Belgium, Chile, France, Japan, New Zealand, Norway, South Africa, the Soviet Union, the United Kingdom, and the United States. Currently, thirty-seven states are parties to the treaty.

6. Edward J. Lacey, "Arms Control and Antarctica: On-Site Inspections on the Frozen Continent" in *New Horizons and Challenges in Arms Control and Verification*, ed. James Brown (Amsterdam, VU University Press, 1994) p. 214.

7. Ibid., p. 216.

8. Pounds, "Proposals for On-Site Inspection" pp. 81–82.

9. Article XII of the Treaty on Principals Governing the Activities of States in the Exploration and Use of Outer Space, Including the Moon and Other Celestial Bodies (Outer Space Treaty), signed January 27, 1967, permits OSI to be carried out in principle, but OSI was never really a central feature of the treaty.

10. The March 1987 U.S. Department of State *Report to Congress on Soviet Noncompliance with Arms Control Agreements* (Washington D.C.: U.S. Department of State p. 6 notes that "in December 1985, the U.S. Government found that: 'Soviet

nuclear testing activities for a number of tests constitute a likely violation of legal obligations under the Threshold Test Ban Treaty.' At present with our existing knowledge of this complex topic, that finding stands."

11. The United States accurately expected a negative Soviet response to its OSI proposals, which were mainly designed to give the appearance of U.S. interest in arms limitations, while satisfying those who wanted no agreement that would restrict U.S. strategic modernization programs. See Pounds, "Proposals for On-Site Inspection," p. 84.

12. SALT I Interim Agreement on Strategic Offensive Arms, Article V.

13. Ralph Earl, II, "Verification Issues from the Point of View of the Negotiator" in *Arms Control Verification: The Technologies that Make It Possible*, ed. Kosta Tsipis, Dave Hafemeister, and Penny Janeway (Washington D.C.: Pergamon-Brassey's, 1986), p. 6

14. Michael Krepon, "The Politics of Treaty Verification and Compliance," in *Arms Control Verification: The Technologies that Make It Possible*, ed. Kosta Tsipis, Dave Hafemeister, and Penny Janeway (Washington D.C.: Pergamon-Brassey's, 1986) pp. 20-21.

15. For a comprehensive discussion of the IAEA safeguards system, see Myron B. Kratzer, *International Nuclear Safeguards: Promise and Performance*, Occasional Paper (Washington D.C.: Atlantic Council, April 1994).

16. In a 1980 joint statement, the parties agreed to allow an unlimited number of requests for on-site inspection, with the challenged party permitted either to comply or explain why inspection was not necessary. In addition, the U.S. and U.S.S.R. had agreed to accept ten tamper-proof unmanned seismic stations on their territories. See *Tripartite Report to the Committee on Disarmament: Comprehensive Test Ban*, July 30, 1980. CD/130. Reprinted in U.S. Arms Control and Disarmament Agency, *Documents on Disarmament* (Washington D.C.: ACDA, 1980), pp. 317–320.

Chapter 2

Development of the Modern OSI Regime

VERIFICATION WATERSHEDS

Changing Standards

The advent of the Reagan administration in 1980 led to demands for much more stringent and intrusive verification regimes than in the past. President Reagan and his advisors rejected the prevailing standard of "adequate verification" and insisted on a more exacting standard termed "effective verification." Part and parcel of this concept was the conviction that the Soviets had taken advantage of loosely drafted treaty language and weak verification provisions to cheat on past arms control agreements. This conviction was reflected in regular reports on Soviet arms control compliance, which began to appear in January 1984 and were issued on an annual basis thereafter. By the mid-1980s, these reports were concluding that the Soviet Union had violated its legal obligations under, or political commitments to, a wide variety of arms control agreements, including the SALT I Interim Agreement and ABM Treaty, the SALT II agreement, the Limited Test Ban Treaty, the Biological and Toxic Weapons Convention, the Geneva Protocol on Chemical Weapons, and the Helsinki Agreement.[1]

The Reagan administration's call for "effective verification" was designed to make it much more difficult for the Soviets to evade treaty commitments and provide increased confidence that the United States would be able to detect, and respond appropriately to, any treaty violation before it could become militarily significant. With this standard in mind, the United States began to insist on more specific, carefully crafted treaty language and on agreements that contained more detailed data exchanges, enhanced national technical means, on-site inspections of unprecedented scope, and various types of technical on-site monitoring.

On-site inspection, in particular, was elevated to the status of a fundamental element of verification. While designed to signal a tougher approach to verification, the insistence on OSI also served useful domestic political purposes. It helped to undercut demands for a nuclear freeze in the early 1980s and to gain support for military modernization. In addition, since many Reagan advisors did not believe that the Soviets would ever accept intrusive OSI, it was seen as a means of slowing the arms control process and keeping the Soviets on the defensive in international fora, while still appearing flexible on arms control issues domestically and with the U.S. allies.

The Stockholm Accords

In the mid-1980s, Soviet First Party Secretary Mikhail Gorbachev, faced with a rapidly deteriorating economy no long able to match U.S. military build-ups and determined to open up Soviet society and reduce confrontation with the West, began to display a new willingness to accept a broader application of on-site inspection in military arms control agreements. The first concrete manifestation of this change was contained in the Document of the Stockholm Conference on Confidence- and Security-Building Measures and Disarmament in Europe (more commonly known as the Stockholm Accords) signed on November 19, 1986. That agreement, negotiated within the framework of the Helsinki Accords, considerably expanded the 1975 Helsinki Final Act by including an unprecedented provision for no-refusal on-site inspections of the military forces of both sides as a confidence-building measure.

While previous provisions under the Helsinki Accords had proposed the invitation of observers to attend military maneuvers, the Stockholm Accord required both the notification and observation of a much broader category of activities and provided for on-site inspection with no right of refusal of military forces. These inspections were not limited to military exercises but applied to other potential military activities as well. The agreement acknowledged the legitimacy of using national technical means (NTM) to monitor military activities and provided for short-notice inspections with tight timelines. These allowed twenty-four hours to respond to a call for inspections, twelve hours to facilitate the start of the inspection, and a forty-eight hour period to conduct the actual inspection. Other provisions permitted the conduct of inspections on the ground and/or from the air and allowed access, entry to, and the unobstructed survey of military areas, with the exception of specified restricted areas whose number and extent were to be "as limited as possible."[2]

THE NUCLEAR ARMS CONTROL TREATIES

The Intermediate-Range Nuclear Forces Treaty

While conclusion of the Stockholm Agreement signaled an important change in the Soviet attitude toward OSI, it was the treaty between the United States and the Soviet Union on the elimination of their intermediate-range nuclear forces (INF Treaty) that marked the true watershed in the acceptance of on-site inspection as a fundamental element, along with NTM, of modern arms control verification regimes. The INF Treaty combined various elements of previous on-site inspection proposals with new OSI concepts to create the basic model for all subsequent arms control treaties. It was followed some four and a half years later by the far more complex Strategic Arms Reduction Treaty (START I), reducing and limiting strategic offensive arms, which added several new types of on-site inspection.

The INF Treaty, signed December 8, 1987, was negotiated to resolve a major East-West confrontation precipitated by the Soviet deployment in the late 1970s of modernized, highly accurate, triple-warheaded SS-20 missiles targeted against Europe and the subsequent NATO decision to counter these deployments by stationing modernized U.S. intermediate-range nuclear missiles in several NATO countries.[3] The treaty went beyond the earlier Strategic Arms Limitation (SALT) Agreements by requiring the actual elimination of missile systems, rather than merely establishing upper limits on their deployment. Specifically, it required the elimination within three years after entry into force (i.e., by May 30, 1991) of all U.S. and Soviet ground-launched ballistic and cruise missile systems with ranges between 500 and 5,500 kilometers (roughly 300 to 3,400 miles).

To verify compliance, the treaty contains an interlocking verification structure designed to help confirm compliance by raising the risks of detection (and hence the cost of cheating) to prohibitive levels. This structure recognizes and enhances the use of NTM, requires comprehensive data exchanges on the military systems covered by the agreement, and includes an array of on-site inspections and procedures designed to confirm that these missile systems and their infrastructure were indeed destroyed and to assist in monitoring treaty compliance for ten years thereafter, i.e, until the year 2001. It also creates a new body—the Special Verification Commission—to monitor implementation and compliance with its provisions.

The unprecedented on-site inspection regime of the INF Treaty provides for five types of inspection: (1) baseline inspections of all inspectable sites were designed to verify the data provided by each side; (2) close-out inspections confirmed that treaty-prohibited activity had indeed ceased at facilities declared to be eliminated; (3) short-notice inspections were instituted to help verify that illegal activity was not occurring at any existing or former INF site; (4) elimination inspections permitted on-site confirmation of the destruction of INF systems in the manner designated in the treaty; and (5) portal and perimeter continuous monitoring of a missile facility on each side was instituted to confirm that all production of INF missiles had ceased at their former production sites.

The acceptance by the Soviet Union of the unparalleled scope and intrusiveness of the INF Treaty's OSI regime extended the newly emerging concepts of *perestroika* (restructuring) and *glasnost* (openness) to the arms control arena. It thus laid the basis for rapid movement across the entire agenda of evolving bilateral and multilateral arms control agreements as the geopolitical sea-change at the beginning of the 1990s unfolded, fundamentally altering the international scene.

The dissolution of the Soviet Union into multiple successor states as part of this change has had some impact on the practical implementation of the INF Treaty. As of this writing, six former Soviet successor states—Belarus, Kazakstan, Russia, Ukraine, Turkmenistan, and Uzbekistan—have inspectable facilities located on their territories. The last two, however, have only a single inspectable facility each and do not participate in on-site inspection activity or inspection-related meetings. In addition, the United States no longer conducts INF inspections at the former Soviet facilities in the newly independent Baltic states of Estonia, Latvia and Lithuania.[4]

The Nuclear Test Ban Protocols

In November 1987, the United States and Soviet Union resumed nuclear testing talks in Geneva in an effort to reach agreement on strengthened verification provisions for the two existing, but unratified, nuclear test ban treaties—the Threshold Test Ban Treaty (TTBT) and the Peaceful Nuclear Explosions Treaty (PNET). New verification protocols, signed in Washington in June 1990, contain provisions to supplement the earlier reliance of these agreements on NTM with the right of each side to employ hydrodynamic yield measurement, seismic monitoring, and on-site inspections in the territory of the testing party to confirm that nuclear testing is within the agreed levels.

The TTBT/PNET protocols permit the United States to make direct, on-site hydrodynamic yield measurements of all nuclear tests exceeding 50 kilotons. This verification method determines the yield of a nuclear test by measuring, at the detonation site, the speed of the supersonic shock wave in the earth caused by the detonation. Under the protocols, the Soviet Union (now Russia) may use its preferred, traditional method of seismic monitoring, which measures the explosion's shock waves as they move through the earth to arrive at an estimate of explosive yield. Each side may undertake on-site inspections to take core samples and rock fragments from the area of the nuclear test to confirm geological and geophysical data associated with each explosion.

These protocols opened the road to U.S. ratification of the two nuclear testing agreements and were a further step toward improving superpower cooperation. But, in practice, the improved verification protocols were moot, since by the time they were agreed at the negotiating table, both sides had introduced nuclear testing moratoria and were giving renewed attention to concepts aimed at achieving a total global ban on all nuclear testing.

The Strategic Arms Control Treaties

The START I Treaty, negotiated over a nine-year period and signed in Moscow on July 31, 1991, by presidents Bush and Gorbachev, is a follow-up to the earlier SALT agreements. However, it goes beyond the upper limits set by those agreements by requiring deep reductions (between 30 percent and 40 percent) in the deployed strategic offensive arms of both sides from the original levels of about 10,500 in each arsenal at the time of signing. It also establishes central limits on the deployed strategic offensive arms of both sides of 1,600 strategic nuclear delivery systems and 6,000 accountable warheads; with sublimits for ballistic missile warheads, warheads on heavy intercontinental ballistic missiles (ICBMs), and warheads on mobile ICBMs.

The verification tasks of the START I Treaty are considerably more complex than those in the INF Treaty and consequently require a much broader range of on-site inspection provisions to confirm compliance. Under the INF Treaty, detection of even a *single* prohibited missile after completion of the three-year elimination period in 1991 would constitute a violation of the agreement. On the other hand, the START verification regime requires the monitoring of *residual limits* on the designated systems. Its task is to confirm that strategic nuclear delivery systems—ICBMs, submarine-launched ballistic missiles (SLBMs), and

Figure 2.1
START Obligations

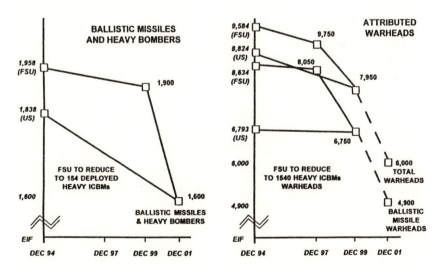

Source: **DynMeridian, Alexandria, Virginia**

aircraft—and accountable warheads are reduced to treaty limits and that the accountable sublimits within each of those categories are observed. In addition, unlike the INF Treaty, which banned only land-based missile systems, START limits apply to land-based and sea-based missile systems and to aircraft.

Thus, although the basic structure of the START verification builds on that of the INF Treaty, the on-site inspection provisions in particular are considerably broader in scope and application. Like the INF Treaty, START has provisions for enhanced NTM and provides for a regime of data exchanges and notifications on strategic systems and facilities covered by the treaty. However, while the INF Treaty has five types of on-site inspection, the START I Agreement gives the parties the right to conduct twelve types of on-site inspections, a number of which break new ground.

In addition to baseline, close-out, short-notice and elimination agreements, and provisions for portal monitoring, START I added the following new types of OSI, explained more fully in subsequent chapters:

- *New Facility Inspections* to confirm data provided on new inspectable facilities that come on-line after entry into force (EIF) of the agreement. Essentially baseline inspections, these can be held within sixty days after a party is notified of a new inspectable facility.

- *Suspect Site Inspections* to help confirm that covert production of mobile missiles is not occurring at specifically listed facilities. These inspections can be held at three missile facilities in the United States and three in the former Soviet Union (FSU) that have the capability to covertly assemble mobile ICBMs or first stages of such ICBMs.

- *Reentry Vehicle Inspections* to "spot check" the data provided by each side on the number of warheads deployed on a specific type of ICBM or SLBM. During these inspections, the inspected party is required to demonstrate that the number of reentry vehicles on these missiles does not exceed the number of warheads attributed to that missile in the treaty.

- *Post-Exercise Dispersal Inspections* (also called post-dispersal inspections) to help confirm that mobile ICBM launchers and their missiles have returned to their bases after completion of a field exercise dispersal, or are otherwise accounted for.

- *Conversion Inspections* to verify that allowable conversions of military equipment are carried out in accordance with the provisions and procedures specified in the treaty's Conversion or Elimination Protocol.

- *Technical Characteristics Exhibitions* to provide an opportunity for each side to verify the data provided by the other party on the technical characteristics of each type and variant of ICBMs, SLBMs, and mobile launchers covered by the treaty.

- *Distinguisability Exhibitions* to provide each Party an opportunity to inspect one of each type, category, and variant of certain bombers to help the inspectors to accurately confirm, during future inspections, the identity of these systems and the number of them that are declared to be present.

• *Baseline Exhibitions of Various Bombers* which are conducted during the baseline inspection period for certain bomber types to confirm that such aircraft meet the standards of conversion contained in the treaty.

In addition to these new types of OSI, the START Treaty also contains a provision for visits with right of special access (SAVs) at any facility or location, whether or not declared as an inspectable site in the treaty, to help resolve compliance concerns. Although SAVs can be refused and their procedures must be agreed on a case-by-case basis in the START Treaty's compliance body—the Joint Compliance and Implementation Commission—the

Table 2.1
START Inspections and Exhibitions

Inspection Type	Annual Quota	Confirm
Baseline	N/A	Data on numbers and types of items in initial data exchanges
New Facility	N/A	Data on numbers and types of items at new facilities
Data Update	15	Data on numbers and types of items in notifications and regular data updates
Suspect Site	(included in Data Update quota)	That covert assembly of mobile ICBMs or their first stages is not occurring
Reentry Vehicle	10	That deployed ICBMs and SLBMs contain no more RVs than the number attributed to them
Post Dispersal	N/A	The number of mobile ICBMs and their launchers located at an ICBM base after an exercise dispersal
Conversion or Elimination	N/A	Conversion or elimination of strategic offensive arms
Closeout	N/A	That elimination of specified facilities has been completed
Formerly Declared	3	That closed-out facilities are not being used for purposes inconsistent with the Treaty
Technical Characteristics Exhibitions	(1 time)	That technical characteristics of ICBMs and SLBMs correspond to the data in the MOU
Distinguishability Exhibitions	(1 time)	Technical characteristics of heavy bombers, the number of LRNA for which they are equipped, distinguishing features, and LRNA technical characteristics
Heavy Bomber Baseline Exhibition	(1 time)	That heavy bombers satisfy conversion requirements and demonstrate the presence of distinguishable features

Source: **DynMeridian, Alexandria, Virginia**

SAV provisions constitute the first agreed version of a challenge inspection regime in a nuclear arms control agreement.

Five months after START I was signed, the Soviet Union dissolved, and four independent states with strategic nuclear weapons on their territory came into existence—Russia, Ukraine, Belarus and Kazakstan. Through the Lisbon Protocol of May 1992, the bilateral START I Treaty was transformed into a multilateral agreement covering these four successor states and the United States. Final ratification of the treaty by the countries of the former Soviet Union was delayed as differences in implementing commitments in the Lisbon Agreement by the Ukraine, Belarus, and Kazakstan were ironed out. These included pledges to adhere to the NPT and to eliminate all nuclear weapons and strategic offensive arms from their territories during the process of START reductions. After protracted negotiations to resolve these remaining issues, all four FSU signatories exchanged instruments of ratification on December 5, 1994, and START I entered into force on that date.

START II

At a June 1990 Washington Summit, the U.S. and USSR committed themselves to consultations without delay on future talks after the START signature to achieve yet further reductions in their strategic systems. Following subsequent high-level exchanges, a "Joint Understanding on Further Reductions in Strategic Offensive Arms" was agreed at the June 1992 Bush-Yeltsin Summit in Washington.[5] The basic elements of the Joint Understanding with some modification of details were subsequently codified in the START II Treaty signed on January 3, 1993, by Presidents George Bush and Boris Yeltsin. Unlike

Table 2.2
START I and II Central Limits

Category	START	START II Phase I	START II Phase II
Strategic Nuclear Delivery Vehicles	1600	START limit applies	START limit applies
Strategic Warheads	6000 accountable	3800–4250 actual	3000–3500 actual
Ballistic Missile Warheads	4900	No sublimit	No sublimit
MIRVed ICBM Warheads	No sublimit	1200	0
Heavy ICBM Warheads	1540	650	0
Mobile ICBM Warheads	1100	START limit applies	START limit applies
SLBM Warheads	No sublimit	2160	1700–1750

START I, START II remains a bilateral agreement in accordance with the provisions of the Lisbon Agreement under which only the United States and Russia will remain nuclear weapons states.

START II contains two central elements. It significantly reduces strategic offensive arms beyond the levels contained in START I, and it requires the elimination of all ICBMs with multiple independently-targetable reentry vehicles (MIRVs)—the missile systems that traditionally have been regarded as the most destabilizing due to their inherent first strike capabilities. In connection with the requirement to eliminate all MIRVs, the treaty modifies some rules in START to allow for reduction to a single warhead ("downloading") of certain formerly multi-warheaded missiles.[6] START II also requires elimination of heavy ICBMs and their launchers, specifically the huge Russian SS-18s that carry 10 warheads. Reductions will occur in two phases. An initial limit of between 3,800 and 4,250 total warheads on deployed strategic offensive arms, with some sublimits, is to be achieved by December 31, 2004. The remaining reductions to a lower limit of 3,000 to 3,500 warheads, of which no more than 1,700 may be SLBM warheads, are to be completed by December 31, 2007.[7] The use of a range of numbers to express limits in START II is unique in strategic arms control and reflects a decision to give each side the freedom to set its own force structure as long as it remains within the overall limits.

START II uses the comprehensive verification provisions of START I and reflects the same assumptions and considerations to verify compliance. It depends on enhanced NTM, supplemented by data exchanges, notifications, and on-site inspections. However, because some START II eliminations have no exact START I counterpart, the new treaty does contain a few new verification measures. It permits on-site observation of SS-18 silo conversions and of SS-18 missile and launch canister elimination. In addition, it provides for exhibitions and on-site inspections of all heavy bombers (including the weapons bay of the B-2 bomber, which is not subject to inspection under START I) to confirm weapons loads and for exhibitions of heavy bombers reoriented to a conventional role to confirm their observable differences.

MULTINATIONAL ON-SITE INSPECTION REGIMES

In addition to the U.S.-Soviet/FSU nuclear arms control agreements, two major multinational arms control agreements, which had proceeded inconclusively for decades, were finalized during the East-West realignments of the early 1990s. These treaties, covering conventional arms control and a ban on chemical weapons created new multinational inspectorates and introduced further variants of on-site inspections, including the first fully developed challenge inspection regimes. The signing in Paris in November 1990 of the Treaty on Conventional Armed Forces in Europe (CFE) by twenty-two members of NATO and the Warsaw Pact marked a breakthrough in decades long efforts to reduce the conventional military confrontation in central Europe, then the most heavily armed area in the world. The thrust of this agreement, which built on the earlier inconclusive Mutual and Balanced Force Reductions (MBFR) talks, was to lower the risk of a conventional attack in the European area by reducing and roughly equalizing the conventional arms holdings of the competing alliances. Three years later, in January 1993, the multinational Chemical Weapons Convention (CWC), which had been under negotiation for twenty-four years, also was opened for signature in Paris. The CWC bans the development, production, acquisition, stockpiling, transfer, and use of chemical weapons—thus, outlawing this entire class of weapons.

The Treaty on Conventional Armed Forces in Europe

As originally negotiated, the CFE Treaty was intended to establish a rough parity in conventional arms between NATO and the Warsaw Pact. However, both the Soviet Union and Warsaw Pact dissolved in the period between treaty signature and its entry into force making the bloc distributions irrelevant. As a result, the focus of the treaty has shifted to establishing maximum holdings for each signatory state of key types of conventional military equipment and of military personnel. In addition, on June 5, 1992, all parties to the CFE Treaty agreed on arrangements by which the eight successor states to the former Soviet Union in the treaty's area of application—Azerbaijan, Armenia, Belarus, Kazakstan, Moldova, the Russian Federation, Ukraine and Georgia—undertook to exercise the full rights and obligations of the CFE and its associated documents. Specifically, it was agreed that the maximum levels of conventional armaments and equipment for all eight of these successor states would not exceed the total ceiling established for the Soviet Union.

The CFE Treaty, which entered into force on November 9, 1992, requires reductions to agreed equal ceilings on the numbers of tanks, artillery pieces, armored combat vehicles, attack helicopters, and combat aircraft in the forces of NATO and those of the former Warsaw Pact (including the former Soviet Union) located in the region from the Atlantic Ocean to the Ural Mountains (Atlantic-to-the-Urals or ATTU). The treaty required implementation of these reductions within forty months and limits former Soviet forces to about one-third of the total armaments permitted for all signatories in Europe.

Follow-up CFE-1A negotiations began immediately after the CFE Treaty was signed, and an agreement was concluded on July 6, 1992. The CFE-1A agreement contained *political* commitments (which unlike the legally binding CFE Treaty are not subject to ratification) by its signatories to limit and, where applicable, reduce their military manpower levels. These manpower levels (e.g., 250,000 for the United States and 450,000 for Russia in the ATTU) were determined separately by each state and subjected to discussion but, as political commitments, not to negotiation. Like the armaments limits, they were to be completed within forty months after EIF and subject to monitoring during CFE on-site inspections.

Verification of the CFE Treaty posed formidable problems. The total land area in the ATTU is over nine million square miles. In comparison with earlier treaties, very large numbers of diverse armaments and manpower had to be removed and monitored. Indeed the treaty required tracking of some 70,000 treaty-limited items and hundreds of thousands of troops with some degree of confidence. At the same time, the individual pieces of military equipment limited by the treaty were of much lower intrinsic value than the nuclear weapons covered by the INF and START treaties. In addition, most of the limited armaments were relatively small and highly mobile. They could be moved easily in a relatively short period of time, and many could be quickly disassembled so that parts could be hidden at diverse locations for later reassembly. Furthermore, the accountable systems were constrained only in the ATTU but not beyond that region, requiring monitoring of movement into and out of the constrained area. Finally, there was a long history of military doctrine, training, and operational experience in the concealment of conventional weapons and in deceptive tactics.

To deal with these problems, the CFE Treaty adopted a verification structure similar in many respects to that of the INF and START treaties but changed the monitoring emphasis. While insisting on the obligation of all parties to abide by the numerical ceilings for all weapons systems, the negotiators recognized that it would not be possible to monitor the data provided by each side to, say, the level of a single tank. Instead, the treaty aimed at ensuring that large violations, especially those involving fully operational and integrated military units, were not occurring or, if taking place, could be detected in early stages.

Like other modern arms control treaties, the CFE Treaty relies on a mix of national technical means, data exchanges, and on-site inspection to verify compliance. As a variant, its NTM provisions sanction the use of both national and international technical means to take into account the possibility of applying multinational technical means, for example, by the NATO allies acting together. The treaty required detailed information exchanges on forces located in the area of application, including details on the numbers, types, and locations of treaty-limited equipment (TLE). Similar data had to be provided on equipment in the area subject to, but not limited by, the treaty, such as combat support helicopters. The on-site inspection regime permits inspections of "Objects of Verification" (OOVs), that is, of units or locations holding treaty-limited equipment at declared sites. Such inspections cannot be refused. In addition, it provides for challenge inspections of suspect activities, although with a right of refusal, at locations other than declared sites. The on-site inspection regime covers brigade- and regimental-level units at declared sites, the destruction of equipment, and the conversion of equipment, such as recategorized multi-purpose attack helicopter and reclassified combat-capable trainer aircraft.

The CFE permitted reductions inspections to be carried out by multinational teams composed of members of various countries. This treaty provision helped spur the creation in Brussels of a NATO Verification Coordinating Committee and a complementary international Verification Support Staff—a new departure in the post-Cold War evolution of NATO. Eventually the multinationalization of inspection teams was expanded to permit members of both former Pacts to serve on a single inspection team. This established an important precedent for future multinational on-site inspection teams.

Table 2.3
Types of Inspections: CFE Treaty

• **Short-notice**

— **Declared sites**

— **Challenge inspections within specified area**

• **Scheduled**

— **Reduction sites (including conversion activities)**

— **Certification of recategorized helicopters and aircraft**

The Chemical Weapons Convention

The devastating effects of gas warfare in World War I, which caused one million casualties, resulted in conclusion of the Geneva Protocol of 1925 banning any future use of lethal or disabling chemicals as instruments of war. However, this protocol did not prohibit the development, production, or stockpiling of chemical weapons, and its provisions were further weakened by reservations imposed by various countries. It proved to be ineffective in halting chemical weapons use. Although chemical weapons were not used in World War II, they have been used repeatedly on a smaller scale since the signing of the Geneva Protocol, fueling demands for a stronger convention.[8] As a result, a strengthened chemical weapons accord was placed on the agenda of the Geneva Disarmament Conference in 1969 and also became the subject of bilateral negotiations between the U.S. and U.S.S.R. in the 1970s and 1980s. These various discussions eventually resulted in the development and conclusion of the multilateral Chemical Weapons Convention (CWC) which was signed on January 13, 1993, in Paris. The treaty entered into force on April 29, 1997.

The CWC bans the development, production, stockpiling and use of chemical weapons by its signatories and requires the destruction of all chemical weapons and production facilities. The United States and Russia are required to destroy between 60,000 and 70,000 tons of chemical agents.[9] The treaty also imposes export controls and reporting requirements on chemicals that can be used as warfare agents and on their precursors. It penalizes countries that do not join by inhibiting their access to certain treaty-controlled chemicals. In addition, the CWC establishes a new multinational organization—the Organization for the Prohibition of Chemical Weapons (OPCW), located in The Hague—to oversee treaty implementation.

To help verify its provisions, the CWC contains the most intrusive OSI regime of any arms control agreement concluded to date, including data declarations and notifications and provisions for both routine and challenge inspections. Its inspection provisions also extend to a vast number of companies in the private sector, rather than to just few such facilities as in the case of the INF and START treaties. The treaty permits monitoring of all chemical industry facilities that produce "dual use" chemicals that have both military and commercial applications to ensure that chemical weapons are not being produced or acquired. The CWC verification regime combines elements of the IAEA safeguards system as well as of the previous nuclear and conventional arms control inspection regimes. It provisions seek a balanced approach which couple inspections of exceptional intrusiveness to ensure compliance with "managed access" provisions to protect confidential private business and national security information.

As part of its verification regimes, the CWC requires all facilities, government or private, that produce, and in some cases process or consume, chemicals on listed schedules above specified quantitative thresholds to submit initial declarations and annual reports to their governments which compile a national declaration for provision to the OPCW.

Certain sites then are subject to initial inspection in the first three years after EIF during which the OPCW and the National Authority—a body established in each country to oversee treaty implementation—work with the inspected facility to develop a facility agreement that lays out such inspection parameters as the sections of the plant to be subject to inspection, the scope of inspection in agreed areas, the storage of confidential information on-site, the taking of samples and their analysis, access to plant records and the use of inspection equipment. All sites receiving an initial inspection are subject to periodic routine inspections, the frequency and intensity of which are determined by the characteristics of the plant site and the risk posed by the activities carried out there to the objectives and purposes of the CWC.

As a unique feature, any facility, whether declared or undeclared, suspected of violating the CWC may be subject to a challenge inspection at the request of another treaty signatory. Potentially highly intrusive inspection measures can be used to support these inspections, including air, soil, and effluent sampling, record searches, and personal interviews. Since all declared industrial facilities are subject to inspection on a routine basis, such challenge inspections are expected to be rare and some checks exist in the treaty to penalize their frivolous use.

The CWC also contains provisions that allow the OPCW to investigate the alleged use, or threat to use, chemical weapons and to take emergency measures to assist a state that is a victim of such use.

The Comprehensive Test Ban Treaty

After three years of intensive negotiations that built on previous proposals, a Comprehensive Test Ban Treaty was concluded at the United Nations in September 1996. The agreement, which bans any nuclear weapons test explosion or any other nuclear explosion, contains a verification regime designed to detect, establish the locality of, and identify clandestine nuclear explosions by utilizing a technical monitoring system supported by a regime of on-site inspection. The technical monitoring system will consist of complementary sensor networks with seismic, radionuclide, infrasound, and hydroacoustic detection devices.

The inspection regime permits on-site inspections at any location where a seismic event is detected. These inspections are designed to clarify any ambiguity about compliance with the agreement. They could involve inspection team access to suspect facilities and authorization to take soil sample collections and photographs at inspected sites. In addition, the treaty establishes a confidence building regime to reduce concerns of possible non-compliance with the Treaty's provisions and reduce the number of on-site inspection requests.

Improving Verification of the Biological Weapons Convention

Efforts, underway since 1980 to improve verification of the Biological Weapons Convention (BWC), have encountered the formidable obstacles posed by the ease and secrecy with which such weapons could be produced. Biological weapons have unique characteristics that distinguish them from other weapons of mass destruction and vastly increase the difficulty of developing effective on-site verification measures to control their production. Unlike the hundreds of tons of agent required to produce a credible chemical weapons threat, only kilograms of agent are required to produce a biological weapon and such a weapon could be produced rapidly (days to weeks) in a small area that does not display any distinctive external signatures readily detectable by NTM. In addition, advances in biotechnology have obviated the need for stockpiling large amounts of bulk agent or specialized production equipment, and much of the technology required to produce biological weapons is already available for a wide variety of legitimate dual-use applications.

Given the difficulties of verifying the BWC, initial efforts at developing a more effective verification regime focused on the development of modest confidence-building measures. The Second Review Conference of the BWC held in Geneva in 1986 agreed on a set of such measures. These included data exchanges on biological research laboratories that met very high national or international safety standards for biological activities; shared information on outbreaks of infectious diseases or similar occurrences caused by toxins that deviate from the normal; increased publication of biological defense research; and the promotion of scientific contacts related to the BWC. But such measures did little to raise confidence in BWC compliance and, in addition, their implementation was spotty.

Accordingly, a Third Review Conference in 1991 established an Ad Hoc Group of Verification Experts (VEREX) to identify, examine, and evaluate stronger measures for verifying compliance. VEREX identified twenty-one potential off-site and on-site verification measures. But the group concluded that, because of the dual-use nature of nearly all biological weapons-related facilities, equipment, and materials, no single approach was sufficient for verification, although some measures had the potential at least to help to differentiate between prohibited and permitted activities and thus to reduce ambiguities about compliance. The Third Review Conference also added two further confidence-building measures: the declaration of past activities in offensive and defensive biological research and development programs and declaration of vaccine production facilities.

In addition, in September 1992, the United States, Great Britain, and the Russian Federation concluded a "Trilateral Agreement" detailing a number of further steps that they would undertake to help ensure compliance with the BWC. These permitted visits to any nonmilitary biological site, including nongovernmental commercial facilities, at any time in order to remove ambiguities, and allowed unrestricted access, sampling, interviews with personnel, and audio and video taping.

A fourth BWC Review Conference held in September 1996 also focused on further verification measures, including mandatory declarations and on-site inspections, as an urgent task for the future. However, the conclusion of a viable on-site inspection regime that effectively verifies compliance with the sweeping BWC without prohibitive costs and the imposition of unusually intrusive inspections on an industry that is now in the forefront of world research faces formidable obstacles. Such verification will be further complicated by existing BWC provisions that specifically allow for the development, production and use of biological agents for prophylactic, protective, or other peaceful purposes.[10]

Other Agreements

While this study concentrates on the on-site inspection regimes of the major arms control agreements, almost all recent arms control agreements concluded in recent years, or still under negotiation, have included some concepts of on-site inspection. As examples, the Open Skies Treaty, concluded in March 1992, establishes a regime of unarmed aerial observation—a type of on-site inspection— over the entire territory of its signatories. The Vienna Documents of the Organization for Security and Cooperation in Europe (OSCE) contain confidence and security-building measures (CSBMs) involving an unprecedented sharing of military information, including visits and inspections of military bases, functions, and activities in member states. The Dayton Accords on Bosnia provide for on-site inspections by OSCE, Serbian, and Bosnian inspectors to collect military exchange data, verify numbers of heavy weapons, and conduct other inspections to confirm compliance.

NOTES

1. U.S. Department of State, *Soviet Noncompliance with Arms Control Agreements* Special Report no. 163 (Washington D.C. U.S. Department of State, March 1987). p. 1.

2. For an inspector's account, see Don O. Stovall, "The Stockholm Accord: On-Site Inspections in Eastern and Western Europe," in *Arms Control Verification and the New Role of On-Site Inspection*, ed. Lewis Dunn and Amy Gordon, (Lexington, MA.: Lexington. 1990), pp. 15-39.

3. A comprehensive treatment of the INF Treaty is contained in George Rueckert, *Double Global Zero: The INF Treaty from Its Origins to Implementation* (Westport, CT.: Greenwood Press, 1992).

4. Arms Control and Disarmament Agency, *Threat Control through Arms Control: Annual Report to Congress 1995* (Washington D.C.:ACDA, July 1996), pp. 64-65.

5. The "Joint Understanding" called for the elimination of all ICBMs with multiple independently targetable reentry vehicles; further reductions in SLBM warheads to 1,750; reductions to 3,000–3,500 deployed warheads during a two-phased elimination period extending to the year 2003; elimination of all heavy ICBMs; and U.S. efforts to facilitate Russian strategic weapons eliminations through the provision of financial assistance.

6. Under START II downloading rules, the three-warhead U.S. Minuteman III ICBM, the four-warhead Russian SS-17 ICBM, and 105 of the six-warhead SS-19 ICBMs will be able to be downloaded to a single warhead. The U.S. Peacekeeper ICBM and the Russian SS-18 heavy ICBM and SS-24 ICBM, each of which carry ten warheads, and the remaining SS-19 ICBMs must all be eliminated in accordance with START procedures.

7. To facilitate Russian ratification of the START II Treaty, the U.S. and Russia signed on September 16, 1997 a Protocol to the Treaty extending the time for implementation of the Treaty from January 1, 2003 to December 31, 2007 and the date by which the interim limitations and reductions must be carried out from December 5,

2001 to January 31, 2004. At the same time they exchanged letters codifying earlier commitments to deactivate by December 31, 2003, the U.S. and Russian strategic nuclear vehicles that will be eliminated under START II so as to realized the Treaty's security benefits as early as possible.

8. Chemical weapons, for example, were used in Ethiopia in the 1930s, in Manchuria in the 1940s and in Yemen in the 1960s. Chemical weapons attacks also were periodically used during the Iran-Iraq war and were used by Iraq against the Kurds in 1989.

9. The United States and Russia are the only two admitted holders of chemical weapons, other than the old or abandoned chemical weapons held by a few signatories, notably Germany.

10. Biological Weapons Convention Article 1 (1) and Article X.

Part II

Fundamentals of On-Site Inspection Regimes

Chapter 3

The Basic Structure of Modern On-Site Inspection Regimes

Although on-site inspection regimes are now used to verify an impressively broad, and steadily expanding, number of modern arms control agreements covering diverse weapons systems, the underlying structures of the on-site inspection regimes concluded since the mid-1980s have many similar basic features.

The template for such regimes was set by the 1987 INF Treaty (Intermediate-Range and Shorter-Range Nuclear Forces Treaty) which incorporated many elements from past agreements. As the last of the arms control treaties negotiated, signed, ratified, and partially implemented during the period of Cold War confrontation and competition,[1] the INF Treaty was the product of adversarial and protracted negotiations lasting just over six years. Although initially a bilateral U.S.-Soviet treaty, the United States closely coordinated its negotiating positions with its NATO allies, since the treaty involved military systems targeted on Europe, and its inspection regime would be implemented in the European INF basing countries as well as in the United States.

In addition, the INF Treaty's on-site inspection (OSI) provisions were negotiated in an atmosphere of mutual distrust. The Soviet Union was suspicious of reasons for the Reagan administration's military build-up and intentions,[2] which it saw as an effort to gain clear military superiority. The United States, on the other hand, was gripped by mounting concern—catalogued from 1984 on in annual reports to Congress—that the Soviet Union was systematically cheating on the legal and political arms control commitments it had made in the past. This concern was encapsulated in the new U.S. emphasis on "effective verification" with its insistence on tightly worded agreements containing tough on-site inspections regimes to supplement monitoring by national technical means (NTM). Indeed, even after the INF Treaty was signed, the United States continued its efforts to further clarify and strengthen the treaty's on-site inspection provisions and procedures.[3] The adversarial atmosphere in which the

INF Treaty was negotiated, the intense U.S. and allied scrutiny to which it was subjected during negotiations, and the demanding U.S. ratification process ensured a carefully crafted and implementable agreement that could be used as a tested model for the future.

THE BASIC MODEL

The verification regime in all modern arms control agreements with on-site inspection provisions is not limited to a single section of the treaty. Rather it is composed of many inter-related elements—sometimes referred to as a "web of constraints"—interwoven throughout the entire treaty text. The main elements of the modern verification regime, each of which is described in greater detail later in the chapter, are as follows:

● an explicit agreement that all signatories have the right to use their own national (or multinational) technical means of verification to confirm compliance.

● the inclusion of additional provisions, such as noninterference provisions, cooperative measures, definitions, counting and type rules, and notification provisions to further enhance the effectiveness of NTM and assist OSI monitoring.

● extensive data exchanges and notifications to provide accurate information for inspectors on the numbers, locations, and types of the weapons systems covered by the treaty.

● a complex series of inter-related on-site inspections designed to accomplish specific tasks, including verifying and tracking treaty-related data, witnessing the destruction or conversion of weapons systems, and helping confirm compliance with treaty provisions.

● a carefully defined system of on-site inspection procedures and timelines regulating the activities of inspectors and escorts and the use of inspection equipment.

● the establishment of formal treaty mechanisms to help improve implementation of the treaty, deal with ambiguities uncovered by the inspectors or NTM, and resolve compliance concerns.

USE OF NATIONAL TECHNICAL MEANS OF VERIFICATION

Historically, countries have always use national means, that is, measures primarily within their own control, including diplomacy, espionage, and other means of information gathering, to monitor treaty compliance. National *technical* means—the application of sophisticated monitoring technologies to verify compliance—is a subset of this activity. Although reliance on NTM for monitoring treaties is usually associated with the development of new monitoring technologies in the late 1950s, technical surveillance has earlier antecedents. For example, electronic collection of information has been used since the last century, and during World War II, it was developed to include the interception of military and diplomatic communications.[4]

Definition of NTM

Virtually all arms control agreements negotiated since the 1960s have relied on some type of technical monitoring for verification purposes. However, in an arms control context, the specific terminology "national technical means" was first used in the Strategic Arms Limitation Talks (SALT) Agreements in the 1970s.[5] Both the Treaty on the Limitations of Anti-Ballistic Missile Systems (ABM Treaty) and the SALT I Interim Agreement on Strategic Offensive Arms specify that "for the purpose of providing assurance of compliance with the provisions each Party shall use national technical means of verification at its disposal in a manner consistent with generally recognized principles of international law."[6]

Most subsequent arms control agreements contain similar language. The stipulation that NTM is to be used in a manner consistent with generally recognized principles of international law explicitly recognizes that, even in this nationally controlled area, nations may not violate internationally accepted norms. For example, they must respect the right of a state not to have its airspace illegally violated.

National technical means was defined in 1983 by the U.S. Department of State as "assets under national control for monitoring compliance with the provisions of arms control agreements. National technical means include photographic reconnaissance satellites, aircraft-based systems (i.e., radars and optical systems) as well as sea- and ground-based systems such as radars and antennas for collection telemetry."[7]

A Senate report on the Conventional Armed Forces in Europe (CFE) Treaty uses this definition and adds specificity by noting that NTM relies on signals intelligence, communications intelligence, electronics intelligence, radar intelligence, laser intelligence, infrared intelligence, and other intelligence gathering methods to provide monitoring information.[8] These technical monitoring systems supplement each other, and their simultaneous application creates an overlap that permits the cross-checking of data for accuracy.

Use of NTM for Arms Control Verification

National technical means are used for many different arms control verification purposes, for example, photo-reconnaissance cameras, carried aboard satellites, allow the monitoring of a large number of militarily significant areas such as missile silo fields, production facilities, and submarine bases, thus permitting close tracking of the military force developments affected by arms control agreements. Radars based on land, at sea, and on aircraft can verify compliance with treaty provisions related to qualitative improvements of ballistic missiles, such as limits on missile throw-weight, missile dimensions, and the number of re-entry vehicles carried. Radars based in space also can supplement optical reconnaissance systems in monitoring ground activities, especially during periods of heavy cloud cover. Electronic surveillance permits the monitoring of transmissions from various radiating sources, including military and civilian communications, test telemetry, and radars.

Telemetry from missiles undergoing flight testing can provide information on such factors as missile fuel consumption, accelerations, and re-entry vehicle performance and reveal design characteristics important to arms control. Above ground and underwater nuclear explosions can be identified with satellite infrared and x-ray sensors, world wide collection of radioactive fallout, and hydrophone acoustic arrays in the world's oceans, while underground nuclear tests can be identified and measured by a network of seismic monitors, thus permitting close monitoring of nuclear testing agreements. In addition, a wide variety of other advanced technologies too numerous and complex to discuss here are available to help judge compliance with arms control agreements.[9]

NTM capabilities are limited and expensive assets and are used for multiple national intelligence tasks in addition to their use for arms control verification. These include applications for general intelligence collection, to provide strategic warning, and to monitor global trouble spots of importance to national security interests. To avoid overtasking these valuable monitoring assets, the Senate Select Committee on Intelligence (SSCI), as early as the hearings for the INF Treaty, flagged the need for additional long-term U.S. investments in NTM to handle the evolving arms control tasks. [10]

Generally speaking, in the past information obtained through national technical means has been closely held and not shared broadly even with allies to protect sources and technologies. However, this now is changing somewhat as arms control treaties have become more multinational and the Cold War confrontation has receded. These factors, in particular, had led to a greater willingness in certain circumstances to share information obtained from national technical means with other countries that do not possess sophisticated collection capabilities of their own. In connection with U.N.-mandated on-site inspection activity in Iraq, for example, the International Atomic Energy Agency (IAEA) and the U.N. Special Commission on Iraq have received intelligence information from a number of member states to assist in identifying and destroying Iraq's weapons of mass destruction.[11] Reflecting the trend toward multinationalization, the CFE Treaty explicitly provides for monitoring both by national and multinational technical means, thus opening the way for the development and use of coordinated monitoring systems by international organizations, such as NATO.

TREATY PROVISIONS TO ENHANCE NTM

In addition to recognizing the use of NTM, all treaties with on-site inspection regimes contain at least some additional provisions designed specifically to enhance the effectiveness of NTM and inspection monitoring. These include provisions that prohibit interference with NTM; cooperative measures to enhance NTM monitoring of specific systems; definitions, counting, and type rules to help resolve potential ambiguities where certain details essential to arms control could not be identified by NTM monitoring; and certain types of notifications, such as those for weapons tests or some kinds of elimination or conversion, to permit the targeting of NTM capabilities for verification purposes.

Prohibition of Interference with NTM

The SALT treaties contained the first provisions against interference with NTM and these have been copied by subsequent arms control agreements. The INF and Strategic Arms Reduction (START) treaties, for example, contain a provision essentially identical to an article contained in the earlier ABM Treaty that stipulates that "neither Party shall interfere with national technical means of verification of the other Party."[12] This stipulation prohibits any party from destroying, blinding, jamming, or otherwise interfering with the NTM of another party, provided, as previously indicated, that such NTM is used in accordance with generally recognized principles of international law.

Several modern arms control agreements also contain additional paragraphs that prohibit the use of concealment measures that impede verification by NTM. For example, START provisions prohibit measures at test ranges that result in the concealment of intercontinental ballistic missiles (ICBMs), submarine-launched ballistic missiles (SLBMs), mobile launchers of ICBMs, or the association between ICBMs and SLBMs and their launchers during testing.[13] These restrictions on concealment measures permit better monitoring of testing programs to confirm that the capabilities in tested systems are consistent with treaty provisions and to associate an ICBM or SLBM with its launcher. START also prohibits efforts to conceal full access to telemetric information during missile flight tests and, with limited exceptions, specifically bans a variety of practices such as the use of encryption, jamming, narrow directional beaming, and encapsulation of telemetric information, all of which are further defined in the treaty's definition annex.[14]

However, treaty obligations not to use concealment measures that impede NTM generally do not apply to cover or concealment practices associated with normal training, maintenance and operations at designated bases or deployment areas, including the use of necessary environmental shelters to protect missiles and launchers from the elements.

Cooperative Measures to Enhance NTM

In addition to restrictions on concealment, modern arms control agreements with on-site inspection provisions contain several or all of the following types of cooperative measures to assist monitoring by NTM.

• *Specific Cooperative Measures* are contained in some treaties to enhance NTM verification. For example, the INF Treaty gave the United States the right, for three years after entry into force (EIF), to request cooperative measures at SS-25 bases that involved opening the roofs of launcher garages to display missiles on their launchers in the open and without using concealment measures.[15] This was designed to help U.S. NTM to confirm that treaty-prohibited intermediate-range mobile SS-20s were not deployed at bases for legal strategic mobile SS-25 ICBMs. In START, a major cooperative measure requires the broadcasting of test flight data—called telemetry—and the exchange of the telemetry tapes after the flight tests to assist monitoring of various quantitative and qualitative limits.[16]

• *Definitions* are also used in all modern arms control agreements to remove monitoring ambiguities. By providing mutually agreed precisely defined terminology, definitions ensure that the meaning of all critical terms in the agreement is clearly understood by all parties. The number of definitions can vary widely from treaty to treaty depending on the complexity of the agreement. The main text of the INF Agreement, for example, contains fifteen definitions, the Chemical Weapons Convention (CWC) twelve definitions, and the CFE Treaty twenty five definitions in their respective definition articles, while the highly complex START Treaty has an entire annex on terms and their definitions, which contains its own preamble and 124 paragraphs, each defining a term. In addition to definitions in the main treaty text, additional definitions usually are found in other treaty documents, particularly in the various inspection and verification protocols. The CFE Inspection Protocol, for example, contains definitions of twenty seven additional terms, two more than are contained in the definitions article (Article II) in the main treaty text.   The CWC's Verification Annex also contains twenty six additional definitions.[17]

• *Counting and Type Rules* essential to verification of the treaty also typically are contained in separate treaty sections. *Counting rules* in arms control agreements provide a formal and legally binding agreement by the signatories that specified items will be counted in a specific way. By way of illustration, a fundamental counting rule in the START Treaty, that serves as a foundation for subsequent counting rules, states that each deployed ICBM and its associated launcher is to be counted as one unit, that each deployed SLBM and its associated launcher is to be counted as one unit, and that each deployed heavy bomber is to be counted as one unit.[18] This means that when a party observes a deployed launcher of an ICBM or SLBM of the other party, the launcher is considered, for counting purposes, to contain a deployed ICBM or SLBM, even if the missile has been removed from the launcher. As another example, the CFE Treaty provides that all battle tanks, armored combat vehicles, artillery, combat aircraft and attack helicopters within the area of application are subject to that treaty's numerical limitations and other provisions, unless they meet explicitly enumerated exceptions.[19]

Table 3.1
Counting Rules: START I and START II

Category	START	START II
Deployed ICBM and associated launcher	1 unit	1 unit
Deployed SLBM and associated launcher	1 unit	1 unit
Deployed heavy bomber	1 unit	*Nuclear-capable:* – 1 unit *Reoriented:* – does not count against limits

Warheads attributed to ICBMs/SLBMs	Number specified in MOU
	
	Downloading rules:
	– Aggregate limits: 1250 total warheads; 500 warheads on all non-MM-III
	– Maximum downloading per ICBM/SLBM: 4 warheads
	– Scope:
	  – US: MM-III + 2 other types
	  – FSU: SS-N-18 + 2 other types
	– RV platform destruction required for MM-III and any ICBM/SLBM downloaded by more than 2 warheads
	– No co-location of downloaded and non-downloaded ICBM/SLBM of same type
		Number specified in MOU
		
		Downloading rules: all START rules apply, with the following exceptions:
		
		– No aggregate limits
		
		– No RV platform replacement requirement
		
		– 105 ICBMs may be downloaded by up to 5 warheads

Warheads attributed to heavy bombers	*Bombers equipped for long-range nuclear ALCMs:*
	– United States:
	  – first 150 bombers: 10 warheads
	  – > 150: number for which bomber is equipped
	– FSU:
	  – first 180 bombers: 8 warheads
	  – > 180: number for which bomber is equipped
	
	Bombers equipped for other nuclear armaments:
	– 1 warhead, regardless of actual loading
		All heavy bombers equipped for any type of nuclear armament:
		– Number of weapons for which bomber is actually equipped

Source: **DynMeridian, Alexandria, Virginia**

● *Type rules* are a formal and legally binding agreement that once a specified item has been counted in a certain way then all objects of that type will be counted in that same way. For example, the difficulty of distinguishing a multiple-warhead from a single-warhead missile by NTM could be solved by counting any missile of a type that has been tested with multiple warheads as one which has multiple warheads, making it irrelevant whether a particular weapon has them or not. In addition, if a weapons system has the general characteristics and appearance of a banned weapon, it is considered to be such a weapon even though shades of difference may exist. In the parlance of arms control negotiators, this is expressed by the phrase "if it quacks like a duck and walks like a duck, it is a duck."

Figure 3.1
Illustrative Type Rule

If it quacks like a duck and walks like a duck...

It's a duck.

• *Notifications*, contained in the notification regimes of modern arms control agreements, also are designed to facilitate the understanding of certain activities as they are monitored by NTM, in addition to assisting on-site inspection activities. For example, there are specific notifications connected with the cooperative measures to enhance NTM verification, with testing of treaty-limited weapons to permit monitoring of telemetry, and with potentially ambiguous activities such as transits, relocations of treaty-limited items, and operational dispersals. These notifications both permit the targeting of NTM assets and assist NTM analysts to interpret suspect activities.

DATA EXCHANGES AND NOTIFICATIONS

General Data Requirements

All modern on-site inspection regimes contain comprehensive provisions designed to identify the numbers, locations, and technical characteristics of all weapons systems and facilities covered by the treaty. Not all signatories may have sophisticated NTM, and the NTM even of the most advanced countries could not be expected to accurately provide data on all of the weapons systems of the other signatories. Accordingly, modern arms control agreements make each party to the treaty responsible for providing its own data and ensuring its accuracy and completeness. Initial data may be required either before treaty signature or upon entry into force of the treaty and is subjected to periodic updating according to provisions that are particular to each agreement. This data then is confirmed by the other party or parties initially by baseline inspections held shortly after EIF, by data update inspections thereafter, and by other elements of the on-site inspection regime.

Data exchanges provide a continuous, evolving, and, in some cases, increasingly extensive data base on the military capabilities of the parties. The essential treaty data usually is contained in a separate section of the treaty—referred to by various terminology, such as the Memorandum of Understanding (MOU) on Data (INF Treaty), the MOU on the Establishment of the Data Base (START I), and the Protocol on Notification and Exchange of Information (CFE). These sections, typically among the most extensive in the treaty, provide the central registry of the data required for effective verification of the agreement. Because some conventional military equipment can be configured for several purposes, the CFE Treaty also has provisions for dealing with "look alikes," which may not be subject to the numerical limitations for that category of equipment.[20]

The information called for in the data annexes varies from treaty to treaty according to the weapons systems to be reduced, limited, or controlled. The INF Treaty lists all INF missiles (including training missiles), launchers and associated support structures and equipment covered by the treaty and their locations. The much more complex START I Treaty includes data on ICBM launchers, SLBM launchers, heavy bombers, intercontinental ballistic missiles, submarine-launched ballistic missiles, long-range nuclear ALCMs, fixed structures for mobile launchers of ICBMs, support equipment, and related facilities. The CFE Treaty provides for an extensive and detailed information exchange by each of the signatories on its forces located in the area of application, including details on the numbers, types, and locations of treaty-limited equipment, and similar information on equipment in the area subject to, but not limited by, the treaty, such as combat support helicopters. The data requirements of the Chemical Weapons Convention, which covers both military and civilian facilities, are so extensive that the agreement, as signed, contains no MOU on data. Instead, the CWC requires that this information be provided separately by each country through its national authority. Separate articles (CWC Article VI and Parts VI-IX) of the CWC Verification Annex set forth the various requirements for declarations of chemicals and chemical facilities.

Site-Specific Data Requirements

All on-site inspection regimes also require the provision of additional site-specific data designed to facilitate the inspection process, such as site diagrams for each facility at which baseline data inspections, data update inspections, and additional specialized inspections are to be held. Site diagrams must be drawn to a specified scale and must include the boundaries of the facility, road and rail entrances and exits, and other detailed facility reference points. For START heavy bomber bases, for example, the site diagrams include depictions of runways, taxiways, parking areas, revetments, shelters, hangers, and other locations where heavy bombers are parked or maintained.

Validation of Technical Data

To assist in validating the technical data provided by each party on specific weapons systems in data annexes, modern OSI regimes often provide for data validation inspections during the baseline period. The pioneering INF Treaty initially had no provisions for data validation inspections, but the necessity to confirm technical details as a means of accurately identifying the missiles systems covered by the treaty quickly became apparent. As a result, such inspections were agreed upon in technical talks in the period between the signing of the INF Treaty and its entry into force. Since it was discovered that the weights and measurements of individual missiles could vary somewhat from the values stated in the treaty's MOU on Data as a result of measurement errors and differences in factory tolerances, both sides agreed to accept technical data measurements within a 3 percent tolerance of the values contained in the MOU. Given the central importance in the INF Treaty of the SS-20 missile system, particularly detailed procedures were worked out to confirm the technical data related to that missile.

Building on the INF Treaty experience, most subsequent arms control treaties have contained specific provisions within the treaty text for special technical or exhibition inspections to confirm the technical data provided by each side on equipment subject to the treaty. These generally contain the 3 percent rule agreed upon for INF missile systems.

Data-Related Notifications

To help track data, on-site inspection regimes contain an extensive array of notification requirements. These often are grouped in a separate section or protocol of the agreement, although they may also be contained in individual provisions throughout the treaty text. Together with the data exchanges, they constitute a core element of the verification regime.

As a rule, modern arms control agreements require that any changes in the original data base be notified. Each party also must notify other signatories of the movement of items subject to locational restrictions and provide basic notifications essential to the inspection process, such as the scheduled dates of elimination and conversion activities and of inspections. A wide variety of treaty-specific notifications also are required. The START Treaty, for example, requires notifications for such specialized activities as certain visits and operations by heavy bombers; departures and returns of deployed rail-mobile test launchers and deployed mobile launchers; exercise and operational dispersals; and on new types of ICBMs, SLBMs, and heavy bombers. The wide-ranging information and notification exchanges required by modern on-site inspection regimes are important adjuncts to verification and constitute major stabilizing measures in and of themselves.

The United States and countries of the former Soviet Union (FSU) receive and transmit all arms control notifications through a central body in each country—for the U.S. and Russia, the Nuclear Risk Reduction Center. Centralized data processing bodies also have been established at NATO, in Vienna, and in the Hague to act as central clearing houses for handling the notifications required by multinational arms control agreements.

Confirmation of the accuracy of the data provided by individual parties to a treaty is at the heart of compliance, and data discrepancies have been a troublesome issue. Data anomalies have been frequently uncovered during inspections and have been found in the implementation of all treaties with on-site inspection regimes. These discrepancies do not necessarily reflect cheating. Most often they are attributable to other factors, including a lack of uniform preparation of required data such as site diagrams, carelessness in preparing and maintaining military data, and the general inability of most countries to provide a precise accounting of all of their treaty-accountable military assets. Indeed, the difficulty of identifying and tracking military weapons, including such major items as missiles, over their entire life cycles, with accountability for factory and operational rejects and discarded systems, has been a problem for all parties to arms control agreements. Major upheavals, such the dissolution of the Soviet Union and the Warsaw Pact, also can confuse and complicate military record keeping and accountability.

A REGIME OF ON-SITE INSPECTIONS

Most arms control agreements concluded since the INF Treaty have contained a comprehensive regime of on-site inspections designed to carry out a number of general tasks, such as the verification of data, confirmation of eliminations and conversions, and monitoring of overall compliance. The INF and START treaties also provide for continuous monitoring of the portals and perimeter of missile productions facilities in the United States, Russia, and Ukraine to confirm that banned missiles are not been produced at those facilities, although the Ukraine portal has been deactivated.

In general, these on-site inspection regimes have become increasingly multinational in make-up since the disintegration of the former Soviet Union. Only a few agreements, notably the Threshold Test Ban Treaty, the Peaceful Nuclear Explosions Treaty, some chemical weapons agreements, the ABM Treaty, and START II, still remain strictly bilateral U.S.-Russian agreements. In addition, some on-site inspection provisions, especially those for challenge-type inspections, have become so complex and potentially intrusive as to raise serious new political, commercial and legal issues and thus new questions about their relative benefit to cost ratios. Because of their complexity and variety, the various categories and types of on-site inspection that have been agreed to date, including portal monitoring, and the issues involved in their implementation are discussed in subsequent chapters.

DEFINED INSPECTION PROCEDURES AND TIMELINES

All modern arms control agreements with on-site inspection provisions also contain a separate section—an inspection annex or protocol—which lays out, carefully delineates, and regulates the procedures for the various types of on-site inspection and for portal monitoring. The annex or protocol sets out general obligations, defines the legal status of inspection personnel, describes the notifications required for inspection and monitoring activities, and sets out arrangements for air transportation. It also establishes maximum timeframes within which the inspections must occur and describes the activities that can be carried out at each stage of the inspection, beginning with arrival at the point of entry and continuing through the conduct of the inspection and continuous monitoring activities. Finally, it regulates preparation of the final inspection reports and sequential (i.e., follow-up) inspections.

While the provisions contained in the inspection annexes or protocols vary significantly from treaty to treaty, in general they have a similar structure and contain a large number of common elements. These are described in detail in the following chapter.

FORMAL COMPLIANCE MECHANISMS

Although modern arms control agreements are highly detailed, they seldom, if ever, define all issues affecting the inspection regime. Often treaty texts are rushed to conclusion to meet politically set signing deadlines at a summit or multinational conference, leaving many technical details to be worked out in follow-up talks.

As a case in point, the INF Treaty, as signed at the Washington D.C. Summit in December 1987, specifies the types of equipment to be used during inspections but contains no provisions on their "use and characteristics" or on a host of other administrative, procedural, and technical details. These initially were dealt with in operational talks that resulted in many precedent-setting agreements on practical implementation matters.[21] At the same time, the INF technical talks revealed continuing differences in approach between the U.S. side, which was intent on exercising the full range of inspection rights under the treaty, and the Soviet side, which was more intent on finding implementation solutions that were simple to implement and minimized costs. As a result of the talks, some issues considered settled during the negotiations had to be returned to higher political levels for further discussion and resolution.[22] The remaining issues were referred, after EIF, to the INF Treaty's newly formed Special Verification Commission (SVC) for further discussion. Many eventually were codified in a separate Memorandum of Agreement on Implementation of the Agreement's Verification provisions concluded by the SVC in December 1989.

With minor exceptions, discussions of technical and operational inspection and escort procedures in all subsequent arms control agreements have been held in the formal implementation and compliance bodies expressly established for that purpose, such as the START Joint Compliance and Inspection Commission (JCIC) and the CFE Treaty's Joint Consultative Group (JCG). These bodies meet either on an established schedule or as required to deal with specific inspection issues. The number of issues raised in them has been surprisingly extensive in content. Indeed, for the most part, these bodies have operated on a nearly continuous basis—allowing for the normal breaks for consultations in capitals—thus underlining the extent to which arms control agreements are "living documents," requiring constant interpretation and fine tuning to ensure continuing smooth operation.

In the United States, the Arms Control and Disarmament Agency, now being integrated into the U.S. Department of State, has generally led the delegation to the meetings of these bodies and chaired the interagency support groups established to develop and coordinate policy issues involving them. To reflect the blend of policy and operational issues involved in such technical issues, discussions in these fora typically are led by policy experts, supported by technical personnel from the on-site inspection agencies to provide operational expertise. A brief description of the bodies established by the various arms control treaties to ensure implementation and compliance during on-site inspections is contained in Appendix 1 to this study.

NOTES

1. The INF Treaty was signed on December 8, 1987. All subsequent arms control agreements have been concluded and implemented under the radically changed geopolitical conditions caused by the dissolution of the Warsaw Pact and of the Soviet Union. The next arms control treaties to be concluded after the INF Treaty were the expanded verification protocols for the Threshold Test Ban Treaty and Peaceful Nuclear Explosions Treaty, which were concluded in June 1990 and ratified in October 1990, a year after the Warsaw Pact had unraveled in Eastern Europe and the same month as the reunification of Germany.

2. This was particularly true of the Reagan administration's Strategic Defense Initiative, which the Soviet Union viewed as an effort to build a unilateral shield against missile attacks. In the Soviet view, this would have altered the strategic balance by giving the U.S. a sword and shield, while the U.S.S.R. possessed only the sword.

3. Numerous INF implementation issues required further clarification in follow-up technical talks after signature and prior to entry into force of the agreement (EIF) and, after EIF, in the treaty's implementation and compliance body—the Special Verification Commission. For details, see George Rueckert, *Global Double Zero: The INF Treaty from Its Origins to Implementation* (Westport, CT: Greenwood Press, 1993), pp. 99–107.

4. William Colby, "The Intelligence Process" in Tsipis et al. p. 9.

5. Edward Lacey, "A United States Perspective on Bilateral Verification," *Disarmament* 14, no. 2, (1991): p. 60.

6. Article XII of the ABM Treaty and Article V of the SALT Interim Agreement.

7. U.S. House of Representatives, Committee on Foreign Relations, *Report, Together with Additional Views, on the CFE Treaty*, Executive Report 102-22 (Washington, D.C.: U.S. Government Printing Office, November 1991), p. 43.

8. Ibid. p. 43.

9. For a more detailed, if already somewhat dated, general exposition of these and other NTM technologies, see Arms Control Association, *Arms Control and National Security: An Introduction* (Washington D.C.: Arms Control Association, 1989), pp. 142–143.

10. The SSCI attached an informal understanding to the INF Treaty to improve NTM capabilities through the launching of additional imagery satellites and urged the intelligence community to continue to make investments helpful in verifying further arms control agreements, especially START.

11. See, for example, Maurizio Ziffero, "Iraq and UN Security Council Resolution 687: The Role of the IAEA and Lessons To Be Learned." in *New Horizons and Challenges in Arms Control and Verification*, ed. James Brown (Amsterdam: VU University Press, 1994) p. 224

12. ABM Treaty, Article XII, Paragraph 2; INF Treaty Article VII, Paragraph 2(a); START Treaty Article IX, Paragraph 2.

13. START Treaty Article IX, Paragraph 3.

14. START Treaty, Article X, Paragraph 2.

15. INF Treaty Article XII, Paragraph 3.

16. START Treaty, Article X, Paragraphs 4 and 5.

17. Additional definitions are found in the CWC Verification Annex, Part I, Article X, paragraph 1 and in Part IV (a), paragraph 12.

18. START Treaty, Article III, Paragraph 1.

19. The enumerated military equipment is exempted from the counting rules under the CFE Agreement if (a) it is in the process of manufacture, including manufacturing-related testing; (b) it is used exclusively for the purposes of research and development; (c) it belongs to historical collections; (d) it is awaiting disposal, having been decommissioned from service in accordance with treaty provisions; (e) it is awaiting, or being refurbished for, export or re-export and temporarily retained within the area of application and meets certain other conditions; (f) it is, in the case of armored personnel carriers, armored infantry fighting vehicles, heavy armament combat vehicles, or multi-purpose attack helicopters, held by organizations designed and structured to perform in peacetime international security functions; or (g) it is in transit through the areas of application from an area of application outside the treaty area to a final destination outside the treaty area for no longer than seven days.

20. Chemical Weapons Convention, Article II, Paragraph 1, Subparagraph S, for example, defines "armored personnel carrier look alike" and "armored infantry fighting vehicle look alike" as an armored vehicle based on the same chassis as, and externally similar to, an armored personnel carrier or armored infantry fighting vehicle, respectively, which does not have a cannon or gun of twenty millimeters calibre or greater and which has been constructed or modified in such a way as not to permit the transportation of a combat infantry squad. The definition further provides that, taking into account the provisions of the Geneva Convention that confer a special status on ambulances, armored personnel carrier ambulances shall not be deemed armored combat vehicles or armored personnel carrier look alikes.

21. INF operational issues initially were dealt with in three rounds of technical talks, held in Moscow, Washington, and Vienna in spring 1988, which resulted in many agreements on the handling of aircraft and air crews, on inspection and escort operations, and on some inspection equipment.

22. Rueckert, *Global Double Zero.*, pp. 103.

Chapter 4

Basic On-Site Inspection Procedures

All on-site inspection regimes include provisions that define the rights and obligations of inspectors and of the inspected party. These are usually found in a separate inspection protocol or verification annex of the agreement. They lay out general obligations and conditions and define acceptable procedures, generally at each stage of the inspection from pre-inspection periods through conduct of the inspection and preparation of the final inspection report. Most on-site inspection (OSI) regimes contain basic procedures along the lines laid out in this chapter, with appropriate variations to reflect the specific requirements of each treaty.

GENERAL OBLIGATIONS

Treaties usually explicitly establish the overarching principle that each signatory has an obligation to facilitate the conduct of inspections. This includes a commitment not to hinder or interfere with inspection activity that is analogous in purpose to the treaty prohibitions against interference with national technical means (NTM). Often this section refers to other overarching responsibilities. For example, in the Intermediate-Range Nuclear Forces (INF) Treaty, the general obligations section refers to commitments that permit inspections in the countries that contained treaty-limited items (Basing Countries) but were not signatories of that bilateral U.S.-Soviet treaty.

LEGAL STATUS OF INSPECTORS

Agreed Inspection Lists

As a rule, only specifically designated personnel—those on agreed lists of inspectors, (portal) monitors, and aircrew members—may conduct inspection-related activities. Inspection personnel must be nationals of the listing country. For inspectors and monitors, these authorizing lists are of sufficient size to contain a pool to select from, but small enough for the inspected party or parties to easily manage background checks and identification tasks. Aircrew lists, due to the frequent turnover of such personnel, usually are not limited in size. Personnel lists usually are exchanged immediately after entry into force (EIF) of the agreement, although some treaties (e.g., the Strategic Arms Reduction Treaty (START)) provided for early exchanges of lists. All lists of designated personnel are updated periodically to account for normal personnel rotation. The multinational Treaty on Conventional Forces in Europe (CFE) provides that once on such a designated list, an inspector is eligible to participate on any state party's inspection team, not just on the team of the listing country. This facilitates the formation of multinational inspection teams.

The lists permit some control over possibly unacceptable personnel and expedite administrative processing of inspection staff before and during the inspection. Within a limited period after personnel are named on the lists, another party to the agreement generally may reject, and remove from the list, a designated person perfunctorily or for cause. "Cause" usually means indictment for, or conviction of, a criminal offense or previous expulsion by the inspected party.[1] In practice, rejections of inspection-related personnel have been relatively rare, although, especially during the period of the Cold War, instances did occur of personnel being rejected and removed from the inspection lists.[2] In the case of some multinational treaties, such as the Chemical Weapons Convention (CWC), the rejection of an inspector by one country does not prohibit the inspector from participating in inspections in other countries that have accepted the inspector. All approved personnel who require visas in accordance with the laws of the inspected country[3] are provided special visas—often two-year visas permitting multiple entry and exit—which, however, must be used only for travel in accordance with the treaty.

Privileges and Immunities

To enable inspection personnel to carry out their activities freely and in confidence, all arms control agreements apply or amplify the provisions of the Vienna Convention on Diplomatic Relations (paragraph 7), which provide personal inviolability to inspection personnel (including observers), their work and living spaces, and their papers. They are subject to routine passport control, agricultural inspections, and export-import laws and regulations when they enter and leave the country but are exempted from host country duties and taxes.

During the early phases of the INF Agreement, a controversy arose over an effort by Soviet personnel to use the basement areas in the housing units erected for the U.S. portal monitors in Votkinsk. The United States objected that this violated inspector immunity, threatened retaliation, and the issue was dropped. As a result of this experience, during the START negotiations, an explicit provision was added to the treaty making clear that attics and basements adjacent to office and living spaces are inherently part of these spaces and thus inviolable. However, operations centers used by inspectors—such as those at a portal monitoring site—are not inviolable. Since the equipment in such centers could be clandestinely configured, after inspection at the border, to assemble data not related to treaty implementation (e.g., intelligence information), the host country has the right to be escorted into such areas whenever it so requests. The host country also has the right to examine the personal baggage—but not papers—of inspectors or monitors during travel to confirm that inspectors are not carrying unauthorized equipment.

For their part, inspectors, monitors, and aircrew must obey the laws and regulations of the state on whose territory the inspection is carried out and refrain from interference in its internal affairs. Violators are subject to immediate removal from inspection activity and deletion from inspection lists.

INSPECTION NOTIFICATIONS, TIMELINES, AND QUOTAS

Notifications

All on-site inspection regimes contain many notifications exclusively connected with implementation of the inspection and monitoring provisions. Some are connected with the sequence of events associated with an inspection, such as initial notification of the intent to inspect or notification by the inspection team at the point of entry (POE) of the specific site it intends to inspect. Other notifications deal exclusively with the administrative aspects of inspections, such as notifications of the diplomatic clearance numbers for aircraft. Such inspection-related notifications usually are contained in the inspection protocol, rather than in a separate notifications annex, for ease of use by those responsible for implementing the inspection provisions.

A series of special notifications apply to perimeter portal monitoring and are discussed in chapter 8. There are also usually separate notifications for the rotation of inspectors and monitors at sites where extended stays are required and for any sequential inspection by teams at such sites. Multinational notifications, such as those for CFE inspections, also contain information on the language to be used by the inspection team and in the inspection report. Like all arms control notifications, inspection-related notifications are transmitted through the Nuclear Risk Reduction Centers or similar centralized notification bodies designated in the agreement, and their receipt is acknowledged.

Figure 4.1
START Notification Format

```
START FORMAT 116

REFERENCE:  INSPECTION PROTOCOL SECTION III PARAGRAPH 3
--------------------------------------------------------------------


SUBJECT:   NOTIFICATION OF INTENTION TO CONDUCT INSPECTION PURSUANT
           TO PARAGRAPH 2, 3, 4, 5, 6, 7, OR 10 OF ARTICLE XI OF THE
           TREATY

1.  ANC  /  STR         /116

2.  REFERENCES:  A)           B)           C)           D)

3.  CONTENT:

    A)  POINT OF ENTRY: [ response ]

    B)  DATE AND ESTIMATED TIME OF ARRIVAL AT
        POINT OF ENTRY:  DD-MMM-YYYY   HH:MM

    C)  DATE AND TIME FOR THE DESIGNATION OF THE INSPECTION
        SITE AND TYPE OF INSPECTION: DD-MMM-YYYY   HH:MM

                  LAST, FIRST, PATRONYMIC              PASSPORT
                     OR MIDDLE NAME                     NUMBER

    D)  NAME OF INSPECTORS:
        1)  [ response ]                            [ response ]
        2)  [ response ]                            [ response ]


    E)  NAME OF AIRCREW MEMBERS:
        1)  [ response ]                            [ response ]
        2)  [ response ]                            [ response ]

    F)  INSPECTION TEAM CONSISTS OF [ response ] MALE AND
        [response] FEMALE INSPECTORS

4.  REMARKS:

5.  END OF ANC  /  STR        /116
```

Source: **U.S. Nuclear Risk Reduction Center, Department of State, Washington, D.C.**

Inspection Timelines

Generally speaking, there are two basic types of inspection: "short notice" inspections in which the speed of arrival of the inspection team at the inspectable site is an important aspect of the verification process (e.g., baseline, short-notice, suspect-site, and challenge inspections); and "scheduled" inspections where speed in reaching the inspectable site is not essential for verification purposes (e.g., conversion or elimination inspections, close-out inspections or exhibitions). The timing and sequence of notifications for inspections within the "short-notice" and for inspections within the "scheduled" categories, respectively, is similar.

The "Short-Notice" Timeline

For "short-notice" inspections, initial notification of an inspection is generally provided only far enough in advance (e.g., sixteen hours) to permit efficient processing of the inspection team by the host country upon its arrival. The notification provides basic information on the arrival time, arrival point (point of entry) in the country to be inspected and on the inspectors and aircrew. It also includes a statement of when, after arrival at the point of entry, the inspection team will reveal the type of inspection to be conducted and the target site. The actual inspection site is designated only after arrival of the inspectors in the country in order to maintain an element of surprise and complicate removal of any illegal items from the site.

Inspectors then must be transported to the named site within a designated short timeframe (e.g., nine hours) after its location is identified. A reasonable amount of time usually is allowed for completion of the inspection (e.g., twenty-four hours), with a proviso that more inspection time (e.g., eight hours) may be permitted if mutually agreed to by the inspection team and the host country escorts. The designation of a specific period within which the inspection must be completed is designed to permit sufficient time for the inspection, including clarification of any ambiguities that may be identified during the inspection process, while restricting opportunities for non–treaty-related information gathering by the inspection team.

Pre-inspection movement restrictions—which are observable by NTM—may be imposed on the site shortly (e.g., one hour) after the inspectable site has been named to ensure that treaty-related items are not moved out of the site. These restrictions remain in effect until the inspection team has arrived at the site and the pre-inspection briefing by the host country, which occurs shortly after arrival at the inspectable site, has been completed and the inspection team deployed. After the inspection is complete, inspectors usually have a set period (several hours) to complete the inspection report and review it with the host country escorts. If there is to be a sequential (follow-up) inspection, this generally is announced after the inspection report has been completed. The host country then has a reasonable (sometimes open-ended) period to transport the inspection team to the next inspection site. There are some variations to this model to accommodate specific circumstances. For example, in the START Treaty there are additional time allowances to permit mobile intercontinental ballistic missiles and certain types of bombers to return to base.

Figure 4.2
INF Short-Notice Inspection Timeline

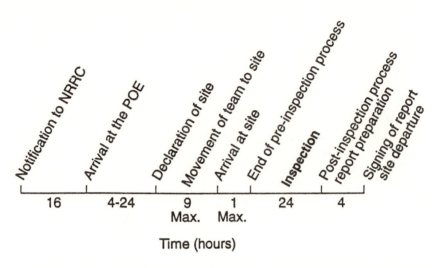

The "Scheduled Site" Timeline

For "scheduled" types of inspection, the notification of arrival of the inspection team is provided further in advance—e.g., seventy two hours prior to arrival—since the element of surprise is not relevant. Unlike short-notice inspections, both the inspection site and the type of inspection are specified in the initial notification, rather than after arrival of the inspection team in the country. A more leisurely time frame is permitted for the transportation of inspectors to the site and the length inspectors remain at the site is related to the activity performed, such as completion of the elimination or conversion process.

Inspection Quotas

Arms control treaties often establish quotas (limits) on the overall number of short-notice inspections that can held in a given time frame, usually a year. Quotas serve three basic purposes. They permit each country to carry out a sufficient number of inspections each year to confirm compliance. They enable the host country to better manage implementation of their obligations to rapidly process the inspection team and transport it to the inspectable site. And they are designed to reduce the temptation to misuse inspections, for example, by scheduling repeated inspections to a single country or base for harassment purposes.

Primarily to permit orderly management, both the INF and START treaties limit the number of inspections that can be carried out during the intensive initial baseline inspection period to confirm data to ten at one time. Another START provision imposes a limit of fifteen data update inspections annually with no more than two at any one facility each year. Some treaties have descending quotas to permit more inspections during especially sensitive periods. For example, the INF Treaty, which has a thirteen year time frame for inspections, established a quota of twenty short-notice inspections per year in the first three years of the treaty during which all INF missile systems had to be destroyed, fifteen annually during the next five years to confirm compliance, and ten annually in the final five-year period. The CFE Treaty bases the quota of inspections that each country must accept on the number of units or locations holding treaty-limited equipment that it possesses. The number of International Atomic Energy Agency and CWC inspections at a facility are based on the sensitivity of the facility for potential violations.

In the case of treaties involving a number of countries, there may also be quotas on the number of inspections that can be held in any one country to reduce the use of inspections for harrasement (or punishment) by one country of another. For example, the INF Treaty stipulates that no more than one-half of the short-notice inspections permitted annually can be held on the territory of any one Basing Country—a provision designed to reduce Soviet retaliation against West Germany for agreeing to the stationing of U.S. INF weapons on its soil. Similarly, the CFE Treaty provides that no country is required to receive more than one inspection team conducting a declared site or challenge inspection at any one time—a provision designed both for orderly management and to prevent harrassment.

ENTRY POINT PROCEDURES AND TRAVEL CONTROLS

As another means of assisting orderly administrative handling and control of inspectors and aircrew by the host country, on-site inspection regimes permit entry into the inspected country only at predetermined points of entry (POEs), sometimes called points of entry/exit,[4] which are listed in treaty documents for each country. For example, for the United States, arms control inspectors for the INF and START treaties must enter at Dulles National Airport, Washington, D.C., or at Travis Air Force Base, San Francisco. For the former Soviet Union, the designated POEs for INF and START inspections are Moscow and Ulan Ude (Siberia) for Russia, Minsk for Belarus, Kiev for Ukraine, and Alma Ati for Kazakstan. For CFE, additional POEs have been designated in the other republics of the former Soviet Union that fall within the CFE Treaty's area of application. Normally, access to each inspectable site or facility may be made only through the POE designated for that site in the treaty. As an exception, the CFE Treaty permits inspectors to "chase" treaty-limited equipment that has been moved from an area covered by one POE to that covered by another POE to confirm its movement.

Treaties also generally list the types of aircraft that can be used by inspectors, including commercial aircraft, which are being used with increasing frequency, and, as applicable, the number of aircrew allowed. There also may be specialized aircraft provisions for unusual types of inspections, such as the START inspections connected with operational dispersements, or for flights involving unusually heavy cargo shipments, such as those connected with portal monitoring or other technical monitoring operations. In addition, treaty provisions normally cover the servicing of aircraft at POEs and the allocation of costs for such services.

ALLOWABLE PROCEDURES DURING INSPECTIONS

The activities of both sides are carefully regulated during the inspection process from the time the inspection team arrives in the country until its departure to ensure that the treaty's inspection objectives are achieved in an orderly and controlled manner. Specific provisions spell out the duties of host country escorts and of inspectors, monitors, and aircrew members; processing procedures at the POEs; the essentials of designating inspectable sites and transporting inspectors to them; the rules of conducting regular and sequential inspections; and the preparation of inspection reports.

Procedures Upon Arrival at the Point of Entry

As a rule, a host country (often called "in-country") escort team—which usually consists of several individuals—meets the inspectors or monitors and aircrew when they arrive at the POE and accompanies and assists them throughout their stay in the country. The escort team may be joined at the inspectable site by representatives of the inspected facility to advise it on local conditions that may affect the inspection. Portal monitors usually also are accompanied by escorts throughout their more prolonged stay, but the host country is not obligated to provide such accompaniment on a continuous basis, for example, during normal monitoring operations at the portal site.

Some on-site inspection regimes (e.g., INF and START) also permit diplomatic personnel from the inspected country's embassy or consulate to meet inspectors and aircrew upon arrival at the POE and to assist them in resolution of any processing issues that may arise. However, diplomatic personnel are not allowed to accompany inspection or monitoring personnel outside the POE. The CFE Treaty permits a third country that has a structure or premise at a site designated for inspection to provide a liaison officer to assist the host country escort team. This provision ensures that no inspection of a third country facility occurs without that country's knowledge and consent.

To permit easier control and identification of inspectors and monitors, on-site inspection teams generally are limited in size, and inspectors are required to wear unique identification badges. Some agreements (e.g., INF and START) require inspectors to wear civilian clothing during their in-country stay, which minimizes the possibility that some inspectors will be treated differently from others based on military rank; other treaties (e.g., CFE) have no such restrictions. CFE also permits multinational inspection teams made up of personnel from several different countries, provided that only a single country has overall responsibility for conduct of the inspection.

Reflecting their diplomatic status, inspectors and monitors are exempted from customs duties and must be expeditiously processed by host country officials at the POE. However, since inspection equipment and supplies in some cases could be configured to obtain non–treaty-related (i.e., intelligence) information, these items are subject to examination by host country officials at the POE or inspection site. Such an examination is carried out, in the presence of the entering inspectors or monitors, each time equipment and supplies are brought into the country, regardless of whether they are brought in with the inspectors or by special cargo flights. Any item that does not meet treaty standards can be impounded by the host country at the examining site and stored, under dual control of the host country and inspection team, until departure of the team from the country. Should there be a dispute over the functioning of equipment and supplies that cannot be resolved at the examining site, the matter most likely be referred to the implementation and compliance body for the treaty concerned for further discussion, although, if the violation were serious, it could be handled through diplomatic channels.

As noted, for "short-notice" inspections, the location and type of inspection to be held must be announced within the notified designated period of time after arrival at the POE. Some agreements, such as the START Treaty, permit the host country escort to inform the inspection team if a facility selected for an inspection has few or no items of inspection present. The team then can choose either to carry out the inspection, select a different type of inspection and site associated with the same POE, or cancel the inspection without penalty.

Treaties also usually specify, either in the treaty text or in subsidiary agreements worked out in their implementation and compliance bodies, the services (e.g., food, lodging, and transportation) that the host country is to provide to the inspectors or monitors and how the costs for these are to be allocated. As a rule, the inspected party pays for all in-country services connected with inspections. There is a tacit assumption that, over time, the services provided by each government will be in rough balance. Continuous monitoring activities are an exception to this rule. Since they involve the erection of complicated infrastructure and are expensive to operate, not all affected parties may want to exercise their portal monitoring rights equally. Accordingly, the inspecting party, not the host country, pays almost all in-country costs associated with such activity.

As a rule, OSI provisions also contain some procedures for regulating activities of the mass media. Generally inspectors and monitors may not disclose information obtained during their activities unless permitted to do so by their governments, which normally treat inspection and monitoring activities as confidential. The host country may provide an opportunity for the mass media to photograph and televise the arrival and departure of inspection teams, but both parties usually must agree in advance, typically through diplomatic channels, to personal interviews. Representatives of the mass media are not permitted to interfere with inspection or monitoring activities nor to accompany inspectors or monitors while they are carrying out their official functions. These restrictions are designed to prevent the sensationalizing of any anomalies that may be found during the course of an inspection and to give the parties a chance to seek to resolve problems in the established manner and fora without haste or undue politicization.

RULES FOR THE CONDUCT OF INSPECTIONS AND MONITORING

All modern treaties contain rules governing the behavior of inspectors and monitors and their host country escorts while performing their duties. These include setting the time for transporting inspectors to the site, the right of the inspectors to obtain all vital data on the site at the time of their arrival, conduct of the inspection according to set rules, establishment of size thresholds for inspection and monitoring, establishment of rules for use of inspection equipment, and procedures for the recording of data and handling of ambiguities.

Transportation to the Site

The host country controls the route and means of travel of inspectors within its territory, but it must transport them to the designated site within specific timelines. While these timelines vary somewhat, as we have noted, they are generally similar in structure for all "short-notice" inspections—inspectors must be transported to the site within a specified early period after the inspectable site has been designated at the POE. Often a somewhat longer or less clearly defined period is allowed for the transport of inspectors from an initial inspectable site to a follow-up inspection from that site in the same country, taking into account that the site may not have the same transportation capabilities at its disposal as the POE. During the period from announcement of the inspected site until the inspection team arrives, treaties usually impose restrictions on the movement of treaty-limited items or of vehicles large enough to contain such items from the site. Compliance with these movement restriction then can be monitored by the NTM of the inspecting party.

An inspection can be canceled if it cannot be carried out due to circumstances brought about by *force majeure*. This term generally is understood to mean a superior or irresistible force beyond the control of a state party that was unforeseeable and could not be avoided by the exercise of due care. It could include, for example, extreme weather conditions, earthquakes and landslides, epidemics, sudden deaths or catastrophic illnesses, strikes and lockouts, riots and civil commotions, or deliberate interference by a third party, such as a guerilla group or insurrectionists. An inspection also can be canceled if more than the designated time is used to transport inspectors to the inspectable site or if *force majeure* requires the removal from an inspection site of any item subject to pre-inspection restrictions. An example of the latter would be if a severe storm forced departure of a ballistic missile submarine from port. In all cases, if an inspection is canceled it does not count against the appropriate inspection quotas.

The Right to Vital Data

The items for which inspectors or monitors are allowed to search during specific types of inspection and at specific facilities are listed in each treaty. The permissible inspection area at a site generally is established by a site diagram contained in the treaty, which shows the boundaries of each inspectable site. These must conform to set standards and include road and rail entrances and exits and key reference points. Normally the entire area within the boundaries set out in the site diagram is inspectable, including the interior of structures, containers, or vehicles. However, in some cases, such as CWC challenge inspections or START visits with right of special access, site diagrams and inspectable areas and procedures may not be contained in treaty documents, but negotiated on a case-by-case basis.

Immediately upon arrival at an inspectable site, the host country escort has an obligation to inform the inspection team of the number of treaty-limited items located there and to provide information on the precise location of such items. Inspectors also must be briefed on any safety concerns at the site and on other relevant factors affecting the inspection in this pre-inspection briefing.

The Inspection Sequence and Rules

The size of inspection teams and the procedures they may use are delineated in treaties. As a rule, only one inspection team is allowed at a site at one time. The team operates under the direction of a team leader and deputy team leader and is limited in size. For example, an inspection team for the INF, START, and CWC treaties generally consists of a maximum of ten persons. However, some variations do exist. For example, START permitted fifteen inspectors for exhibition inspections during the baseline period due to the number and diversity of the systems exhibited.

Figure 4.3
INF Site Diagram: Missile Operating Base Saryozek

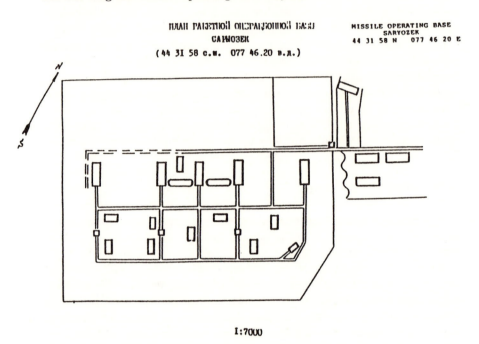

1:7000

Source: **INF Treaty Memorandum of Understanding on Data**

At the site, inspection teams may break into subgroups, each of which must contain at least two people. The disposition of these subgroups is the responsibility of the inspection team chief who must ensure the most effective deployment of the team during the inspection. As a rule, during short notice inspections, inspectors can be posted at any building with an exit large enough to permit passage of a treaty-limited item. Subgroups also may be used to patrol the perimeter of an inspection site and monitor the exits of the site.

Inspectors generally have the right to inspect any vehicle capable of carrying a treaty-limited item at any time during the inspection. Such a vehicle may not leave the site until an inspector has inspected it. Site diagrams may have two or more separated inspectable areas, and special provisions apply to roads joining non-contiguous areas in such cases. As a rule, during an inspection, an item is not inspectable while on such a road, but it is inspectable if it enters an inspectable area within the site diagram.

To minimize disruption of normal operations, inspectors and monitors may interfere with on going activities at an inspection site only to the extent necessary to carry out agreed inspection procedures. They may not hamper or delay operations or compromise safety. In controlled environments or where special safety hazards exist, the host country must provide protective gear. For safety reasons, inspectors must obey normal precautions, such as prohibitions against touching items sensitive to electrostatic impulses, while the host country must ensure adequate conditions for the inspection, such as sufficient lighting for inspection and photography. If either party—an inspector or escort—takes an action that is not in accordance with treaty procedures, the inspection and escort team chiefs must first consult before taking punitive measures in response to the action. Unresolved matters are included in the inspection report.

The host country normally controls communications at the inspection site, subject to treaty provisions. These often require the host country to provide a means for the inspectors or monitors to communicate with their embassy at any time and for inspectors to communicate with each other when divided into subgroups. Usually inspectors have a right to establish a link with their embassy as soon as they arrive on-site. During early INF implementation, U.S. inspectors experienced some difficulty exercising this right due to the poor condition of the Soviet public ground communications system. Accordingly, subsequent treaties permit the use of satellite communications systems, subject to some restrictions.[5]

The period of inspection is carefully delineated. Most treaties specify that pre-inspection procedures, including safety briefings and information on how the inspection will be conducted, must begin upon arrival of the inspection team at the site and be completed within a specified period, which ranges from one hour (INF, START) to three hours (CWC). Unless otherwise specified by the team chief, the inspection must begin immediately upon completion of these procedures. For many types of arms control inspection, the period allowed for inspection after completion of pre-inspection procedures and the beginning of post-inspection procedures is twenty four hours, although it may be considerably longer for the inspection of large facilities, such as chemical plants under the CWC or nuclear facilities under inspection by the International Atomic Energy Agency. The base inspection period may be extended (usually by 8 hours) by mutual agreement or ended early at the discretion of the inspection team leader. However, certain types of inspection that may be particularly complex, such as START baseline data inspections, new facility inspections, exhibitions, and re-entry vehicle inspections, can be extended as long as necessary to complete the inspection process. Conversion or eliminations inspections can continue for weeks or months as is necessary to accomplish their purpose and do not have a specified time limit for their completion.

Size Thresholds and Viewing Restrictions

Arms control procedures often impose size thresholds and other viewing limitations designed to protect sensitive or classified information, while permitting inspectors to carry out their legitimate duties. A common threshold is to limit inspections only to those structures or containers large enough to contain a treaty-limited item. A structure large enough to hold the smallest inspectable item is inspectable, but not if its interior is so divided as demonstrably to be too small to hold the item or if the item could not pass through any of its entrances or exits. If an individual container or canister is too small to hold the smallest inspectable item, it likewise is not inspectable.

To protect classified items or information, the host country can cover or shroud sensitive items, but such items are still inspectable if they are large enough to contain the smallest treaty-limited item (TLI). It is up to the host country to show that a shrouded or environmentally protected object is not a treaty-limited or banned item. This can be done by any method acceptable to the inspectors, including partial removal or lifting of the shroud or cover, or by measuring or weighing the item. If any question about whether the item is treaty-limited remains after such measures are taken, an ambiguity is declared and details of the incident and a photograph of the shrouded object is included in the inspection report. A suspected violation would then be subject to discussion in the treaty's implementation body or in diplomatic channels.

As a further restriction on inspection activity, inspectors and portal monitors, in discharging their duties, often are required to communicate with personnel of the host country, including personnel working at the site, only through the host country escorts. However, some treaties, such as the CWC, permit the inspection team to ask spot questions of site management personnel and workers and even request formal interviews. CWC inspectors also can inspect plant records, although proprietary records can be isolated or masked to protect confidential business information as long as inspectors can be satisfied that the plant is not engaged in illegal activity.

Delineation of Inspection Equipment

Inspectors are not free to use any equipment they desire. All of the equipment that can be used during an inspection is delineated in treaty documents. As a rule, inspection equipment carried by on-site inspectors is carefully tied to the inspection task. For most on-site inspections, basic equipment consists of photographic equipment, nonsparking flashlights (to protect against igniting missiles or other munitions by static emissions), measuring tapes or poles of various sizes, compasses and, for elimination sites, binoculars. The host country may also require the wearing of special clothing for safety reasons. The CFE treaty further permits inspectors to use portable passive night vision devices, binoculars, videotapes, dictaphones, and laptop computers. The CWC allows various items of inspection equipment for detection, safety, sampling and analysis, communications and administrative support that has been preapproved, certified as reliable, electrically safe, and tamper free, and can be examined by the host government. Beyond treaty-specified equipment, inspectors may also wear radiation or similar detection devices for safety and carry water and first aid kits.

Depending on the inspection, specialized technical equipment may be required. For example, the INF Treaty permits the use of radiation detection equipment to assist in determining whether canisterized missiles are legal single warhead SS-25 ICBMs or banned triple warhead SS-20 intermediate-range missiles. Portal monitoring and other types of on-site monitoring equipment are subject to special rules described in the section on monitoring.

Right to Use Inspection Equipment

The right of inspectors to bring in and use cleared inspection equipment and supplies is usually specified in the treaty. Inspectors are allowed to bring in the maximum permissible amount of such equipment, even though only some of it may be used at any one time, to allow for the possible naming of a sequential inspection.

Even after inspection equipment has been cleared, treaties often levy some restrictions on its use, mainly to ensure that it is used solely for legitimate treaty-related purposes. In particular, special restrictions apply to photography of sensitive military equipment or areas. Photographs can be taken only to document possible ambiguities. Under all treaties, inspectors may request that such a photograph be taken during the inspection. However, often photographs are not freely taken by inspectors but rather are taken by a host country escort using an approved instant camera provided by the inspection team. Two identical photographs are taken—one for each party—of the ambiguous object or building, and the inspector's photograph is included in the final inspection report along with a description of the possible ambiguity. Under the CFE Treaty, which deals with less sensitive conventional armaments, inspectors may take some photographs themselves, but they are required to consult with host country escorts before photographing sensitive areas. In the case of the CWC, a facility can request that the inspection team take a substitute photograph if it believes the initial photograph compromises trade secrets or other sensitive information.

The taking of measurements also is controlled. In the case of particularly sensitive equipment, some treaties provide that such measurements be taken by the host country escort, although they can be supervised by the inspectors and must meet the inspector's specifications. Measurements taken during inspection or monitoring activities are contained in the final inspection report and must be certified by both Parties to be recorded officially.

Handling and Reporting of Ambiguities

On-site inspection regimes usually contain the principle that, if an ambiguity arises during the course of an inspection, the host country escort has an obligation to try to satisfy the concern through clarifications on the spot. Only if these clarifications do not resolve the ambiguities are they documented by photographs and recorded in the inspection report. The common inspection provision that at least two inspectors or monitors on each team must speak the language of the inspected party is designed partially to ensure that there is clear communications on the discussion and recording of any ambiguity.

Inspection reports are designed to be strictly factual in nature, that is, to contain statements of fact that lead to opinions or conclusions rather than contain the opinions or conclusions themselves. Generally treaties list the specific points that must be included in the report. Inspectors observe, state the facts and substantiate ambiguities with all available evidence, such as supporting photographs, site diagrams and maps. However, the final judgments about whether a treaty violation has occurred at the site are not made by the inspectors in the field, but by analysts in capitals after consideration of all relevant information, including the inspection report.

Inspection reports generally are prepared in two languages with the language of the inspecting party considered to be the official translation. Post-inspection procedures, including completion of the inspection report take place at a location designated by the host government and must be completed within a limited time frame, often four hours after arrival at that location.

Sequential ("Follow-up") Inspections

If a sequential inspection is requested after completion of an inspection, but before departure of the inspecting team from the country, it usually may take place only at facilities associated with the same POE originally used by the inspecting team. The inspection team chief must announce the intention to carry out a sequential inspection prior to completion of the pre-inspection period. The type of inspection and site to be inspected then must be revealed prior to completion of post inspection procedures or no later than one hour after return of the inspection team to the POE. For a "scheduled" inspection (e.g., an elimination inspection) notification of intent, type, and site of the sequential inspection must be given reasonably in advance (usually, at least twenty-four hours) before the planned commencement of the inspection to permit orderly host country arrangements for the inspection. If there is no sequential inspection, the inspection team must return to the POE and leave the territory of the inspected party within a set period, often twenty-four hours.

NOTES

1. Because of their continuous presence over an extended period of the territory of the inspected Party, portal monitors may be rejected for any reason without explanation.

2. Under the INF Treaty which was implemented during the Cold War, the United States rejected seven people on the original list of portal monitors submitted by the Soviet Union, all of whom had been previously identified by various countries as having engaged in unacceptable (espionage-related) behavior. The United States also rejected one person on the initial INF inspector's list who, as a Soviet diplomat, had previously been expelled from the U.S. Although reciprocity on treaty implementation issues was then the rule, the Soviets did not reject any U.S. inspectors on the initial INF lists, possibly due to fortuitous timing; U.S. rejection of the Soviets personnel came after the Soviets already had approved all U.S. inspectors. Later the Soviets did reject a United States inspector, without providing a reason, probably as a retaliatory measure.

3. Reflecting the general easing of visa requirements in Europe for residents of neighboring or allied countries, many CFE inspectors do not require visas, and in those cases where visas are required, they can be obtained upon entry into the inspected country. This is a good example of finding a practical solution to an otherwise potentially confusing and distracting inspection issue.

4. These are designated points of entry/exit in the CFE Treaty given the large number of facilities that are inspectable in certain countries and the possibility that, with sequential inspections, inspection teams may enter the country at one point and exit it at another.

5. For example, under START, portal monitors can use satellite communications only if facsimile communications through their embassy cannot be achieved within twenty minutes.

Part III

Types of On-Site Inspection

Chapter 5

Routine Data and Compliance Inspections

There are over twenty distinct types of on-site inspection (OSI) included in the arms control agreements signed since the Intermediate-Range Nuclear Forces (INF) Treaty was concluded in December 1987. Each type of inspection has its own peculiarities crafted to accomplish a specific, sometimes highly technical, verification task. In general, however, the inspections in the major arms control agreements fall within four broad categories. They are designed to: 1) assist in confirming treaty-related data during the baseline period and thereafter; 2) help verify that all parties are complying with treaty provisions at declared sites, that is, those sites that are listed in the treaty or related documents; 3) confirm that the required destruction or conversion of military weapons is being carried out strictly in accordance with the agreed procedures; and 4) help resolve ambiguous situations, or detect cheating if it is occurring, at a suspected site whether or not the site is listed in treaty documents. Data and routine compliance inspections are discussed below; elimination and conversion inspections are covered in chapter 6; and suspect-site and challenge inspections are presented in chapter 7. Perimeter and portal continuous monitoring and other on-site monitoring regimes have unique qualities and are dealt with in chapter 8.

Inspections designed primarily as confidence- and security-building measures (CSBMs) are not covered in this study. These include overflight inspections under the Open Skies Agreement; the inspection of member state military force structures and activities codified in the Vienna Document 1994 and its predecessors developed by the Organization for Security and Cooperation in Europe (OSCE); and the inspections contained in the Dayton Accord on Bosnia.

Data inspections, routine compliance inspections, and elimination and conversion inspections employ mutually agreed procedures contained in the treaty text. Such inspections typically take place at sites listed in the treaty, called declared sites. These are primarily military or government operational, storage, repair, training, or destruction facilities, although private industrial facilities may also be affected.

By way of contrast, suspect site or other challenge inspections may occur at sites not listed in the treaty (i.e., undeclared sites), as well as at declared sites, and they are as likely to affect privately owned industrial facilities as military sites. Some such regimes have open-ended inspection provisions that may require site-specific negotiations prior to, or during, the inspection process to agree upon the procedures to be used and the degree of access inspectors will have during the inspection. Because they can involve highly intrusive inspections of private facilities, such inspections raise potential legal and constitutional concerns not normally present in other types of inspection regimes.

BASELINE AND OTHER DATA INSPECTIONS

Providing and Confirming Data

All on-site inspection regimes require each party to provide data on its own military equipment and facilities that are regulated by the treaty. This is the only feasible way of establishing an accurate treaty data base, since no other country —not even one with highly developed national technical means (NTM)—could be expected to have completely accurate information on the treaty-limited items or equipment of the other treaty signatories. During any given period large amounts of military equipment normally would be located inside buildings at military production, storage, repair, and training facilities. Moreover, even some of the military weaponry located in the open at military sites could be expected to be camouflaged or concealed in accordance with routine military practices, rendering it difficult to find or identify. Highly mobile equipment, such as mobile missiles, also is very difficult to locate and track with NTM.

The data provided by each signatory in accordance with treaty provisions is typically assembled in a separate section of the treaty—generally a memorandum of understanding (MOU) or protocol on data or information exchange.[1] These data bases contain the information essential to carrying out the treaty, including the number, location, and technical characteristics of all weapons systems regulated by the treaty. The data section of the treaty is updated upon entry into force (EIF) of the agreement and periodically thereafter and serves as the central repository of information on its evolving status.

The accuracy of the data provided by each party to an arms control agreement must be independently confirmed by the other party or parties. This is accomplished in a variety of ways. Baseline (or, in the case of the Chemical Weapons Convention (CWC), "initial") inspections to confirm the accuracy of the date provided at EIF are held within an established period immediately after entry into force of the treaty and during any residual level validation period that may be established. Data update inspections then are held at established intervals after the baseline inspections to confirm notified changes in the data during the course of the treaty. In addition, technical characteristics and/or other technical distinguishability inspections are held during the baseline period, or as necessary, to help confirm the data provided by each party. These also assist inspectors to distinguish between "look alike" items that are covered by the treaty and those that are exempted. New facility inspections, which are essentially baseline data inspections for inspectable facilities that come into being after entry into force, are required by some treaties to track new facilities as they come online and are added to the treaty's data base. Some specialized inspections, such as re-entry vehicle inspections under the Strategic Arms Reduction Treaty (START) to confirm the number of warheads deployed on a specific type of intercontinental ballistic missile (ICBM) or submarine-launched ballistic missile (SLBM), also are designed to "spot check" data.

General Provisions

The INF Treaty was the first to require comprehensive baseline inspections of all declared sites. Provisions in that agreement required baseline inspections to begin at all declared locations in the treaty's MOU on Data shortly (thirty days) after EIF and be completed within a specified time frame after the inspections begin (sixty days). The INF Treaty also established the precedent for permitting baseline (and other) inspections of facilities of the signatories located in third countries, that is, of the U.S. and Soviet INF sites in the Western and Eastern European Basing Countries.[2]

The time frame for the baseline inspection period varies from treaty to treaty in accordance with the complexity of the task. The START baseline period, for example, was 120 days, beginning 45 days after EIF. The Treaty on Conventional Forces in Europe (CFE) also allowed a 120-day period for both its initial baseline validation inspections, held 45 days after EIF, and for the residual level inspections—essentially second baseline inspections—held three years after the initial baseline inspections. The initial on-site inspections held to confirm CWC data vary in time, with the earliest on-site inspections—those to verify the declarations of chemical weapons production facilities—beginning ninety days after EIF and continuing for a thirty-day period.

Baseline, data update, and new facility inspections generally follow the "short notice" model. This enables inspectors to arrive promptly at the site, thus complicating the inspected party's ability to remove treaty-prohibited items. In addition, since baseline inspections involve a period of intensive inspection activity within a restricted time frame, there are normally limits on the number of baseline and related data inspections that can be held simultaneously. This ensures that the baseline inspections can be carried out in an orderly manner without overtaxing the ability of the host nation to provide the required escort services. Both the INF and START treaties, for example, limited the number of baseline inspections to ten at one time.

Modern arms control treaties usually also contain provisions to help inspectors verify data during baseline and other data inspections. These include an obligation of the host country escort to inform the inspecting team upon its arrival at the site how many inspectable items of each type are present, indicate where on the site diagram they are located, and provide any other specialized information required by the treaty. This data then is confirmed during the inspection process, using the agreed inspection procedures. If an inspectable item is absent from the inspectable site at the time of inspection, including on a road between two non contiguous inspectable sites, the inspection team leader must be informed of this fact and the reason for the absence. A brief account of the practical experience in implementing baseline inspections and in procedures which vary somewhat from treaty to treaty follows.

INF Baseline and Other Data Inspections

The INF Treaty pioneered modern baseline inspections. Under that agreement, 117 U.S. and 26 Soviet baseline inspections were held at all INF facilities listed in the MOU (with the exception of missile production facilities) in July and August 1988. The INF Treaty exempted declared former INF missile production facilities from interior inspections, but not the less sensitive former INF launcher production facilities. Later this was modified by the START I Treaty, which permits suspect site inspections at specified areas within a few missile production plants. Despite the continuing Cold War confrontation and the unprecedented intrusiveness of the inspections, the INF baseline inspections were marked by a high degree of mutual cooperation,[3] proceeded smoothly, and were completed within the scheduled time frame.[4]

The INF Treaty does not have separate data update inspections or new facility inspections. Since the treaty outcome was the complete elimination of all treaty-limited items (TLI), the task of inspectors was simply to maintain an accurate count as facilities were closed out and TLI eliminated. INF data was updated on a periodic basis and "short notice" (vice data update) inspections were used to confirm that data.

START Baseline and Data Update Inspections

START baseline inspections generally followed the INF model, with the addition of specialized provisions for aircraft and mobile launchers. START I entered into force on December 5, 1994 with each party having the right to begin baseline inspections within forty-five days thereafter. Although START baseline inspections actually began late—on March 1, 1995 (vice January 19, 1995)—for weather-related reasons, they were completed, with one exception,[5] on June 28, 1995, within the prescribed 120 days. The United States conducted seventy-five baseline inspections in the former Soviet Union (FSU), while personnel from the FSU conducted thirty-seven baseline inspections at U.S. facilities.

START baseline, data update. and new facility inspections can be conducted at any of the following facilities: ICBM and submarine bases; ICBM and SLBM loading and repair facilities; ICBM, SLBM, heavy bomber, and former heavy bomber storage and training facilities; conversion or elimination facilities; test ranges; and airbases for heavy bombers (with some exceptions) and for former heavy bombers. In addition, baseline inspections can be held, solely for the purpose of inspecting weapons storage areas, at some air bases not otherwise subject to START inspections.

A number of separate provisions apply to aircraft data inspections. There is a separate quota on the number of alert heavy bombers (i.e., those actually armed with nuclear weapons) subject to inspection, and the treaty requires the host country escort to provide information, including the identity and location of such bombers at nuclear air bases. Alert heavy bomber inspections also are limited, with only one airplane of each type inspectable each year. In addition, for heavy bomber and former heavy bomber facilities, the categories of absent aircraft must be given, including their "general location" (e.g., Middle East) outside the territory of the inspected party.[6]

With some exceptions,[7] all aircraft at a base of the type specified in the MOU for that base are inspectable. However, visiting heavy bombers of a type not listed for that base are not inspectable, since equipment to support that type of inspection may not be present. For baseline and new facility (but not data update) inspections there is a call-back for airplanes based at the facility, which have twenty hours from the beginning of the inspection to return. There is a similar call-back provision for launchers at road-mobile ICBM bases, which must return to their bases unless they are in restricted areas, being relocated, or cannot return due to *force majeure*. Even in those circumstances, they must be accounted for in explanations.

The START Treaty provides for data update inspections to be held after the end of the baseline data inspections. As an anomaly, the START Treaty provides that air bases may be exempted "temporarily" from data update inspections, with the understanding that this exemption is to be used only infrequently and not for purposes "inconsistent with the treaty." This provision was added, after intensive negotiations, to permit the United States to use its heavy bombers for conventional missions outside the context of the U.S.-Soviet strategic relations, for example, for such operations as the Gulf War.[8]

START also requires notification of any new facilities subject to START provisions that come online after EIF. The other party then has sixty days to conduct a new facility inspection. Such inspections, however, cannot begin sooner than forty-five days after EIF and no other inspection can be conducted at the facility until the new facility inspection is complete or the sixty days allowed for the inspection expires, whichever comes first.

CFE Baseline and Other Data Inspections

The multilaterally negotiated CFE Treaty has two baseline periods. The first occurred during the four-month period after EIF to validate a baseline of data for the future. The second occurred at the forty-month mark to help verify that the signatories had reached their ceilings for the long term. The initial CFE baseline inspections began on July 17, 1992, and were completed on November 13, 1992, within the 120-day period allowed for such inspections. During this period, the United States conducted forty-four inspections in the former Soviet Union and the territory of other former members of the Warsaw Pact, including German territory that formerly was part of the German Democratic Republic. The United States also led or participated in sixteen inspections of reduction activity during the baseline period. The residual level validation inspections of all sites began in November 1995 to verify the disposition within the treaty area of application of the military forces of the thirty CFE States Parties and ensure that all were complying with the treaty-limited equipment (TLE) limits. These second baseline inspections also were completed on time.

CWC Initial Declarations and Inspections

The Chemical Weapons Convention uses a combination of the older International Atomic Energy Agency (IAEA) and more modern arms control treaty regime provisions in compiling and verifying data. It imposes substantial new reporting requirements even on the already heavily regulated chemical industry.[9]

Chemicals controlled by the CWC are listed on three "schedules" in a Treaty Annex. Schedule 1 covers known chemical warfare agents and their immediate precursors; Schedule 2 covers toxic chemicals and precursors produced in small quantities for non prohibited purposes; and Schedule 3 covers toxic chemicals and precursors produced in large qualities for non prohibited purposes. Facilities that produce, and in some cases, process or consume chemicals on the Schedules are required to submit declarations and reports. The amount of information that a facility must declare depends of its industrial activities and the types and quantities of CWC-relevant chemicals involved. Some, but not all, of this information is subject to verification after EIF.

Four types of data submission are required. An *initial declaration* containing combined industry information relevant to the CWC must be provided to the Organization for the Prohibition of Chemical Weapons (OPCW) by the National Authority within thirty days after EIF. An *annual anticipatory report* on treaty-related activities planned for the next calendar year must be provided to the OPCW sixty days before the end of the first year after EIF. A *change report* also must be filed with the OPCW during the next calendar year if a facility's activities diverge significantly from those stated in the anticipatory declaration.

A change report would be required, for example, if a facility began production of a new scheduled chemical or if the volume of production exceeded the anticipated level or range. Finally, an *annual retrospective report* on CWC-relevant activities during the previous calendar year must be provided to the OPCW ninety days after the end of that year.

The data obtained is subject to CWC initial inspections. These vary somewhat from other baseline inspections in that they are not only intended to verify the data provided in the declarations, but also to develop additional information needed for planning future verification activities at the facility and to work out facility agreements. Initial inspections are not held at all facilities that provide data—only the most vital to operation of the treaty. They are conducted at chemical weapons (CW) production facilities; single small-scale facilities for production of Schedule 1 chemicals; declared plant sites that process, produce or consume Schedule 2 chemicals; and CW storage facilities. Similar inspections, termed "initial visits," are held at CW destruction facilities. Initial inspections also are conducted of any old chemical weapons declared by a state party or discovered by a state party after EIF but are optional at Schedule 3 or other relevant facilities.

While most initial inspections are to be conducted "promptly" after a facility is declared, the CWC specifically establishes a thirty-day period beginning ninety days after EIF for CW production facilities. The schedule for an initial visit to a CW destruction facility is based on when destruction operations are initiated.

All plant sites that produce, process, or consume Schedule 2 chemicals in quantities above the inspection threshold[10] must undergo an initial inspection during the first three years after EIF, unless the state concerned and OPCW agree to waive it. During this inspection, the OPCW and the state concerned, with the direct participation of the inspected facility, negotiate a facility agreement that defines the verification procedures on a plant-specific basis. The facility agreement lays out basic inspection procedures including which parts of a plant site are subject to inspection, the scope of inspection in agreed areas, the storage of confidential information on-site, the taking of samples and their analysis, access to records and the use of inspection equipment.[11] Whether any additional inspection activities are conducted during an initial inspection depends on the type of facility being inspected. Additional inspection activities, for example, might be required at a CW production, storage, or destruction facility.

Initial inspections are scheduled and monitored by the OPCW's operational body—the Technical Secretariat—which carries out the verification measures of the CWC, based upon the number of facilities to be inspected and the resources that OPCW has available. For such inspections, the country to be inspected is notified by the Technical Secretariat's director-general seventy-two hours in advance of the arrival of an inspection team at the point of entry (POE). The inspection then is carried out according to the agreed procedures contained in the treaty.

Baseline Inspections in Practice

The baseline and other data inspections conducted to date have worked well on the whole. They have successfully identified both data and procedural problem areas and surfaced treaty-related ambiguities requiring subsequent resolution.

The INF baseline inspections revealed problems on both sides in compiling precise data. Soviet inspectors found several factual errors in U.S. site diagrams that required later changes in U.S. data.[12] In addition, discarded, only partially complete, missile stages were listed by the United States in the MOU on Data as complete stages, later causing accounting problems during eliminations when the missiles did not meet the dimensions specified in the treaty. There also were problems with data on the weight of the Pershing missile. Some Soviet data also was found to be incomplete or inaccurate. For example, it was discovered during U.S. inspections that the Soviets had two SS-20 missile canisters of different sizes—a "normal" canister and a shortened version—and dimensional data on Soviet SS-12 and SS-23 ballistic missiles and on the weight of the SSC-X-4 cruise missile were found to be inaccurate. In addition, some Soviet missiles and various other pieces of INF equipment were found by U.S. NTM at undeclared locations.

The INF data anomalies of both sides were corrected in subsequent exchanges of data and did not impede basic implementation to the treaty, but data anomalies were cited as INF Treaty violations by both sides. In addition, the problems on both sides in measuring the precise weights of missiles led arms control negotiators to move away from weight as a vital data factor in later arms control agreements.

Despite the INF experience and the long preparation time between treaty signing and EIF (over three years), The START baseline inspections also surfaced both procedural and data-related problems. A number of procedural questions required consideration in the START Treaty's implementation body, the Joint Compliance and Inspection Commission (JCIC), including Russian charges that U.S. escorts had improperly prevented Russian inspectors from directly measuring the external dimensions of a covered object at Vandenberg Test Range. The United States also raised concerns about data accountability, the most serious of which was resolved on September 28, 1995, when the parties formally acknowledged that space launch vehicles using the first stage of an ICBM or SLBM remain accountable under the Treaty as an ICBM or SLBM of that type.

Significant data problems also were encountered during CFE inspections, especially in connection with site diagrams. Inspectors found, for example, that site diagrams often did not include the entire site, had inaccurate coordinates, did not define specific boundaries for each Object of Verification (OOV) within the site, and did not incorporate areas at the site common to several OOVs. These CFE data problems were attributed both to poor preparation by the inspected country and to spotty implementation by poorly trained escorts. The problems with site diagrams were sufficient to result in the declaration of several ambiguities in CFE inspections.[13]

Some of the problems encountered with Soviet and Eastern European CFE data during the baseline inspections can be attributed to the disarray caused by the breakup of the Warsaw Pact and the Soviet Union. The movement of TLE by former Soviet states following the apportionment of former Soviet conventional arms and equipment by the Tashkent Accord[14] and similar apportionment problems after the break-up of Czechoslovakia complicated baseline inspections. There also were problems with the use by escorts of old data that had been subsequently updated by data declarations and with poorly prepared site diagrams. In addition, the deterioration of some inspectable military facilities, particularly previous Soviet military assets in former basing countries, created unsafe conditions for inspectors, while poor transportation systems led to some delays in moving inspectors from the POE to sites. [15]

Serious CFE data problems also surfaced when the final reduction period ended and treaty limits took effect in November 1995. These included the failure of some newly independent countries (NIS) to complete their required reductions, violations of the national TLE limits by several states, Russian violation of limits in several categories of TLE there were permitted to have in flank areas, and Russian failure to meet some other obligations, separate from but related to the CFE Treaty.[16]

SPECIALIZED TECHNICAL DATA INSPECTIONS AND EXHIBITIONS

INF Technical Inspections

The INF Treaty contains no provisions for confirming technical data. Accordingly, in the period between signature to the INF Treaty and EIF, a separate agreement was reached to permit one-time "data validation" inspections to be carried out during the baseline inspections. The agreed procedures required that at least nine of each specified TLI be displayed at an elimination site. Inspectors then were permitted to select samples at random to verify the technical data provided in the MOU on each system, with agreement that measurements and weights would be acceptable within 3% percent tolerances from the values contained in the MOU. The INF data validation inspections surfaced a number of the data discrepancies noted previously, including the two versions of the SS-20 and problems with weighing TLI in field conditions.

START Technical and Distinguishability Inspections

Building on the INF experience, the START Treaty contains specific provisions for technical characteristics and distinguishability exhibitions and inspections and specifies the required procedures in an annex to the Inspection Protocol. The START *technical characteristics exhibitions* permit inspection of each type and variant of ICBM and SLBM and each version of a mobile launcher of ICBMs to confirm the MOU data for these systems. START *distinguishability exhibitions* allow inspection of one of each type, category, and variant (as applicable) of heavy bomber,[17] former heavy bomber, and long range nuclear air-launched cruise missile (ALCM) to observe the technical characteristics specified in the MOU and confirm distinguishing features. These help inspectors, during future inspections, to accurately identify the individual weapons and the number declared to be present.

Since the TLIs covered by START technical and distinguishability exhibitions were subjected to prior inspection before EIF under a separate Agreement on Early Exhibitions, START established only a brief period (between thirty and forty-five days after EIF) for such exhibitions and waived further inspections of items already satisfactorily exhibited under the early exhibition agreement. New systems, however, must be exhibited. Specialized Treaty provisions were provided for some missiles scheduled for early elimination.[18] The Treaty specifies how each item is to be exhibited, but leaves the sides free to chose their own exhibition site.

Procedures for exhibition and distinguishability inspections are relatively simple. The inspection team arrives at the site one to three days before the exhibition date and is transported to the site "in a timely manner." During the pre-inspection procedures, host country escorts identify the exhibited items to the inspectors by type, variant, and version using visual aids (photographs, slides, drawings, or the like) to point out the distinguishing features or external differences. The escorts also designate where measurements can be made on each exhibited item, using sketches or diagrams if needed. The measurements taken by inspectors are certified by both parties immediately after they are taken, and the certified data is entered into the inspection report. Inspectors are allowed to take three photographs of each variant in a technical or distinguishability exhibition with their own cameras. Additional photographs may be taken where ambiguities exist, with the difference that photographs of ambiguities are taken by the host country (not the inspectors) using the inspection team camera.

Specialized provisions exist for dealing with new types of ICBMs and SLBMs. The procedures for exhibiting new types of mobile ICBMs are particularly rigorous, involving both a regular exhibition and one with additional procedures. This is because a new type mobile ICBM might have a different number of re-entry vehicles (RVs) than an existing type. It also must be established that neither the new type nor the existing type mobile launcher can launch a missile of the other system. Mobile ICBM launchers of each new type must be distinguishable from previously declared types both with and without their associated missiles installed and the host country must demonstrate those distinguishing features. Heavy bombers, former heavy bombers, and long-range nuclear ALCMs also are subjected to inspections to confirm technical character-istics, illustrate distinguishability, and demonstrate the maximum equipage for long-range nuclear ALCMs.

One-time *baseline exhibitions* of certain types of bombers began only after the completion of distinguishability inspections, where examples of the systems had been exhibited. Baseline exhibitions also are required for each heavy bomber equipped for non-nuclear armaments, each training heavy bomber, and each former heavy bomber declared as of EIF. These exhibitions permit inspectors to confirm that these aircraft meet the standards of conversion contained in the treaty. Subsequent baseline inspections also are required when a long-range ALCM is first flight tested from a deployed type of bomber from which no long-range nuclear ALCM previously has been flight tested.

Table 5.1
Bomber Exhibition Requirements under START I and START II

START	START II
Distinguishability Exhibitions: - confirm technical characteristics, distinguishing features - may inspect HB equipped for LRNA, HB/FHB used to test LRNA, and LRNA	*Weapons Loading Exhibitions:* - confirm weapons loadings (per START II MOU data) on one HB of each type and variant of type - demonstrate change in weapons loadings
Baseline Exhibitions: - confirm HB for non-nuclear armaments, training HB, FHB satisfy conversion requirements - verify distinguishability of HB equipped for (non-LRNA) nuclear weapons from HB of same type equipped for LRNA	*Reoriented HB Exhibitions:* - demonstrate observable difference on reoriented HB or reoriented HB returned to a nuclear role - only required if not all HB of a type/variant of that type are reoriented/returned to a nuclear role

HB = heavy bomber
FHB = former heavy bomber
LRNA = long-range nuclear ALCM

Source: **DynMeridian, Alexandria, Virginia**

DECLARED SITE INSPECTIONS TO CONFIRM COMPLIANCE

A second major category of routine inspections is designed to confirm that signatories are abiding by the provisions of the treaty and that no illegal activity is occurring at sites declared in the treaty. With the exception of the older IAEA safeguards inspections, declared-site compliance inspections as a rule have "short-notice" timelines to ensure that inspectors can arrive promptly at the site and pre-inspection movement restrictions to complicate removal of any illegal items from the site prior to arrival of the inspection team. To guard against frivolous use, there also are quotas the number of such inspection that can be held annually.

IAEA Safeguards Inspections

Since its conclusion in 1968, the Nuclear Non-proliferation Treaty (NPT) has been the centerpiece of multinational efforts to control the spread of nuclear weapons. To verify compliance, it relies on the oldest of the declared site inspection regimes—the IAEA's safeguards system.

Safeguards agreements are negotiated and concluded individually by the IAEA with each state or group of states, based either on Information Circular (INFCIRC) 66—the safeguard system for states not party to the NPT—which involves application of safeguards to specified equipment or material, or INFCIRC/153—the model agreement for comprehensive safeguards involving full scope safeguards, which extend to all peaceful nuclear activities and materials in the state. Since the safeguards agreements approved by the IAEA's Board of Governors are drafted in relatively general terms, they are usually supplemented by more detailed documents known as *subsidiary arrangements*, which describe specific safeguards activities, such as the frequency of routine inspections and reports, in more detail on a facility-by-facility basis.[19]   As a rule, the frequency and intensiveness of routine safeguards inspection is related to the amount and type of nuclear material at the inspected facility, ranging up to continuous inspection for large and complex facilities containing large amounts of weapons-usable material.

Routine safeguards inspections utilize *material accountancy*—measures to establish through sampling and physical measurement that all nuclear material supposed to be present is in fact accounted for—supplemented by *containment and surveillance* measures designed to provide evidence of diversion of safeguarded nuclear material.[20] The primary thrust of the IAEA safeguards regime has been to track and account for nuclear material in a manner that increases the intensity of the inspection process as the material approaches a condition where it could be used directly in a nuclear explosive, so as to detect in a timely fashion if any material is being diverted and to provide warning.

Under the agreed rights of access, IAEA inspectors regularly visit nuclear facilities to verify records that state authorities keep on the whereabouts of nuclear material under their control, check IAEA-installed instruments and surveillance equipment, and confirm physical inventories of nuclear materials. During inspections, IAEA inspectors conduct independent measurements for on-the-spot confirmation of the enrichment level and content of nuclear material. They also collect samples of certain types of safeguarded nuclear materials that are later tested and measured at the IAEA's Safeguard's analytical laboratories and at a cooperative network of other laboratories in various parts of the world.

INF Short-Notice Inspections

INF short-notice inspections were designed both to track data on the remaining INF missile systems during the three-year period for elimination of all such missiles and to be used as compliance inspections to confirm that no prohibited activity occurred at any declared INF site. These inspections began immediately after completion of the INF baseline inspections (August 1988) and will continue until the thirteen-year INF inspection period ends on May 30, 2001. The annual quota on the number of INF short-notice inspections that can be held annually decreases over the life of the treaty, since the complete elimination of all INF missiles and infrastructure in the first three years of the treaty makes it easier to monitor the treaty by NTM after that period. Twenty short-notice inspections could be held in the first three years; fifteen in the next five years; and ten in the last five years of the on-site inspection regime. The treaty does not differentiate between INF short-notice inspections in the European Basing Countries and in the United States and former Soviet Union.

INF and START Close-out Inspections

The INF and START treaties both contain inspections to help confirm that treaty prohibited activity has indeed ceased at sites declared to have been "closed-out." Only one such inspection is allowed for each declared facility, and it must be held within a specified period (sixty days) after notification of elimination of the facility. INF close-out inspections also could be conducted during the baseline inspection period at facilities that had been closed-out between treaty signature and EIF. Once a site has been eliminated and subjected to a close-out inspection, it is still subject to short-notice inspections (INF) or formerly declared facility inspections (START) to ensure that no prohibited activity is occurring at the site.

Since close-out inspections simply confirm the elimination of a facility as notified by the inspected party, they do not use a "short notice" timeline, but instead permit transportation of inspectors to the eliminated facility within a more leisurely forty-eight hours after arrival of the inspection team at the POE. During a close-out inspection, the entire site is subject to inspection, and normal inspection procedures are used.

START Formerly Declared Facility Inspections

Under START provisions, formerly declared facility inspections are used (vice short-notice inspections in INF) to help confirm that the eliminated facilities are no longer being used for purposes prohibited by the treaty. Each party has the right to conduct a total of three formerly declared facility inspections each year, of which no more than two per year can be held at any one facility. START formerly declared facility inspections have a "short notice" timeline. Pre-inspection restrictions are imposed, the entire area within the site diagram is inspectable, and normal inspection procedures are used.

START Re-entry Vehicle Inspections

START has overall restrictions on the number of warheads permitted on specific missiles. The treaty provides for re-entry vehicle inspections at declared sites, after the baseline period, to help confirm that missiles are not deployed with more re-entry vehicles than the number attributed to them in the data declarations. These inspections cover ICBMs deployed in silos, on road-mobile launchers in restricted areas, and on rail-mobile launchers in rail garrisons. They also cover SLBMs that are deployed on submarines at submarine bases. During these inspections, the inspected party is required to demonstrate that the number of re-entry vehicles does not exceed the number of warheads attributed to that missile.

Because of their specialized nature, a number of restrictions are placed on these inspections. There is an annual quota of ten such inspections with no more than two per year at any one base. In addition, there can be no more than one inspection at a time; the inspection cannot be held at the same time as another type inspection at the facility; and no more than one missile can be inspected, unless a launcher declared to be empty is found to contain a deployed missile.

Re-entry vehicle inspections are "short notice" inspections with highly specific pre-inspection procedures designed to preclude altering the front section of the deployed missiles before the inspectors can arrive. These procedures also apply to submarines not only at bases, but in waters within five kilometers of the site diagram for the submarine base. The pre-inspection procedures remain in effect until the inspection team leader has designated all launchers to be inspected—including those that the host nation has declared to be empty—and an inspection subgroup has arrived at each of those locations.

If an emergency situation does not permit the required pre-inspection procedures to be implemented, the inspectors can cancel the inspection. After completion of the pre-inspection procedures, the inspection team chief designates in writing the specific launcher or fixed structure to be inspected. The inspection team then must be transported, within a specified time frame, to the designated launcher.

START Postexercise Dispersal Inspections

Because of the difficulty of locating and inspecting mobile ICBMs, the START Treaty requires that at both the beginning and the end of an exercise dispersal of mobile ICBMs be notified to the other party, which then has the right to conduct a postexercise dispersal inspection to confirm that the exercise is indeed over and that all mobile launchers and missiles are accounted for in compliance with the treaty's locational restrictions. Up to 40 percent of the bases involved in an exercise dispersal may be selected at random for inspection, including at least one base for each type of mobile missile that took part in the dispersal.

After completion of the exercise, movement restrictions are imposed on the mobile launchers and missiles that participated in the dispersal, which must remain in specified restricted areas. Postexercise dispersal inspections are conducted on a "short notice" basis with pre-inspection restrictions remaining in effect until inspectors arrive. Host country escorts must inform the inspectors of the number of mobile launchers and missiles at the base and provide an annotated site diagram showing their current location, including those that have not returned to the restricted area of the inspected base. Inspectors may inspect all restricted areas and maintenance facilities and read the "unique identifier" tag (described later) on each ICBM. They can inspect the entire inspection site to ascertain that the total number of mobile launchers and their associated missiles at an inspection site and the number that have not returned there after the dispersal does not exceed the number specified for that base.

CFE Declared Site Inspections

The CFE Treaty permits a specified number of inspections without a right of refusal at all declared units or locations in the area of application reported to be holding treaty equipment. These are defined in the treaty as "objects of verification," or OOVs. Inspectable sites generally include those containing conventional armed forces units down to the brigade/regiment or separate battalion/squadron level; designated permanent storage sites; repair and maintenance facilities where TLEs are found; and military training establishments. The quotas on such inspections differ for each period of treaty activity, and no party is required to accept more than 50 percent of its quota of declared site inspections from a single country. Unless otherwise agreed, inspectors can remain in an inspected country for a total of ten days, of which forty-eight hours can be used for the first inspection and thirty-six hours for each sequential inspection.

Inspection procedures for CFE declared site inspections generally follow the "short-notice" model, with some variations. They permit considerable flexibility to accommodate the range of size and complexity of inspectable areas. When designating the site, the inspection team can specify whether the inspection is to be conducted on foot, by cross-country vehicle, by helicopter, or by a combination of these methods. The inspected party then must provide appropriate transportation for the inspection team. This includes cross-country vehicles and

Figure 5.1
CFE Declared Site Inspection Timeline

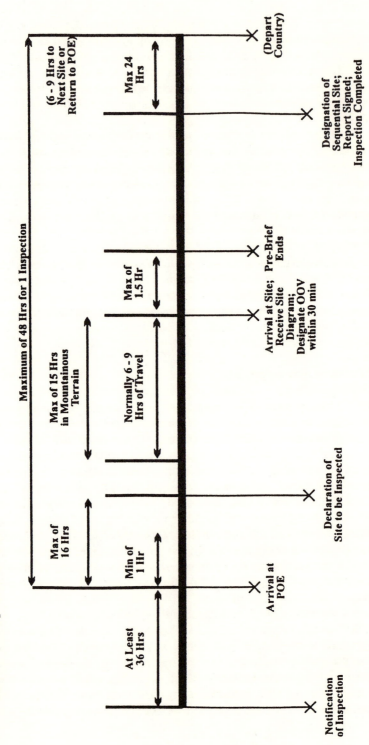

Note: Changes and variations may occur upon mutual agreement.

Source: DynMeridian, Alexandria, Virginia

helicopters for inspection team overflights of one hour duration at inspection sites larger than twenty square kilometers.

Like other declared site inspections, the inspection team has the right to inspect all of the territory delineated on the site diagram but can be denied access to sensitive points and containers with any dimension of less than two meters, unless the inspected party declares TLE or a "look alike" to be present. To ensure compliance, the inspection team also may request that doors and hatches of armored personnel carrier and armored infantry fighting vehicle "look-alikes" be opened to permit visual inspection of the interior and confirm that the vehicle is not capable of transporting combat infantry squads. Inspectors also may look into hardened aircraft shelters to ascertain the presence of TLE, but require permission to enter the shelter. If entrance is denied, the inspected party, on request, must display outside the shelter any TLE contained in the area to which access has been denied.

Given the less sensitive nature of conventional armaments, CFE declared site inspections also have more liberal photography rules than INF or START inspections. Inspectors (not just escorts) have the right to take photographs and videos to record the presence of conventional armaments and equipment subject to the treaty, including within designated permanent storage areas containing more than fifty such items. However, inspectors still must inform the escort in advance of plans to take photographs, still cameras are limited to 35 mm cameras and to polaroid-type cameras, and sensitive points and interiors can be photographed only with the cooperation of the escort team, including during helicopter overflights.

CWC Systematic Verification Inspections

The CWC provides for a variety of routine compliance inspections, termed *systematic verification inspections*, at declared sites. These can be held both at facilities that are subject to initial inspection and at those where no initial inspection is required. They vary in purpose, frequency, and timeline and for each type of facility. The CWC systematic verification inspections have roots in IAEA, as well as more modern declared site, inspections. In general, the more sensitive the facility, the shorter is the notification period prior to arrival of the inspection team and the longer inspectors may stay at the plant. A brief description of the CWC's systematic verification inspection provisions, by type of facility, follows:

CW production facilities must be closed no later than ninety days after EIF. In addition, agreed measures must be taken to render these facilities inactive, such as prohibiting occupation of facilities, disconnecting equipment, decommissioning protective and safety equipment, and interrupting access to the site. After closure and until the CW production facility is destroyed, up to four inspections per year can be conducted at each facility to confirm there is no resumption of activity or removal of declared items. Once the facility is nonoperational, a forty-eight hour notification period is allowed before the inspection team's planned arrival at the facility. When the CW production facility has been destroyed, inspections confirm that the facility has been eliminated in accordance with the treaty provisions. After all declared inventory at the facility has been destroyed and this has been duly declared by the state party, inspectors confirm the accuracy of the declaration after which further systematic verification ceases.

CW storage facilities are also subject to systematic inspections to ensure that no undetected removal of chemical weapons takes place. Normally, these inspections must be notified at least forty-eight hours before the planned arrival of an inspection team at the facility, but if the inspection or visit is to resolve an urgent problem, this period can be shortened. Once all chemical weapons have been removed from a storage facility and this is declared and confirmed by the OPCW, systematic verification of the facility is terminated.

CW destruction facilities are subject to continuous physical presence by inspectors and monitoring with on-site instruments. Following each period of destruction, inspectors confirm the report of the complete destruction of the designated quantity of chemical weapons. A storage facility located at a destruction facility is subject to systematic verification as soon as, and as long as, chemical weapons are located there.

Facilities with Schedule 1 chemicals are subject to several types of inspections. The number, intensity, duration, and mode of inspections for a particular facility is based on the characteristics of the facility, the relevant chemicals produced, the nature of the activities carried out there, and the overall risk to the CWC. Countries that produce Schedule 1 chemicals for research and medical, pharmaceutical, or protective purposes must limit such production to a single small-scale facility (SSSF). In addition, production at the facility must be carried out in reaction vessels in production lines not configured for continuous operation; the volume of such a reaction vessel must not exceed 100 liters; and the total volume of all such vessels with a volume exceeding 5 liters must not to exceed 500 liters. The systematic verification inspections at these plants verify that the quantities of Schedule 1 chemicals produced have been correctly declared and that their aggregate amount does not exceed one ton. They involve both on-site inspection and monitoring with on-site instruments. Only twenty-four hours notice is required for such an inspection to preserve the element of surprise and complicate potential cheating. The duration of each inspection, the degree of access permitted, and the maximum number of such inspections is based on the characteristics of each individual facility and specified in the facility agreement that each such facility must sign.

A state may also maintain other Schedule 1 facilities subject to inspection. These include a single, state party-approved facility other than an SSSF that produces Schedule 1 chemicals in aggregate quantities not exceeding ten kilograms per year for protective purposes; and state party-approved facilities other than SSSF producing Schedule 1 chemicals in quantities of more than 100 grams per year for research, medical, or pharmaceutical purposes in total quantities not exceeding ten kilograms per year per facility. Inspections at these facilities are designed to confirm that the quantities of Schedule 1 chemicals produced, processed, or consumed are correctly declared and consistent with needs for the declared purpose and that Schedule 1 chemicals are not diverted or used for other purposes. These inspections follow the same timeline as inspections for an SSSF.

Declared facilities with Schedule 2 chemicals also are subject to on-site inspections if they comprise one or more plants that produced, processed, or consumed during any of the three previous years or are anticipated to produce, process, or consume in the next calendar year schedule 2 chemicals above a certain threshold. The frequency and intensity of these inspections is based on assessments by inspectors conducting the initial inspection of the potential for violation of the CWC given the characteristics of the plant site and the nature of the activities carried out there. The inspections verify the absence of Schedule 1 chemicals, especially their production; confirm the accuracy of previous declarations on the levels of production, processing, or consumption of Schedule 2 chemicals at the plant; and ensure that there is no diversion of Schedule 2 chemicals for activities prohibited by the CWC.

There is a quota of not more than two inspections annually at any one Schedule 2 plant, although the OPCW has the option to also schedule a challenge inspection (without quota limitation) to investigate any suspect activity at the plant. At least forty-eight hours notification must be provided before the arrival of an inspection team at the plant site, and the period of inspection is not to exceed ninety-six hours unless an extension is mutually agreed between the inspectors and the inspected state party.

Declared facilities producing Schedule 3 chemicals which produced, during the previous calendar year, or are anticipated to produce in the next calendar year, in excess of 200 metric tons aggregate of any Schedule 3 chemical above the declaration threshold of thirty metric tons also are subject to on-site inspections. Such inspections are limited to two (challenge inspections excepted) at any plant. At least 120 hours notification before arrival of the inspection team is required and the period of inspection is not to exceed twenty-four hours unless an extension is agreed upon. These inspections verify that activities at the facility are consistent with information provided in declarations and that no Schedule 1 chemicals are present.

Inspections also are conducted at plant sites that, during the previous calendar year, produced by synthesis more than 200 metric tons of unscheduled discrete organic chemicals containing the elements of phosphorous, sulfur, or fluorine to ensure that plant activity is consistent with the information provided in the declarations. Inspections at these facilities are not scheduled to begin until the fourth year after EIF.[21] They require a 120-hour notification period and the inspections are limited to twenty-four hours unless an extension is agreed to by both parties.

NOTES

1. The data bases for the major agreements are the Memorandum of Understanding (MOU) on Data (INF), the MOU on Establishment of the Data Base (START), the Protocol on Information Exchange (CFE). Chemical Weapons Convention (CWC) data is collected and transmitted through National Authorities in each signatory country. Since issues of business confidentiality are involved, the CWC maintains only the minimum amount of information and data needed to carry out its obligations. An Annex on the Protection of Confidential Information regulates the handling of this data.

2. U.S. INF missiles were based in the United Kingdom, Italy, West Germany, Belgium, and the Netherlands. Soviet INF missiles were based in the German Democratic Republic and Czechoslovakia. A separate Basing Country Agreement between the United States and the European basing countries permitted conduct of INF inspections in Western Europe, while recognizing the sovereignty of the individual countries. The Soviet Union also had agreements with its basing countries.

3. Multiple small gestures, such as the provision by the Soviets of separate bathrooms for U.S. female inspectors at normally all-male military sites, and a serious effort to resolve inspection-related problems as they arose typified a mutual desire to ensure smooth implementation of the treaty.

4. The INF baseline inspections were aided by good summer weather, which particularly helped U.S. inspectors at the more remote Soviet inspection sites.

5. A START baseline inspection, at Mozdak, was postponed by mutual agreement until January 1997 because of safety hazards existing at that site.

6. As an interesting anomaly, because of the wording of the inspection provisions, until such time as the United States tests a long-range nuclear air-launched cruise missile for a B-2, B-2 bases are not inspectable, except for their weapons storage areas.

7. The exceptions are for alert heavy bombers, test heavy bombers, and types never listed with long-range ALCMs.

8. The United States insisted during the START negotiations that the preparations for such conventional missions should not be subject to interruption for START inspections. The United States offered during the negotiations to restrict the frequency and duration of such exemptions, but the Soviets refused to accept implementing language that they believed would be tantamount to their concurrence, before the fact, on U.S. military operations against third parties. As finally agreed, the START Treaty requires an explanation of the planned operations, but not a specific description of the planned operations, thereby protecting operational inspections. See U.S. Arms Control and Disarmament Agency Treaty Doc. 102-20, *Article by Article Analysis of the Treaty Text; Treaty with the Union of Soviet Socialist Republics on the Reduction and Limitation of*

Strategic Offensive Arms (Washington, D.C.: U.S. Government Printing Office, 1991), p. 191.

9. For an excellent synopsis of current chemical industry reporting requirement and the new CWC reporting obligations, see U.S. Congress, Office of Technology Assessment, *The Chemical Weapons Convention: Effects on the U.S. Chemical Industry* (Washington, D.C.: OTA, 1994), pp. 19–24.

10. The threshold quantities that trigger inspections generally are ten times higher than those that trigger the initial declaration requirement.

11. The Preparatory Commission of the OPCW has worked out a sample facility agreement to assist this process.

12. For example, errors in the compass azimuths and other technical details of site diagrams and in the depiction of roads that would be subject to movement restrictions during inspection required changes in U.S. site diagrams.

13. For a summary of the various ambiguities surfaced each year in connection with arms control agreements, see the annual assessments of the adherence to and compliance with arms control agreements by the United States and other parties provided in the U.S. Arms Control and Disarmament Agency's annual report to Congress through 1996, entitled *Threat Control Through Arms Control: Annual Report to Congress* (Washington, D.C.: ACDA).

14. The Tashkent Accord was signed on May 15, 1992, by the FSU successor countries within the CFE area of application to allocate division of the CFE Treaty obligations and entitlements of the former Soviet Union. A description of events leading to the agreement and of its results can be found in Joseph Harahan and John Kuhn III, *On-Site Inspection under the CFE Treaty* (Washington, D.C.: On-Site Inspection Agency, July 1996), pp. 88–90.

15. See ACDA's *Threat Control Through Arms Control: Annual Report to Congress 1995* (Washington, D.C.: ACDA, July 1996), pp. 68–70.

16. Ibid., p. 69.

17. Heavy bombers never tested with long-range nuclear ALCMs, such as the B-2, are exempted.

18. Specialized provisions cover the SS-N-17, which is not subject to technical inspection, and the SS-11, SS-17, and SS-19 ICBMs, which had to be exhibited only during a year after treaty signature during the first elimination of the systems.

19. Myron B Kratzer, *International Nuclear Safeguards: Promise and Performance*. Occasional Paper Series (Washington, D.C.: The Atlantic Council, April 1994), p. 20.

20. Ibid. pp. 26–31

21. Unless the Conference of States Parties decides otherwise at its regular session in the third year after EIF.

Chapter 6

Elimination and Conversion Inspections

The verification regimes of all modern arms control treaties permit on-site inspections of elimination and conversion activities to confirm that relevant weapons systems are destroyed or rendered incapable of performing their military functions and that this is done in the manner set out in the treaty. The Intermediate Nuclear Forces Treaty (INF) and the Chemical Weapons Convention ban entire categories of weapons and thus contain only elimination provisions.[1] The Strategic Arms Reduction Treaty (START) and Treaty on Conventional Forces in Europe (CFE) have provisions that permit lower residual levels of some weapons systems and have both elimination and conversion provisions.

Elimination inspections are held for the purpose of confirming that treaty-limited items and equipment (TLIs; TLEs) have been destroyed in accordance with treaty provisions. In general, these provisions ensure that destruction has been carried out in such a manner that the item or equipment either could not be restored at all or only at a prohibitively high cost, that is, at a cost well above normal manufacturing costs. Once eliminated in accordance with treaty provisions, such items or equipment are no longer subject to treaty constraints and numerical limitations and are removed from further accountability under the treaty.

Conversion inspections help to confirm that an item, which can be legally converted under the provisions of a treaty, has been converted in accordance with established procedures so that it is no longer capable of performing its previous military functions. Converted items remain subject to certain treaty constraints and numerical limitations even after the appropriate conversion procedures have been completed.

The general provisions governing eliminations and conversions are set out in the treaty text. The specific elimination and/or conversion procedures for each weapons system are listed in a separate section or protocol. The INF Treaty has a Protocol on Elimination; while the START I Treaty has a Protocol on Procedures Governing the Conversion or Elimination of the Items Subject to the Treaty. The CFE Treaty has three relevant protocols: a Protocol on Reductions, a Protocol on Aircraft Reclassification, and a Protocol on Helicopter Recategorization. The specific provisions in the CWC related to destruction of chemical weapons facilities are contained in the treaty text and in a separate Annex on Implementation and Verification. In addition, the sites where elimination and conversion activities can occur are specified in each treaty's data section.

BASIC ELIMINATION INSPECTION PROVISIONS

General Provisions

The inspection procedures for elimination and conversion activities generally follow a similar pattern. Elimination and conversion inspections are not subject to any quota limitations, and there is no right of refusal for such inspections. As a rule, elimination and conversion inspections begin at the start of the baseline inspection period. There often is a limitation (usually two) on the number of sites at which such elimination or conversion activities can take place simultaneously during the baseline period to avoid overstraining the host country's escort abilities during this period of particularly intense inspection activity.

Like other inspection teams, there is a limit (usually twenty) on the number of inspectors on elimination teams, although in practice the numbers can vary somewhat depending on circumstances. During the INF elimination inspections, for example, both sides decided that, in some cases, smaller inspection teams were sufficient to confirm the elimination process, especially when eliminations took place during the course of a normal working day and week, rather than on an around-the-clock basis, making it unnecessary to set up inspection shifts. Accordingly, INF elimination teams of both sides typically averaged only ten inspectors, with an occasional increase of up to fourteen to accommodate training of new inspection personnel.

Since eliminations require substantial advance planning and can be programmed well in advance, elimination inspections have "scheduled," rather than "short notice," timelines. Usually a notification of the systems to be eliminated and the date and place of the elimination activity is provided by the host country to the inspectors a full month in advance to permit ample time to prepare to send an inspection team. Similarly the inspection team notifies the host country at least seventy-two hours ahead of time of their arrival at the point of entry (POE) in the country of the inspected party. If there is a short delay (less than five days) in the initiation of elimination activity after the inspectors have departed their home base, they have their choice of remaining at the POE or the inspection site. If the delay is longer than five days, the inspectors return home, unless otherwise agreed. Once transported to the elimination site, inspectors are housed for the period of elimination or conversion activity at, or in reasonable proximity to, the inspection site.

Inspection Procedures at the Site

In general, modern arms control treaties follow the principle that, in eliminating or converting treaty-accountable items, each side is free to use its own destruction technology, provided the country complies fully with the destruction or conversion procedures stipulated for each item in treaty provisions. Inspectors are obligated to ensure that the inspections do not interfere with on-going activities at the site or unnecessarily hamper, delay, or complicate the elimination or conversion process.

The steps for preparing individual pieces of equipment for on-site inspection and inspection procedures are delineated in the treaty. Before elimination or conversion activity begins, the inspection team confirms and records the type and number of TLIs or TLE to be destroyed or converted. Inspectors may take measurements and observations to confirm this data, including, in the case of START, reading and inspecting the individual identification numbers (unique identifiers) required to be placed on each mobile missile. Host country representatives are obligated to assist this process including, in the case of canisterized missile systems, permitting the viewing of the insides of canisters or removing the missile from the canister, although this latter procedure is not mandatory.[2] If a canisterized missile is involved, inspectors are permitted to open the canister and visually inspect the missile to confirm that a treaty-limited missile, and not some other object, is in fact destroyed. In the case of elimination of heavy bombers, inspectors have the option to confirm that a heavy bomber said to be equipped to carry long-range nuclear air-launched cruise missiles (ALCMs) is actually so equipped before the elimination begins.

If dangerous activity is involved, such as the destruction of missiles by explosive demolition, igniting the missile in a fixed stand (static burn) or launch to destruction, inspectors observe the elimination process from a viewing site located a safe distance from the place of elimination. In such cases, inspectors must be able to keep the item in sight at all times and be provided with binoculars.

The results of the elimination or conversion process are duly recorded in an inspection report filled out by the inspection team leader and a member of the in-country escort. Like other inspection reports, this report does not make judgements about whether the inspected party has fully complied with its obligations. It records the facts observed, points out any anomalies that may occur, and notes efforts made to resolve them. Like other inspection reports, a final determination of compliance with all treaty-mandated elimination requirements is made only after the report has been analyzed in the capitals.

Since the elimination process may take place over an extended period, some treaties, such as the INF and START agreements, permit the rotation of inspectors during the elimination process. However, to ensure the orderly management of transfers at the elimination sites—which because of the very nature of the elimination process often are located in remote areas—the frequency of replacements is limited, typically to once every three weeks with at least half of the inspectors being replaced during the changeover. Moreover, the changeover must be carried out in a manner that ensures that the number of inspectors at the site does not exceed the allowable quota. This provision is to accommodate potentially limited accommodation and transportation arrangements at the site and to avoid overburdening the host country escort team.

Special provisions often apply to the rotation of inspection team chiefs at elimination sites. To ensure continuity and accuracy in the tracking of eliminations, the team chief generally is required to see through to completion, and duly record, any elimination activity begun under his or her surveillance. In addition, there are often provisions for a short hiatus (three hours or so) in elimination or conversion activity during the changeover period to permit pre-inspection procedures for the new inspectors to be completed.

METHODS OF ELIMINATION AND CONVERSION

Eliminations and conversions can be carried out in a number of different ways, depending on the treaty. The usual method is to move items to be elimination or converted to designated elimination or conversion sites specified in the MOU on data and to destroy them there by cutting, crushing, static testing, burning, demolition or other method. If an item to be destroyed is a fixed or immovable structure, such as a concrete launch silo, it can be destroyed where it stands—*in situ*. In some cases, missiles can be eliminated by launching them to destruction or destroying them by flight tests. Some conventional items can be destroyed by using them as targets. Elimination also can result through accidental loss or disablement beyond repair. An accountable item also can be "destroyed" by rendering it inert and using it for static display, that is, for museum or other exhibition-type purposes. Finally some equipment can be removed from accountability under a treaty by being converted, reclassified, or recategorized, permitting its use solely for civilian or military training purposes. Each of these methods of elimination or conversion is verified by its own procedures. Some are confirmed by on-site inspection, others by national technical means (NTM), and still others by a combination of both types of verification.

Elimination and Conversion at Designated Sites

Most routine elimination and conversion activity takes place at sites that have been previously listed in the treaty's data section. The data on these sites is periodically updated as activity is completed at a site or a new site is designated. The restriction of most elimination or conversion activity to designated sites simplifies the handling of logistics for on-site inspection and facilitates monitoring by NTM.

Routine INF Eliminations at Designated Sites

The INF Treaty required the two signatories (the U.S. and U.S.S.R.) to destroy all ground-launched INF missile systems with ranges between 500 and 5,500 kilometers. This included their infrastructure but not nuclear warheads, guidance systems, and certain other designated salvageable items. Nuclear warheads and guidance systems were exempted, since their elimination posed verification difficulties that were insurmountable at that time, including the problem of differentiating INF warheads and guidance systems from those for other missile systems. Their verification also would have required highly intrusive inspections of sensitive nuclear and other military production facilities which neither side was then prepared to accept. The INF Treaty also permitted the salvaging of some items that could be used for legitimate civilian purposes, notably transporter-erector vehicles for the eliminated missiles, provided these were modified to prevent their use for purposes prohibited by the treaty. This pattern of permitting salvageable items during the elimination process has persisted in follow-up arms control treaties.

In general, INF cruise missiles were destroyed by having the front section removed and cut up, crushed, or flattened. The cruise missile then was sliced longitudinally and its wings and tail section were severed at points other than the normal assembly joints. Liquid fueled missile systems were eliminated by draining the liquid propellant and cutting up the missile bodies. Solid propellant missiles either were blown up, eliminated by static fire, burned, or launched to destruction.

During static fire the missile stage is anchored on a fixed stand in a horizontal position and ignited, burning virtually all of its propellant. The blown out missile casing then is crushed and disposed of in a landfill. To prevent misuse of the static fire process for missile test purposes, the INF Treaty prohibited instrumentation during firing. Old or defective INF missiles, which could not be safely destroyed by static fire, were cage burned. This involved placing a missile stage horizontally in a partially enclosed "cage" and igniting a linear shaped charge placed along it. The cage contained debris should the missile explode. Components such as canisters, rocket nozzles, and motor cases not destroyed in the elimination process were burned, crushed, flattened, or destroyed by explosion. The preferred Russian method of INF missile elimination was explosive demolition, which involved simply grouping and detonating the missiles.

Routine START Eliminations and Conversions at Designated Sites

The START I and II treaties require reductions and limits on the strategic offensive forces (intercontinental ballistic missiles (ICBMs), submarine-launched ballistic missiles (SLBMs) and manned strategic bombers and their weapons) of the United States and the four nuclear successor states of the former Soviet Union, including elimination of all multiple warhead ICBMs.

Given their special importance in treaty provisions, stringent accountability procedures govern the elimination of mobile missiles. START requires notification of the transit and arrival of such missiles at the conversion or elimination site. At the site, the main elements of the mobile missile launcher, including the erector-launcher and leveling supports, must be destroyed and the vehicle chassis reduced in size. A railcar or flatcar for a rail-mobile missile must be cut in half to render it useless. Also reflecting their special status, verification of the elimination of mobile missiles is by on-site inspection, rather than NTM.

The mobile missile stages can be removed from accountability in a number of ways. The treaty provides for destruction by explosive demolition, if the solid fuel is not removed, but leaves open the option of removing the propellant and destroying the casings. This permits possible reuse of the propellant for other than military purposes, e.g. as a fertilizer or mining explosive. However, missiles also can be destroyed by static testing at designated destruction sites, involving both the ground-based firing of first stages and other means of destructive ground-based testing that may be required for research and development or force reliability purposes. Notification must be provided prior to such static testing and the remains of the missile are subject to on-site inspection before final elimination.

SLBM launch tubes also must be destroyed at designated elimination and conversion facilities, but this time consuming and highly observable elimination process is verifiable by NTM. The elimination process begins when a ballistic missile submarine is positioned at an elimination site with all missile launch tubes empty and hatches opened or removed. SLBM launchers are considered eliminated when either the missile section or missile launch tubes and structures are removed from the submarine. The submarine must remain visible to NTM during the entire elimination process to confirm complete dismantlement. Retired ballistic missile submarines may be converted for purposes not inconsistent with the treaty, including conversion to cruise missile submarines incapable of redeployment of SLBMS, but any permissible refurbishment of the dismantled missile compartment may not begin before the end of the observation period.

The elimination of heavy bombers and former heavy bombers, provided for in START, also takes place at designated elimination or conversion facilities and is subject to verification by both NTM and on-site inspections. The elimination of heavy bombers equipped for long-range nuclear ALCMs, which has an impact on the treaty's aggregate limitation on warheads, is subject to an initial on-site inspection to confirm that the heavy bombers being eliminated are actually of the type and category declared and not of one with no attributed warheads. The completion of the elimination process then also can be verified by on-site inspection. The entire bomber elimination process is not observed by on-site inspection because the length of time involved makes this impractical, and once the type and category of heavy bomber has been confirmed by inspectors, NTM can effectively observe the remaining procedures.

Figure 6.1
Russian SSBN Elimination Process

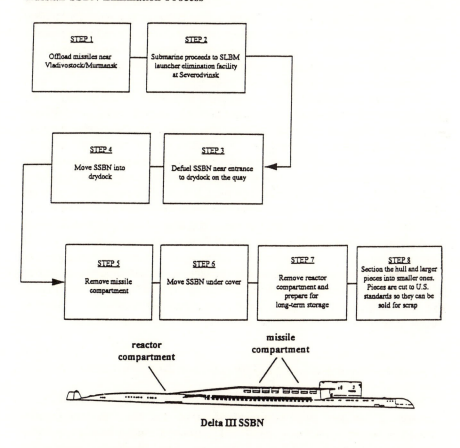

Delta III SSBN

Source: **Jean Laybyle Couhat, ed.** *Combat Fleets of the World 1986/87* **(Annapolis, MD: Naval Institute Press, 1986) p. 493**

As in other eliminations, the bomber elimination process is carefully defined, including salvageable equipment and the point at which the elimination process begins and ends. To eliminate a heavy bomber the tail section must be severed from the fuselage at a location obviously not an assembly joint; the wings are separated from the fuselage; and the remainder of the fuselage is cut in two in the area where the wings are attached. Eliminations must be notified, and the entire process then completed within sixty days to ensure that once elimination begins and the item is removed from accountability, the elimination is completed promptly. The bomber also must remain visible to NTM during the entire process and the remains of the airframe for ninety days thereafter.

Under START, heavy bombers also can be converted in a number of ways: Heavy bombers equipped for long-range ALCMs can be converted into heavy bombers equipped for other nuclear armaments or non-nuclear armaments or into training or former heavy bombers; heavy bombers equipped for nuclear armaments other than long-range nuclear ALCMs can be converted into heavy bombers of non-nuclear armaments or into training or other former heavy bombers; and heavy bombers equipped for non-nuclear armaments can be converted into training or other heavy bombers.

Procedures for each type of conversion are defined in the treaty. These include, where appropriate, the inspection of weapon bays and external attachment points and pylons to confirm that the bombers have been properly converted. A converted bomber may not be immediately flown, but must be moved directly to a viewing site at the conversion or elimination facility, after proper notification that the conversion process has been completed.[3] Inspectors then have the right, within twenty days after arrival of the plane at the viewing site, to inspect the aircraft and confirm that proper conversion has taken place.

Heavy bombers or former heavy bombers can be converted to ground trainers by the removal of at least one-third of each wing or the entire vertical stabilizer after which the item ceases to be accountable under the treaty. Notification of this change must be provided, and after completion of the change, the converted bomber or former heavy bomber must remain visible to NTM for ninety days. When no longer used as a ground trainer, the item can be eliminated either *in situ* or at a conversion or elimination facility using applicable procedures.

Routine CFE Eliminations and Conversions at Designated Sites

The CFE Treaty embodies a complete set of ceilings on those categories of conventional military equipment and weapons that most directly support offensive operations, including battle tanks, armored combat vehicles, artillery pieces, combat aircraft, and attack helicopters. It also establishes upper limits on the amount of equipment that any single state may hold in the treaty's region of application—the Atlantic to the Urals. Equipment in excess of treaty limits had to be destroyed, with the reductions carried out so that the agreed limits on equipment were reached forty months after entry into force of the treaty, that is, by November 1995.

Like INF and START, the CFE Treaty contains detailed provisions on how equipment was to be destroyed or converted in order to ensure that it was effectively deprived of its military capability. The treaty permitted destruction by cutting, exploding, deforming, or smashing. An example of deforming was the elimination of an aircraft by compressing the fuselage to reduce its height, length, or width by at least 30 percent. Smashing, a cost-effective destruction method used by Poland, involved the destruction of TLE by dropping an eight-ton wrecking ball on the equipment from a crane.

Figure 6.2
CFE Armament Reduction Timeline

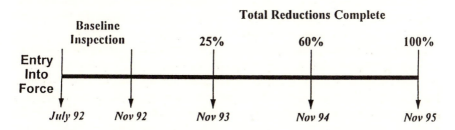

In general, battle tanks, armored combat vehicles, and artillery had to be reduced by destruction, placement on static display, or used as ground targets. Tanks and armored personnel carriers also could be converted for nonmilitary purposes. Some aircraft and helicopters could be reclassified or recategorized in a manner that ensures that their attack capability is eliminated. Combat aircraft could be destroyed (including by use as target drones), placed on static display, used for ground instructional purposes, or, in the case of a limited number of specific older models or versions of combat capable trainer aircraft, reclassified into unarmed trainer aircraft.[4] In addition, multipurpose attack helicopters could be recategorized.

The process of reductions of TLE to established ceilings was subject to on-site inspection, with only one inspection team at a site at one time. In practice, CFE reduction inspections were carried out by multinational teams, generally coordinated through the NATO Verification Coordinating Committee. Because a number of CFE signatories have served, or continue to serve, as basing countries for the military forces of third countries, the CFE Treaty provides that several parties could use a single reduction site. If two states parties notified reduction schedules calling for simultaneous reduction activities at the same site, there still could be only one inspection team at the site at any one time, but that team could inspect the reductions of both countries. Each reduction period had to be notified separately.

Under CFE provisions, each signatory was notified of the specific conventional armaments and equipment to be reduced at each reduction site during a calendar reporting period. The reduction period had to be at least thirty days, but no longer than ninety days, in duration. Further notifications had to be provided to all signatories at least fifteen days before the reductions began. These notifications had to provide information on the designation and geographic coordinates of the reduction site; the scheduled dates for beginning and completing the reductions; the estimated number and type of conventional arms to be reduced; the objects of verification (sites) from which the items to be reduced were withdrawn; the reduction procedures to be used for destroying each type of armament and equipment; the POE to be used by the inspection team; and the date and time by which the inspection team were to arrive at that POE.

The CFE Treaty gave inspectors the right to remain at a reduction site through one or more calendar reporting periods, provided the periods were not separated by more than three days. At the reduction site, inspectors could observe all reduction procedures. However, because some reductions were more time consuming or of less military importance than others, inspectors were free to come and go as many times as they wished through the specified reduction process. They had the option to remain at the reduction site and continuously observe the entire notified reduction process; inspect the beginning of the process, depart (including to inspect other reductions or recertification) and return at the end or at a time of their own choosing during the process; or inspect only part of the particular notified reduction process at that site. During the inspection, inspectors could either freely record the serial numbers from the conventional armaments and equipment to be reduced, or place special markings on such equipment before initiation of the reduction process and then confirm those serial numbers or markings at the completion of the process.

Figure 6.3
CFE Reduction Inspections Timeline

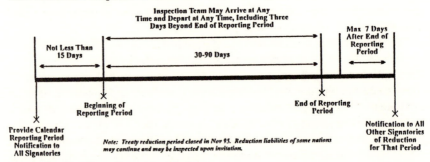

Source: **DynMeridian, Alexandria, Virginia**

The treaty also required that certain items be made available by the inspected party for inspection at least three days after the end of the calendar reporting period unless inspection of the items had already been completed. These included the essential components of the conventional armaments and equipment subject to reduction procedures, such as the hull, turret, and integral main armament of a battle tank and, in the case of conversion, the vehicles converted for nonmilitary purposes.

To help inspectors track reductions and assist preparation of the inspection report at the end of each inspection period, the treaty required a "working register" to be maintained at each reduction site and made available to the inspection team for the period of the inspection. The register had to contain a record of factory serial numbers for each item to be reduced, the dates on which the reduction procedures were initiated and completed for each item and the aggregate data for each calendar reduction period. After conclusion of the inspection period, inspectors had the option to either depart the territory of the inspected party or conduct a sequential inspection. The reducing party was obligated to inform all other State Parties of the completion of reductions for each calendar reporting period, providing particulars of the reductions.

In-Situ Elimination

Most treaties permit buildings, silos, and other fixed structures slated for elimination to be destroyed where they stand (*in situ*) since moving them at a designated destruction site would be impossible or impractical.

Fixed support structures and shelters for INF missiles and equipment were eliminated in place by destroying the superstructure and excavating or blowing up its base or foundation. The destruction had to be notified in advance and the destroyed base or foundation then had to remain visible to NTM either for six months or until completion of an optional on-site inspection.

START also permits *in situ* elimination of major elements of infrastructure at declared facilities, including bases, loading facilities, repair facilities, storage facilities, training facilities, conversion or elimination facilities, and test ranges. Verification of this destruction is by OSI. The *in situ* elimination of all other declared facilities, including silos, is subject to verification by NTM, with the exception of conversion of silos for heavy ICBMs. A declared facility is considered to be eliminated under START when all strategic offensive arms specified for the facility, and all support equipment, has been removed and when silo launchers and fixed structures for mobile ICBMs have been destroyed in accordance with treaty provisions.

Elimination of START "soft-site" launchers, that is fixed land-based launchers other than silos, is accomplished by removal of all key equipment at least 1,000 meters from the launcher to be eliminated and excavation or explosion of the site to a depth of at least two meters.[5] The soft-site launcher must remain visible to NTM during the entire elimination process.

Elimination *in situ* of START "hard-site" launchers, which include such readily observable structures as missile silos, training silos, and the fixed structures used by mobile launchers of ICBMs, is verified solely by NTM. To aid NTM, the destroying party must provide notification of its intention to eliminate hard sites thirty days before beginning the process and remove all missiles, containers, and support equipment at least 1,000 meters from a silo to be eliminated.[6] The elimination process must include the removal, dismantlement, or destruction of the silo door and destruction of the silo headworks and silo by excavation to a depth of at least eight meters or explosion to a depth of at least six meters. Once this is done, preliminary safety measures can be taken to reduce hazards, such as backfilling, but the hole cannot be filled until at least ninety days have passed to assist NTM observation. The entire silo elimination process must be competed within 180 days of notification, and the silo must remain visible to NTM during that entire period.

Special provisions exist for the elimination of silos used for heavy ICBMs (the huge SS-18s). These large silos may be converted to permit their use by smaller missiles, provided this is done in a way that precludes any re-use by SS-18s. This is done by requiring that the base of the silo be filled with at least five meters of concrete and that a restrictive ring be installed in the silo, which restricts its use only to missiles with a diameter significantly smaller than that of the SS-18. These measures can be verified by on-site inspections to ensure that they are done properly and in an non-reconvertable manner.

Elimination by Launching to Destruction or by Flight Tests

The INF Treaty provided that up to 100 missiles on each side could be destroyed by launching from existing test ranges within the first six months after EIF. Missiles launched to destruction could be visually inspected by inspectors just before launch to confirm that they were treaty-limited missiles (not substitutes), and the launching was observed from an area that permitted the launch site to be under constant surveillance. Such launches had to be from designated elimination facilities to existing impact areas, and the launched missiles could not be used as target vehicles for ballistic missile interceptors. To permit better coverage of the launches by NTM, only one launch was permitted at a time and the launch intervals had to be separated from each other by a time interval of at least six hours. All missile stages had to be ignited during launch to destruction. To prevent use of the launches for testing purposes, no data, other than unencrypted data for range safety purposes, could be transmitted or recovered from the missiles.[7]

Under START, ICBMs for mobile launchers also may be removed from accountability by flight tests. The procedures require advance notification of the test, and the ICBM is removed from treaty accountability when the flight test has been completed. Verification is by NTM. As a variant on this type of elimination, CFE permitted the use of aircraft as target drones as an approved method of reduction.

Elimination by Static Display

Most treaties permit a limited number of treaty-limited items (up to fifteen each for START and INF) to be eliminated by "static display," that is, by making them museum or display pieces. To be removed from accountability by static display, the item must first be visibly rendered inoperable and unusable for purposes inconsistent with the treaty and (with the obvious exception of silos) transported to a location where it can be inspected. Once these procedures are complete, a notification is sent. An on-site inspection then can be held within thirty days after the notification is received. When the thirty day period expires, the item is considered on static display whether or not the other party has exercised its right of inspection. If an item subsequently is removed from static display, it either can be destroyed at the site of static display or transported to a designated elimination facility, where it must use the applicable procedures agreed to in the treaty.

Accidental Loss or Disablement Beyond Repair

Under several treaties (INF, START), TLIs can be removed from accountability if they are accidentally destroyed or disabled beyond repair. In the case of a TLI destroyed by accident, the other party must be notified of the particulars of the accidental loss, including the date or assumed date of the loss, its approximate or assumed location, and the circumstances of the loss or destruction. Inspectors then have the right to inspect the accident site to confirm destruction.

If, in the judgment of the possessing party an item accountable under the treaty is disabled beyond repair, a notification to that effect must be provided, and the item then is destroyed either at the site of disablement or at a conversion or elimination facility where it is subject to the applicable elimination procedures, including on-site inspection.

Conversion of Vehicles for Non-Military Purposes

While the INF Treaty has only an elimination (not conversion) protocol, the treaty nonetheless did permit the conversion and reuse of some equipment. The German-made ten-ton tractors that pulled the erector-launcher trailers for U.S. Pershing missiles were standard commercial vehicles, indistinguishable from other readily available, commercially sold tractor cabs. Thus there was no rationale for destroying them. On the basis of reciprocity, the Soviets insisted that their missile transporter-launcher vehicles, which were integrated units without separate cabs, also should be exempted from elimination—after being

Figure 6.4
START Notification Format for Static Display

```
START FORMAT 55

REFERENCE:  NOTIFICATION PROTOCOL SECTION IV PARAGRAPH 1
------------------------------------------------------------------


SUBJECT:  NOTIFICATION OF INTENTION TO PLACE AN ITEM ON STATIC
          DISPLAY

1.  ANC  /  STR         /55

2.  REFERENCES:  A)          B)          C)          D)

3.  CONTENT:

    A)  TYPE, CATEGORY (AND VARIANT OR VERSION IF APPLICABLE) OF
        ITEMS:  [ response ]

    B)  NUMBER OF ITEMS:  9999

    C)  UNIQUE IDENTIFIER FOR ICBM FOR MOBILE LAUNCHER OF ICBMS:
        1)  [ response ]
        2)  [ response ]

    D)  LOCATION OF ITEMS:
        [ response ]  DD-MMD, DDD-MMD

    E)  PROCESS LOCATION:
        [ response ]  DD-MMD, DDD-MMD

    F)  DATE OF SCHEDULED INITIATION:  DD-MMM-YYYY

    G)  PROCEDURES ASSOCIATED WITH PLACING AN ITEM
        ON STATIC DISPLAY:

4.  REMARKS:

5.  END OF ANC  /  STR         /55
```

Source: **U.S. Nuclear Risk Reduction Center, U.S. Department of State, Washington, D.C.**

rendered incapable of further military use—so that they could be used for civilian purposes. The United States accepted reuse of the vehicles provided their launcher mechanism was destroyed, their stabilizers removed, and the vehicle chassis shortened to preclude any use as a launcher platform. During the INF inspection process, however, U.S.inspectors discovered that the Soviets had welded a rear portion of the chassis back on to a number of transporter-launcher vehicles that had been designated as "eliminated," ostensibly to make the vehicles watertight so that they could be used as amphibious vehicles for civilian use. The U.S. inspection chief declared an anomaly, and the Soviets subsequently recut the chassis, completing the elimination process in the prescribed manner.

Like INF, START also permits the reuse of military vehicles previously used as launcher platforms for ICBMs once the erector launcher mechanism and leveling supports, together with their mountings, have been destroyed. However, as a result of the INF experience, there is a specific provision in the START Treaty stipulating that removed pieces of a vehicle chassis may not be reattached.

CFE also permits conversions of military vehicles into vehicles for nonmilitary purposes subject to inspections. Certain tanks and armored combat vehicles could be converted to nonmilitary equipment, such as bulldozers, firefighting equipment, and rescue vehicles. In these cases, the inspection team had the right to arrive at the reduction site during the three days after the end of the notified completion date of conversion. This enabled inspectors to validate only the completion, rather than the entire process, of conversion to ensure that vehicles had been converted into the declared specific types of vehicles for nonmilitary purposes.

Reclassification of Aircraft

The CFE Treaty also gave each state party the right to reduce no more than 550 combat-capable trainer aircraft by reclassification into unarmed trainer aircraft. To implement this provision, it established specific procedures for (1) disarming and certifying specified combat-capable trainer aircraft and (2) for simply certifying models or versions of specified combat-capable trainer aircraft that have never been armed, based on whether or not the aircraft had certain components. All states parties had to be notified of each certification. Each party then could inspect the certification using the specified certification procedures in the Inspection Protocol to confirm that the combat-capable trainer aircraft had been reclassified in accordance with treaty provisions. The actual process of disarming was not inspected, but inspectors could confirm at its conclusion that the conversion process had been carried out properly. Such inspections could not be refused and were not subject to quotas.

Recategorization of Multipurpose Attack Helicopters

Special CFE provisions applied to inspections of multipurpose attack helicopters, that is, helicopters that performed multiple military functions and employed guided weapons. By removing their weapons systems, mounting points, fire control systems, and wiring, the helicopters could be recategorized as combat support helicopters not limited by the treaty. Inspectors had the right to inspect internally any helicopter found at an inspection site that was declared to be either a combat support helicopter of a type that was, or had been, on the multipurpose attack helicopter list to ensure that it remained incapable of employing guided weapons or remained equipped for the stated purpose of reconnaissance, spotting, or sampling.

Figure 6.5
CFE Certification Inspection Timeline

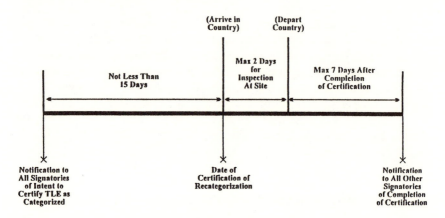

Source: **DynMeridian, Alexandria, Virginia**

NOTES

1. The CWC also provides for the conversion of CW production facilities, but, as of this writing the specific rules and modalities have not been determined. These may eventually be addressed on a case-by-case basis.

2. During the INF and START negotiations, the Soviets insisted that many of their missiles and canisters constituted a single missile system and that removal of the missiles from their canisters, outside of production or repair facilities, was dangerous. The United States agreed to make removal optional as long as it could otherwise confirm the type of missile contained in the canister.

3. To expedite movement of the converted bomber to the viewing site and allow inspectors to prepare for an early inspection, the START Treaty also provides for a voluntary additional notification of the planned date of arrival of a converted bomber at the viewing site.

4. Only certain Soviet-produced aircraft are on the list of aircraft eligible to be reclassified, since no other signatory nation chose to reclassify any aircraft.

5. The term "soft site" is somewhat of a misnomer since such sites typically have a reinforced concrete slab base, often of considerable thickness.

6. Except for training silos.

7. The United States elected not to eliminate any of its INF missiles by launch to destruction, largely for reasons of cost and to avoid overtasking the launch facilities at Cape Canaveral. The Soviet eliminated seventy-two SS-20s by launch to destruction, with only a single failure down range, underscoring the reliability of that missile system.

Chapter 7

Suspect Site Regimes

Most arms control inspections designed to ensure compliance with treaty provisions take place at previously declared military-controlled or- related sites and facilities, using well-established procedures laid out in treaty documents. But what if a party to a treaty has strong reason to suspect—perhaps through information gained by its own national technical means (NTM), by defectors, or by reports from other countries—that a treaty violation is occurring at an undeclared, perhaps privately owned, site not normally subjected to inspection under any arms control regime?

Under most early arms control agreements, countries had little recourse but to raise such issues through diplomatic channels. To provide an alternative expert forum for raising arms control compliance issues, The Strategic Arms Limitations Treaty (SALT) established a separate body—the Standing Consultative Commission (SCC)—to discuss such matters. Early experience with using that body to deal with problem areas was relatively positive, but the cooperative atmosphere in the SCC deteriorated as serious compliance concerns were raised during the Reagan administration. There was no way of compelling a satisfactory answer to these concerns, which, more often than not, were dismissed by the Soviets in the SCC as "groundless," answered with unsubstantiated "assurances" that no violation had occurred, or tied up in endless fruitless discussions.

To improve the investigation and resolution of compliance issues that can not be resolved in the established treaty compliance bodies, many modern arms control agreements also contain specialized procedures that permit "suspect site" inspections. Some of these inspections are limited to designated sites, but others permit inspections at any location, whether or not listed in the treaty text, and at privately owned facilities as well as government sites. Among the various types of suspect site inspections are International Atomic Energy Agency (IAEA) special inspections—an early type of suspect site inspection; suspect site inspections under the Strategic Arms Reduction Treaty (START), which permit short notice inspections at a few designated missile sites; START "visits with right of special access" (SAVs), which establish a mechanism for negotiated access anywhere a treaty violation is suspected; and challenge inspections under the Treaty on Conventional Forces in Europe (CFE) and the Chemical Weapons Convention (CWC). Because of their potential intrusiveness and application to privately owned industrial facilities, suspect site inspections raise important questions of how trade secrets and other confidential proprietary or security information is to be protected, while still permitting inspectors to resolve their compliance concerns. Some also raise legal and, in the United States, even constitutional questions not encountered to the same degree by other types of on-site inspection.

IAEA SPECIAL INSPECTIONS

General Provisions

The IAEA safeguards system has a two-tiered inspection regime: "routine inspections" carried out to verify non diversion under normal circumstances, and "special inspections" that can be invoked when the director general concludes the IAEA cannot meet its verification responsibilities on the basis of information available from its routine inspections. In recent years, as attention has focused on nuclear proliferation in Iraq, North Korea and elsewhere, the IAEA has demonstrated an increased readiness to apply its special inspection authority.

The heart of the IAEA's current capability to discover or confirm undeclared nuclear material or activities in non-nuclear states party to the Nuclear Nonproliferation Treaty (NPT) is found in the provisions of United Nations Information Circular (INFCIRC) 153, which authorize the agency to call for special inspection whenever it "considers that information made available by the state is not adequate for the Agency to fulfill its responsibilities under the Agreement." Thus the IAEA must have a good faith reason to request a special inspection, but the grounds on which it can do so are extremely broad and decided on by sole discretion of the director general.[1]

Special inspection can involve access to locations or information not available through routine inspections. Thus the agency can request a special inspection even if it cannot specify the location of the suspected undeclared nuclear material or activity. When the location of suspected undeclared nuclear material or activity is unknown, the director general can request a special inspection to provide access to any information necessary to determine that location and the purposes of the suspected activity. The IAEA's special inspection demand to North Korea in 1992 made use of this feature, calling for access both to additional locations and to additional information.

A state may reject a request by the IAEA for a special inspection or other special steps, but if it does so this can be overridden by the agency's Board of

Governors, who must find that the inspection is "essential and urgent." While this procedure involves a number of steps, there are no minimum times specified for each step; they can be telescoped to permit prompt agency response.

In addition to special inspections, in case of verification of initial inventory, the agency may conduct inspections as a matter of right, without consultation and without limit as to the number of inspections, at any location where the initial report or its initial inspections indicate nuclear material may be present.[2]

Use of IAEA Special Inspections in North Korea

Both IAEA routine and the previously rarely used special inspection procedures were applied in an effort to clarify ambiguities in a 1992 case involving North Korea. North Korea acceded to the NPT in December 1985, but it found a variety of excuses over the next six years not to complete its required safeguards agreement with the IAEA.[3] During this period it became apparent that North Korea was operating a nuclear reactor and constructing what appeared to be a nuclear fuel reprocessing plant and other associated fuel cycle facilities in violation of its NPT commitments to have IAEA safeguards on nuclear material in all of its peaceful nuclear activities.

In April 1992, after concluding a bilateral denuclearization agreement with South Korea, which included a renunciation of the production of fissile materials on the Korean peninsula, and under international pressure, North Korea finally brought into force its IAEA safeguards agreement. It declared various nuclear facilities at Yongbyon, and IAEA inspections of those facilities began.[4] After six IAEA inspections in 1992, evidence collected by the IAEA, and intelligence information made available to it, the IAEA concluded that additional nuclear sites beyond those declared by North Korea could contain evidence of North Korean nuclear reprocessing activities.

When extensive discussions between IAEA and North Korea failed to resolve these discrepancies, the IAEA Director General formally requested a "special inspection" of two suspected North Korean waste sites in February 1993. This request was refused by North Korea. Accordingly, the IAEA's Board of Governors adopted a resolution formally requesting access to the sites and gave the North Koreans a month to comply. North Korea responded by declaring that it was exercising its right of withdrawal under the NPT. The IAEA Board of Governors then declared North Korea in noncompliance with its NPT safeguards agreement and affirmed that the agency could not verify nondiversion of nuclear material. It so advised the U.N. Security Council. In May 1993, the Security Council adopted Resolution 825, with China and Pakistan abstaining, calling on North Korea to reconsider its withdrawal from the NPT and to honor its obligations under the treaty and its safeguard agreement. The resolution urged the IAEA to continue consultations with North Korea to resolve the issues and asked member states to encourage a positive North Korean response. More decisive Security Council action was prevented by China's insistence that North Korea not be sanctioned and that further dialogue be encouraged.[5]

Following the Security Council action, The United States initiated a direct bilateral dialogue with North Korea to resolve a broader complex of issues, with the primary objective of obtaining North Korean compliance with the NPT and its IAEA safeguards agreement. In October 1994, the United States and North Korea signed an Agreed Framework, which requires North Korea to freeze its nuclear program and ultimately comply with its NPT safeguards agreement. North Korea subsequently froze construction and work on the two suspect reactors and allowed a continuous IAEA presence at Yongbyon but did not permit IAEA special inspections, leaving unresolved a definitive answer by the agency of whether it had violated the NPT.

START SUSPECT SITE INSPECTIONS

Initial Proposals

During the START negotiations, the United States introduced various verification proposals calling for "anywhere, anytime" suspect site inspections both with and without a right of refusal. Over time, however, ambivalence grew within the U.S. government regarding the potential costs, both financially in preparing a large number of facilities for such inspections and in the potential loss of confidential proprietary and security information, of "anywhere, anytime" on-site inspections. By the late 1980s, U.S. military technology had far outstripped that of the Soviet Union, giving the United States more to lose by intrusive inspections of sensitive facilities. In addition, the capabilities of NTM to detect violations had further improved reducing the risks that violations would go undetected.

These factors led to modifications in the U.S. negotiating proposals that eventually evolved into two separate provisions in the START Treaty. One provision was aimed at confirming that the declared missile production facilities of both sides were complying with START provisions. This was accomplished by requiring "suspect site inspections" (SSIs) at a few particularly important missile production facilities specified in the treaty.[6] The other provision called for a mutually agreed "visit with right of special access" to provide a mechanism for resolving compliance concerns at any facility, whether declared or undeclared, where suspect activity might be occurring.[7]

START Suspect-Site Inspections

The START Treaty provides for suspect site inspections of the final assembly areas for mobile Intercontinental ballistic missiles (ICBMs) to be conducted after completion of the baseline inspections to help confirm that there is no covert assembly of mobile ICBMs or of the first stages of such ICBMs at locations known to have produced such missiles. In the negotiating process, agreement was reached on permitting "suspect site" inspections at three sites on each side, which then were listed in the treaty.[8] In the United States they are located at Hill Air Force Base in Ogden Utah and at missile plants in Magna, Utah and Sacramento, California. In Russia, the missile production facilities subject to suspect site inspections are located in Zlatoust, Bershet', and Petropavlovsk. Additional facilities can be added to this list, provided they meet specifically defined criteria.[9] Should suspicious production activity be detected at other locations, the matter would be raised as a compliance concern in the treaty's Joint Compliance and Inspection Commission (JCIC), opening the way for resolution of the matter through other treaty provisions, including special access visits.

The combined quota for suspect site inspections and data update inspections is fifteen per year; with no more than one suspect site inspection at a time or two inspections each year at any one facility. All areas within the SSI site diagram, which generally focus on missile final assembly areas within the missile production facility, are inspectable. During inspections, pre-inspection restrictions similar for those for other types of "short notice" inspection apply to vehicles, containers, and launch canisters large enough to conceal any item of inspection. Normal inspection procedures apply "unless otherwise agreed." This caveat provides flexibility to develop specialized or tailored inspection procedures if these should be deemed necessary to deal with unusual circumstances at these missile production sites.

START Visits with Right of Special Access

In addition to suspect site inspections, the START Treaty provides for "visits with right of special access" (hereafter called special access visits, or SAVs) at any facility or location, declared or undeclared, to help resolve a compliance concern. START SAVs are part of a flexible procedure to help resolve compliance issues. This procedures allows signatories to call a special session of the treaty's compliance body—the JCIC—should a compliance question arise. In this body, they are free to explore various options for resolving the compliance concern that balance the need for clarification by the requesting side with legitimate concerns of the inspected party to maintain sufficient control of the fact finding process to protect classified and proprietary information unrelated to the issue at the suspect facility. The special session process, of which SAVs are a part, was agreed upon late in the negotiations. To allow adaptable approaches, an inspection visit to the site can be refused and alternative means of resolving the issue proposed. To this end, the START Treaty defines JCIC procedures for the resolution of compliance issues only in

Figure 7.1
SSI Site Diagram: Petropavlovsk

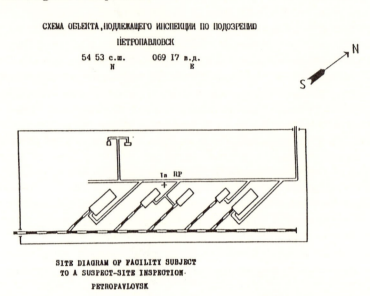

СХЕМА ОБЪЕКТА, ПОДЛЕЖАЩЕГО ИНСПЕКЦИИ ПО ПОДОЗРЕНИЮ

ПЕТРОПАВЛОВСК

54 53 с.ш.   069 17 в.д.
N   E

SITE DIAGRAM OF FACILITY SUBJECT
TO A SUSPECT-SITE INSPECTION·
PETROPAVLOVSK

SCALE
МАСШТАБ I:5000
50   0   50   100 150 200 250 м

Source: START Treaty

general outline, with the exception of comparatively stringent timelines to force the sides to deal with these issues expeditiously. This provides flexibility and allows the sides to work out the specific methods and procedures to be used in resolving each compliance concern on a case-by-case basis.

Treaty Provisions

Section III of the JCIC Protocol lays out basic modalities and timelines for requesting a "special session" of the JCIC to deal with "urgent compliance concerns." Any signatory of the START Treaty (the United States, Russia, Ukraine, Belarus, or Kazakstan) may request such a special session. The treaty specifies only that the request must provide details of the compliance concern, including the kind and, if applicable, the type of strategic offensive arms involved, name the chief representative of the requesting party, and specify a proposed date and location for the special session. The request may also propose a way to resolve the compliance concern, including a special access visit to the suspect facility or location, or an alternative solution. An example of an alternative method might be a request to display suspicious items in the open for a specified period to enhance NTM coverage or Open Skies Treaty overflights.

To require a party to deal with the concern immediately, a specific timeline for responding begins as soon as the request for a special session is made. A reply must be provided no later than seven days after such a request is received. The response must either accept the proposed data and location of the special session of the JCIC or propose an alternative date and location no later than ten days after the date originally proposed. The response may also accept the specific method proposed for resolving the concern, including a special access visit if one is requested and any proposed date, location, and procedures for the visit. If the parties can agree immediately on a special access visit or an alternative method for resolving the concern, the JCIC special session is waived. In such a case, the visit is conducted in accordance with the accepted procedures for implementing on-site inspections laid out in the START Treaty's Inspection Protocol.

Any party also can request additional information to clarify issues raised in the request for a special session. The party receiving the request for clarifying information must respond within seven days, but this process does not affect the timeline for convening the special session. When a special session of the JCIC is held, it can last no more than thirty days—an additional provision intended to force constructive engagement.

How a SAV Might Work

As of this writing, neither a JCIC special session nor an associated START SAV has ever been requested, perhaps reflecting a tacit understanding that these specialized provisions will be exercised only for the resolution of compliance concerns of an exceptionally serious nature. Nonetheless, both sides must be prepared to implement a special session, including a SAV, should one be requested. This is a formidable task. The side receiving the request must carefully evaluate it, determine its accuracy, assess alterative means of responding and formulate a reply within the tight seven day-deadline stipulated by the treaty.

One possible method of doing this, which has been explored by U.S. decision makers, would be to send a special evaluation team to the suspect site named in the request, if the site were a U.S. government installation or a defense contractor. Such a team would evaluate the situation on the spot and develop critical information needed by policy makers, including possible alternative methods of resolving the compliance concern. Given the treaty requirement to respond to the request within seven days, the action agency—most likely the U.S. Department of Defense—must be prepared to provide its recommendations on a response to the U.S. National Security Council within as little as five days to allow time for final decision making.

A SAV request processed by the U.S. Department of Defense (DoD) probably would be reviewed initially by the START Compliance Review Group

Figure 7.2
Visit with Special Right of Access Timeline

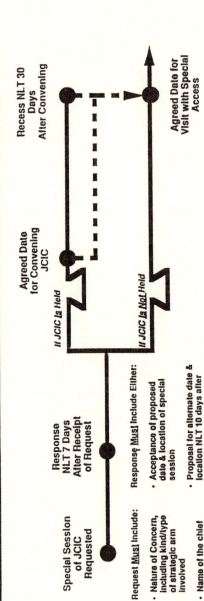

Special Session of JCIC Requested

Response NLT 7 Days After Receipt of Request

Agreed Date for Convening JCIC

Recess NLT 30 Days After Convening

Agreed Date for Visit with Special Access

If JCIC Is Held

If JCIC Is Not Held

Request <u>Must</u> Include:

- Nature of Concern, including kind/type of strategic arm involved

- Name of the chief representative of the requesting party

- Proposed date & location of the special session

Request <u>Can</u> Include:

- A specific method for resolving the concern, including a visit with right of special access

Response <u>Must</u> Include Either:

- Acceptance of proposed date & location of special session

- Proposal for alternate date & location NLT 10 days after requested date

Response <u>Can</u> Include Either:

- Acceptance of the proposed method for resolving the concern, including the proposed, date, location, & procedures if for a visit with special access

- An alternate method for resolving the concern, including the proposed date, location, & procedure if for a visit with special access

Parties <u>Can</u> Agree Not to Hold a JCIC Session if any of the Proposed Alternate Methods of Resolution are Agree Upon

NOTE:

Either Side may Request Additional Information or Clarifications from the Other Party during this period, with a 7 days' response requirement, without affecting the agreed or required timelines

Source: DynMeridian, Alexandria, Virginia

(CRG)—a body established within DoD to develop a coordinated position on START compliance issues.[10] The review group would determine whether additional information or clarifications are necessary, evaluate relevant information on hand, and make a preliminary judgment on the merits of the request and on possible U.S. responses. Should it deem it useful to do so, DoD might then send a suitably composed site assessment team to the facility named in the request on an urgent basis to work, in cooperation with plant officials, on developing critical information. If a private industry were involved, the United States would have to inform, and gain the cooperation of, senior management and key personnel of the facility to ensure the assessment team is able to carry out its analysis freely and thoroughly. If a facility proved uncooperative, the U.S. government might be compelled to take legal measures to ensure that it could meet its treaty obligations.

Possible Activities of a Site Assessment Team

Careful consideration would have to be given to the composition of any site assessment team (SAT). Its leader ideally would have to be of decision making (senior) rank, have START Treaty expertise and be drawn from the military service having cognizant responsibility over any defense contractor facility identified in the SAV request, since questions of security and possible funding for the visit might be involved. The remainder of the team ideally would be composed of representatives with the specialized expertise needed to develop a response to the compliance concern. The SAT team would need to be able to work closely with facility representatives to develop the information needed to respond to the SAV request. It would have to be capable both of developing recommendations on how a SAV should be carried out, should such a visit be determined to be the best means of resolving the concern, and suggesting alternative means of resolving the compliance concern short of an actual site visit.

Among other factors, the team would have to consider the potential costs of hosting a site visit. A visit that is sufficiently intrusive to satisfy the requesting party that no illegal activity is occurring could also result in the loss of proprietary or classified information. The financial costs of hosting such a visit also must be considered, especially if a visit would require extensive shrouding or other protective measures such as a partial or full shut down of operations. Granting a visit to a sensitive facility also could be viewed as establishing an undesirable precedent for the future.

In connection with its evaluation of a possible SAV, a team would have to develop details on the most effective way to carry out a visit so as to resolve the concern while protecting vital national security information. Such information could involve the formulation of specific recommendations on possible timeframes, routes, and procedures for the visit. For example, the SAV could be planned for a holiday, weekend, or after hours to avoid costly shutdowns of operations during the visit; routes could be proposed that would allow resolution of the concern, while limiting access to areas of particular national security or proprietary sensitivity; or specialized procedures, not otherwise authorized under START, such as interviews with site personnel or access to relevant records, could be proposed.

In developing possible alternatives to a visit, all courses that might resolve the concern would have to be evaluated. These could include such measures as verbal or written explanations or assurances; the submission of relevant diagrams, photographs, videotapes, or maps; technical data exchanges to clarify ambiguities; the presentation of models or mockups; access to technical experts or records; or steps to enhance the ability of the requesting party to verify by national technical means or overflights that no violation had occurred.

Information developed during the SAT visit would then assist formulation of the recommendations to senior U.S. policy makers. The information also would be a resource for U.S. negotiators at any JCIC Special Session in dealing with the compliance concern and suggesting modalities for any visit that may be decided upon. The JCIC also would decide, on a case-by-case basis, the procedures to be used for any visit. These could be either the procedures used for the more routine inspections at declared sites or new procedures especially tailored to address the compliance concern. In general, a SAV team probably would enter at a designated POE and follow normal POE processing procedures. It probably also would travel to the site under normal host country escort. The remainder of the visit then would proceed according to the specific procedures, conditions and timeframes agreed upon in the JCIC.

Site Preparations

Should a SAV be agreed upon, the site would have to be prepared for the visit in accordance with the decisions made by the U.S. government and agreed to in the JCIC. One way of handling this would be to dispatch a site preparation team to the facility to assist preparations for the visit. The main responsibilities of such a team might include assisting the site to develop a planning document for the visit; working out all logistical operations for the visit, including transportation, communications, translation, housing, feeding, safety clothing and similar requirements; planning government and plant escort procedures; training personnel to ensure that visit protocol and agreed procedures are scrupulously followed; determining security requirements and steps, such as shrouding, to be implemented on the day of the visit; and dealing with public affairs, contractual and legal issues that may arise.

CFE CHALLENGE INSPECTIONS

The CFE Treaty was the first to provide for challenge inspections. These allow for the inspection of specific and limited areas, whether or not they are declared sites, to investigate possible noncompliance. The boundaries of areas subjected to challenge inspections have to be so delineated that they do not exceed sixty-five square kilometers with no more than sixteen kilometers between any two points within the area. In general, the procedures for these challenge inspections are similar to those for declared sites. They are subject to quotas and have short-notice timelines to complicate cheating.

There are, however, several important differences. Unlike declared site inspections, CFE challenge inspections could be refused within two hours after the challenge inspection request was received. Such refusals were supposed to be based solely on considerations of safety or security, but they clearly provided a hedge against misuse of the challenge inspection process. If a challenge inspection request were refused, the challenged state was obligated to provide reasonable assurance that the area concerned did not contain treaty limited equipment. Following a refusal, the inspection team could designated another challenge or declared site inspection. During the reduction period, CFE challenge inspections were used sparsely, but they did take place throughout the treaty area, including in Belarus and England.

CWC CHALLENGE INSPECTIONS

The Chemical Weapons Convention (CWC) contains the most intrusive provisions for on-site inspections of suspect facilities of any arms control agreement concluded to date. The treaty allows any signatory to request a challenge inspection of any suspect facility or location on the territory, or any other place under the jurisdiction or control of, any other state party, solely to clarify and resolve any question of possible noncompliance with the provisions of the CWC.[11] The challenge inspection then can be conducted at the site without delay by an international inspection team designated by the CWC Technical Secretariat's director general, unless the treaty's Executive Council should decide not to carry out the inspection.

The procedures for challenge inspections proved to be among the most sensitive and difficult to develop during negotiation of the CWC, since they required a delicate balance between the need for sufficient intrusiveness to address compliance concerns and the need to protect sensitive proprietary and national security information in the highly competitive chemical industry. To meet these concerns, the Treaty requires a State Party to accept a challenge inspection and make every reasonable effort to satisfy the compliance concern. At the same time, it provides, like a START special access visit, for a system of managed access that gives the inspected party flexibility in dealing with national security and constitutional concerns.

How a CWC Challenge Inspection Would Work

Requesting an Inspection

Challenge inspections can be requested at any facility in a signatory country by any state party to the Chemical Weapons Convention. Since such inspections could be requested for spurious reasons (e.g., political harassment or retaliation) as well as legitimate purposes, the CWC contains provisions to deter abuse. Both the requesting and the inspected parties have the right to have their concerns about compliance and possible abuse of the system addressed by the Organization for the Prohibition of Chemical Weapons's (OPCW) Executive Council at both the beginning and conclusion of the inspection.

The request for a challenge inspection must be submitted to the Executive Council and the director general of the Technical Secretariat. Should either consider the request to be frivolous, abusive, or clearly beyond the scope of the convention, the council can decide—within twelve hours of having received the request—by a three-quarter majority vote of all of its members against carrying out the challenge inspection. After a challenge inspection is completed, the Executive Council reviews the final report of the inspection team and, in addition to addressing concerns about whether any noncompliance has occurred, further addresses whether the inspection was within the scope of the convention and whether the challenge inspection request was abusive. Should it decide there was abuse, it can recommend to the conference that punitive measures be taken against the requesting party, such as requiring it to bear some or all of the costs of the inspection.

Inspection Procedures

If the inspection request is not rejected, the party to be inspected must be informed of the pending challenge inspection location at least twelve hours before the planned arrival of the inspection team at the designated point of entry into the country. The OPCW ensures that international inspection team dispatched for the challenge inspection has the necessary qualifications, experience, skill, and training to conduct the inspection. There are different procedures for challenge inspections of declared and undeclared facilities. Inspections of declared facilities, on which extensive information already is available from the required declarations, are both shorter and less extensive in scope. Challenge inspections of undeclared facilities contain the following more comprehensive elements.

Upon arrival at the POE, the inspection team informs the inspected party of the inspection mandate and (if it was not already included in the inspection notification) designates the *requested perimeter*, that is, the area at the suspect facility that it wishes to inspect, providing a site diagram that is as precise as possible and has geographic coordinates. The requested perimeter must run at least ten meters outside any buildings or other structures and not cut through existing or requested security enclosures. If the inspected party finds this area unacceptable, it can propose an *alternative perimeter,* which then is subject to negotiation between the inspection team and the inspected party at the POE. An alternative perimeter must include the whole of the requested perimeter and be closely related to it, taking into account the terrain at the location and man-made boundaries such as security fences. The inspection team must be transported to the inspection site within thirty-six hours of its arrival at the POE. If no agreement has been reached on a perimeter, the alternative perimeter becomes the final perimeter.

While the inspection team is at the POE, actions also are taken to secure the site. No later than twelve hours after the inspection team arrives at the POE, the inspected party must begin monitoring all vehicular traffic (road, air, and water) exiting the challenged site. The affected facility may be asked to assist in this process by using traffic logs, photographs, or video recordings. When the inspection team arrives, it may continue exit monitoring under its control.

Upon arrival at the site, the inspectors also are permitted to verify the geographic location of the site, go to any point on the perimeter and take wipes, air, soil, and effluent samples within a fifty-meter band around the final perimeter or the alternative perimeter, if no agreement has been reached by that point on the final perimeter. The inspectors and inspected state officials negotiate an inspection plan. To facilitate this process, inspectors are to be provided with a pre-inspection briefing on safety and logistics issues that may affect the process of the inspection.

If no agreement is reached within seventy-two hours (and no later than 108 hours after arrival at the POE), inspectors must be allowed access to the inspectable area. The period of inspection lasts up to eighty-four hours, extendable by mutual agreement, during which inspectors are permitted access to areas within the agreed perimeter and are allowed to conduct personal interviews and examine records. The requesting party can request to have an observer accompany the inspection team, but the inspected party has the right to disapprove this participation or, if the participation is allowed, to limit access and activities at the site.[12] Upon completion of inspection activities, the inspection team has up to twenty-four hours to meet with representatives of the inspected party and the inspected site to review its findings and clarify any ambiguities.

Figure 7.3
CWC Challenge Inspection Timeline

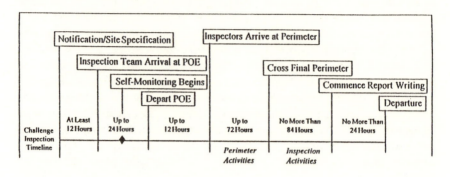

Source: **DynMeridian, Alexandria, Virginia**

Managed Access

Although inspectors are granted full access within the agreed perimeter, the inspected party has the final say in determining the extent and nature of access within the challenged site, through a concept called managed access. Managed access is designed to protect legitimate sensitive proprietary or national security information at the site during the inspection process. It permits the host country to designate the entry/exit points for access to the inspectable site and negotiate the extent of access to any particular place or places within the final and requested perimeters, the particular inspection activities (including sampling) to be conducted by inspectors, the performance of activities requested by the inspectors, and the provision of particular types of information.

Specifically, the inspected party has the right to take measures to protect sensitive installations and prevent disclosure of confidential information and data not related to chemical weapons. These measures may include the removal of sensitive papers; the shrouding of sensitive items; the shutdown of computer systems and data indicating devices; the restriction of sampling to the presence or absence of treaty-listed chemicals; the use of random selective access techniques, such as requesting inspectors to select a given percentage or number of buildings of their choice to inspect; and, in exceptional cases, the limiting of access to certain (usually hazardous) parts of the inspection site to only one, or a few, inspectors. However, if the inspected party provides less than full access to places, activities, or information at the inspectable site, it has an obligation to make every reasonable effort to provide alternative means to clarify the compliance concern. This could be accomplished, for example, by the partial removal of shrouds or environmental covers or by visual inspection of an enclosed space from its entry way.

CWC Investigations of Alleged Use

In addition to its challenge inspection regime, the CWC also permits "investigations" by its inspectors to determine whether chemical weapons or riot control agents prohibited for use in war have been used against a state. The OPCW also may investigate threats of such actions.

A request for an investigation of this sort, submitted by a state party and substantiated by relevant information, must be transmitted by the OPCW director general immediately to the OPCW Executive Council and to all parties to the convention. An investigation must be initiated within twenty-four hours of receipt of the request and the report completed within seventy-two hours. An extension of an additional seventy-two hours is permitted, if required, but in this case an interim report must be prepared following the initial investigation period.

The purpose of the investigation is to establish the relevant facts and the type and scope of any supplementary assistance and protection that may be needed by the victim state. Once the report of the investigation has been evaluated by the OPCW, a decision is made whether to forward it to all parties to the CWC and to relevant international organizations for consideration of an international response. If the report establishes that chemical weapons have been used, the OPCW also takes emergency measures of assistance, using all resources at its disposal, until other parties to the convention can provide additional help.

NOTES

1. Myron B. Kratzer, *International Nuclear Safeguards: Promise and Performance* (Washington, D.C.: The Atlantic Council, April 1994), p. 53

2. Ibid. p. 54.

3. This put North Korea in technical violation of its agreement with the IAEA within eighteen months after accession to the safeguards provisions.

4. Ira N. Goldman, "NPT Verification and Enforcement: Problems and Prospects," in *New Horizons and Challenges in Arms Control and Verification*, James Brown, ed. (Amsterdam, VU University Press, 1994), p. 126.

5. Ibid. p. 127.

6. START Treaty, Article XI, Paragraph 5, provides for suspect site inspections. Specific implementation provisions are contained in the Protocol on Inspections and Continuous Monitoring Activities, Section VIII.

7. The provisions governing START special access visits are contained in the treaty's Protocol on the Joint Compliance and Inspection Commission. The enabling provision for the JCIC is Article XV of the treaty.

8. These facilities are listed in the START Treaty's Memorandum of Understanding on Data, Annex I, Paragraph 12.

9. To be added to the list of final assembly areas, a facility must be "a production facility not subject to continuous monitoring that begins to produce ballistic missiles as large or larger than any mobile ICBM, unless otherwise agreed, or a previously-monitored production facility that did produce mobile ICBMs, but ceased production."

10. Operation of DoD's Compliance Review Groups is discussed in chapter 9.

11. The basic provisions for CWC Challenge Inspections are contained in CWC Article IX, Paragraphs 8–25.

12. The role of the observer is to ensure that the inspectors conduct their activity in a way that satisfies the inspecting state's compliance concerns. The observer therefore is likely to want access to the inspection team throughout the inspection.

Chapter 8

On-Site Monitoring Regimes

Several on-site inspection regimes include provisions for the on-site monitoring by inspectors of particularly sensitive facilities or sites to confirm that they are complying with treaty requirements. Monitoring differs from other types of on-site inspection in that it involves a protracted or "continuous" presence of the monitoring team and/or technical monitoring equipment at a specific location on the soil of the inspected party. The technical monitoring equipment can range from seismic monitoring equipment emplaced to monitor a specific test to the emplacement and continuous observation of an array of technical sensing and measuring equipment located at the portal and around the perimeter of a facility.

The earliest long-term monitoring regimes involve containment and surveillance measures developed as part of the International Atomic Energy Agency's (IAEA) safeguards regime. The strengthened verification provisions added to the agreements to monitor the Threshold Test Ban Treaty (TTBT) and the Peaceful Nuclear Explosions Treaty (PNET) provide for on-site yield measurements of nuclear explosions and the establishment of seismic stations on Russian and U.S. territory for on-site monitoring. However, these new verification provisions were used only once early on, since, after their signature, both sides first adopted nuclear testing moratoria, then signed the Comprehensive Test Ban Treaty (CTBT) which establishes a global nuclear test ban.

The most elaborate and complex long-term on-site monitoring regimes developed and implemented to date are the portal and perimeter continuous monitoring (PPCM) systems established by the Intermediate-Range Nuclear Forces (INF) and Strategic Arms Reduction (START) treaties. These are designed to continuously monitor missile production at designated missile plants in the United States and the former Soviet Union (FSU). Conceptually, they use a team of on-site monitors, supported by monitoring equipment, to continuously observe shipments leaving the monitored facility to confirm that they are in accordance with treaty provisions. The monitoring equipment is located at the portal, exits, and around the fenced perimeter of the facility. Under the INF Treaty, portal monitoring helps to confirm that the banned missiles, especially the SS-20 IRBM and Pershing II missile, are no longer being produced at their former production sites. Under START, PPCM is used to monitor the production level of mobile missiles systems limited (but not banned) by the treaty.

IAEA CONTAINMENT AND SURVEILLANCE MONITORING

The IAEA safeguards system, used as the verification system for the Nuclear Nonproliferation Treaty (NPT), is so constructed that the intervals and intensiveness of inspections at any specific facility depend on the size and nature of the nuclear activity there. Inspections extend along a continuum from limited, periodic inspections of lesser nuclear facilities to the continuous inspection of large and complex nuclear facilities containing large amounts of weapons-usable material. The safeguards structure identifies *material accountancy* as the "safeguards regime of fundamental importance" (U.N. Information Circular INFCIRC/153), while *"containment and surveillance"* are characterized as "important complementary measures."[1] The terms "containment" and "surveillance" are customarily coupled and the techniques overlap and work in tandem. They belong to those safeguards measures designed to ascertain directly whether nuclear material has been removed from a known location without appropriate measurement and reporting.

Containment

Containment is ensured to a considerable degree by the very nature of the structures and containers in which the nuclear material is stored. The walls of both the building itself and the containers are typically strong and of high structural integrity. In addition, nuclear material usually can be removed from such facilities only through a very limited number of exit routes. As a result, containment of the nuclear materials within these structures often can be effectively accomplished by placing seals on the limited exit routes or on individual nuclear containers. These seals are designed to indicate to an inspector, carrying out periodic on-site visits, whether any unreported removal of nuclear material could have taken place since the previous inspection. As an example of the extent to which such seals are used in practice, 23,877 affixed seals were verified by IAEA Inspectors in 1995 alone.[2]

Surveillance

Surveillance most commonly refers to visual observation of an exit or other pathway that, for operational or structural purposes, cannot be sealed. It also includes observation of numerous other operations at the facility that might indicate an unusual departure from normal operational practice and thus signal possible attempted diversion. This type of monitoring—known as "process monitoring"—can be accomplished by observation by an inspector or by continuous monitoring by optical or other equipment. Radiation detectors, for example, could detect radiation in a location where it would not ordinarily be present.

Optical observation by cameras of reactor-spent fuel storage areas is the best known application of surveillance. Often, reactor facilities contain only a single portal through which large spent fuel transport casks can enter and leave. Continuous surveillance of this opening by a stationary tamper proof camera provides a highly effective (although not infallible) means of verifying that spent fuel has not been diverted. Instrument monitoring both contributes to the effectiveness of the safeguards system and allows for a reduction in the level of on-site inspections beyond what would otherwise be required. In practice, optical surveillance has become the key measure in verifying that no diversion of plutonium-bearing spent fuel has taken place.[3]

Assessment of Containment and Surveillance

Containment and surveillance monitoring add complementary verification means to back up and support the material accountancy aspects of the IAEA safeguards regime. These monitoring measures help to confirm that diversion from a specific nuclear facility has not occurred, even if the precise nuclear material content of the facility should come into question. But, while containment and surveillance monitoring potentially could provide direct evidence of unreported transfers of nuclear materials, it is unlikely that a country intent on cheating would allow direct observation of a diversion either by an inspector or by any surveillance device or monitoring system known to be present at the nuclear facility. The primary usefulness of these monitoring methods, rather, is in revealing anomalies such as broken seals or obscured vision of the cameras which—like nuclear material that has not been accounted for—would spark further investigation of compliance by on-site inspectors or other means. Such anomalies may fall short of producing a "smoking gun" direct observation of a violation, but they still can be less ambiguous in triggering a further investigation than the findings of material accountancy.

Containment and surveillance, like other methods of monitoring, have limitations. They are dependent on observing the proliferation pathway. Unknown portals may exist. In addition, containment and surveillance devices can be violated, spoofed (deceived), or simply fail. For example, the lighting required for proper camera functioning can be extinguished for limited periods, either accidently or deliberately. Extraneous items, such as the placement of large pieces of equipment, can obscure a camera's field of vision, deliberately or not. In addition, containment and surveillance, unlike material accountancy can provide no indication of the quantity of material, if any, that might be missing, if a suspicious event is indicated, or determine whether an indicated event was deliberately caused or inadvertent. For these reasons, indications of containment and surveillance failure ideally should be followed up by material accountancy.   As one expert concludes, "Either material accountancy or containment and surveillance alone, if infallible and complete, would be sufficient to verify non-diversion or detect diversion. Since both have strengths and weaknesses, there is broad agreement among safeguards experts that a practical, effective and efficient safeguards system must include both categories of measures."[4]

ON-SITE MONITORING OF NUCLEAR TESTING

General Concepts

The verification regimes of both the TTBT and the PNET contain elaborate provisions for on-site monitoring. In both cases, however, this monitoring is permitted only during periods of nuclear testing, not on a continuous basis. In practice, the TTBT/PNET on-site monitoring regime has only been used only in connection with Joint Verification Experiments (JVCs) held in 1988 by scientists from the United States and the Soviet Union at the Nevada Test Site and Semipalatinsk. These monitoring regimes currently are moot since both sides have signed the Comprehensive Test Ban Treaty banning all further nuclear testing at any level. They therefore are covered only in a cursory manner in the following paragraphs.

For many years, the U.S. apparatus for detecting and identifying nuclear weapons tests has been a network of seismic electromagnetic and acoustic sensors called the Atomic Explosion Detection System (AEDS), which has over twenty stations ringing the former Soviet Union. The backbone of this system is a small set of highly specialized seismometer arrays oriented toward the known Russian test sites.

This system basically senses teleseismic waves traveling through the earth's interior. Analysis of the wave attributes can help distinguish nuclear tests from earthquakes or other events such as chemical explosions or industrial accidents. However, this type of remote monitoring involves assumptions about the local geology of test locations and about the modes by which signals travel to the seismic stations that, in the past, have made possible relatively large inaccuracies in the yield determination and lowered the confidence level of the measurements.

In addition, there are various methods for possibly reducing a seismic signal, including muffling, decoupling, and masking.[5] A test, for example, can be muffled by holding it in a geologic medium that reduces its seismic signal. Decoupling involves conducting tests in large cavities that can substantially reduce the seismic signal of the test if the space is big enough to prevent the blast from fracturing the surrounding walls. Masking is the term for hiding the signs of small nuclear explosions among other seismic noises. This might be done, for example, by conducting small nuclear tests in an active seismic region and timing them so that the signal from the test is masked by earthquake activity. In any event the inaccuracies and uncertainties inherent in the AEDS system led to charges during the Reagan administration that the Soviet Union was testing above the TTBT's 150 kiloton limit in violation of the treaty, although there were differences within the various U.S. government intelligence agencies on this point.

The proposals for strengthening the TTBT and PNET verification protocols, therefore, concentrated on constructing a verification structure that would avoid potential problems by permitting actual on-site monitoring of nuclear tests over certain yield thresholds. This regime permitted on-site yield measurements and seismic monitoring.

Monitoring of Yield Measurements

During the negotiations for improved TTBT/PNET verification protocols, the United States sought the right to verify the yields of nuclear tests by using direct on-site methods of yield measurement that would be near the source of the explosion, not at a remote location, and resistant to manipulation by the other side. This goal was achieved by provisions permitting direct on-site hydrodynamic yield measurements in a satellite hole at the test site for all nuclear tests declared to have a planned yield over fifty kilotons. The U.S. method, called CORRTEX—an acronym for Continuous Reflectometry for Radius versus Time Experiments—is a faster, more accurate method for measuring yields of underground nuclear explosions than remote monitoring.

The CORRTEX system consists of an electronic unit, coaxial cables and a microcomputer for data collection. In use, the battery-operated electronic units remain above ground and can be remotely controlled. Coaxial cables attached to the units are inserted into holes extending from ground level to a point near the nuclear explosion. Repetitive electrical impulses, sent down the cable at intervals of ten to ninety millionths of a second, reflect from the end of the cable and return to the source. When the nuclear device explodes, the shock wave travels outward and progressively crushes the cable, producing a fast-moving short circuit picked up by the electrical pulses from the surface. By determining the speed at which the cable is shorted out, the yield of the explosion can be calculated, since large explosions produce shock waves that travel faster than do those from small explosions.[6]

Figure 8.1
CORRTEX Yield Measurement Concept

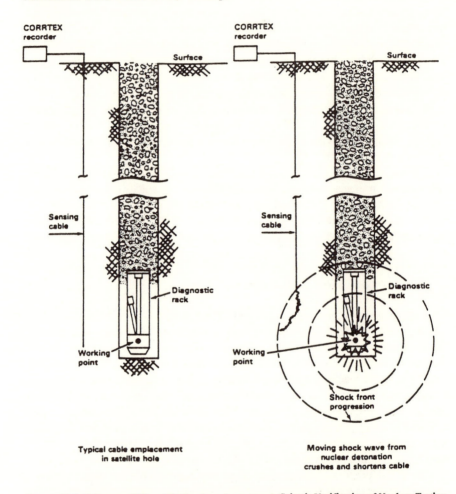

Typical cable emplacement
in satellite hole

Moving shock wave from
nuclear detonation
crushes and shortens cable

Source: U.S. Congress, Office of Technology Assessment, *Seismic Verification of Nuclear Testing Treaties* (Washington, D.C.: U.S. Government Printing Office, May 1988) p. 131

CORRTEX works best when used in the "strong shock" region closest to the explosion. Placing the CORRTEX cables in a satellite hole parallel to the hole for emplacement of the nuclear device permits accurate measurements, without revealing weapon design and diagnostic information. However, since CORRTEX requires prior emplacement and is only useful for tests that have been previously announced, it is not suitable for monitoring a CTBT.

Because of the highly intrusive nature of CORRTEX monitoring and the need to drill an auxiliary hole near the actual test emplacement hole, the TTBT/PNET protocols closely regulated this type of on-site monitoring.[7] Notification of the test was required at least 200 days in advance, and at least 120 days prior to the test, highly specific and detailed information had to be provided to the verifying party on the test and test-site geology. Testing equipment was subject to prior evaluation by the testing party. In addition, the set-up and operation of equipment at the test site, as well as all other on-site activities by monitoring personnel at the test site, were to be closely supervised and regulated to ensure that procedures and operations would be strictly in accordance with treaty provisions.

To assist the accuracy of the tests, the TTBT/PNET verification protocols permitted on-site confirmation of the geology near an emplaced nuclear device and of test emplacement conditions. They also allowed monitors to observe emplacement of the nuclear explosive canister for all tests declared to have a planned yield greater than thirty-five kilotons. For tests conducted in so-called non standard conditions (those not optimal for CORRTEX), the parties had the right to carry out hydrodynamic measurements on a "reference test" and to deploy an extended hydrodynamic technique. As additional measures to protect the accuracy of the data collected at the site, monitors were allowed to install anti-intrusiveness devices and to protect them from interference. Agreed procedures were to be used for recovering and authenticating data, and identical copies of the data recovered from the test were to be provided to both parties immediately after the test.

In-Country Seismic Stations

While the United States insisted on CORRTEX monitoring during the negotiations of the TTBT and PNET verification protocols, the Russians preferred to use more conventional seismic measurements to determine nuclear test yields. Thus, in reciprocity for agreement to permit hydrodynamic yield measurements, the United States accepted Soviet proposals for the presence of on-site monitors at in-country seismic stations during the nuclear test period.[8]

The TTBT permitted the collection of regional seismic data from temporarily deployed seismic equipment at three existing stations on the territory of the testing party for all tests declared to have a planned yield over fifty kilotons. These seismic monitors were designed to measure the distant shock wave produced by the nuclear test explosion to arrive at an estimate of its explosive yield. The Russians were granted sites in Oklahoma (Tulsa), in South Dakota (the Black Hills), and in the State of Washington (Newport). The United States was permitted to have sites near Moscow (Arti), in the Ural Mountains (Obninsk), and in Siberia (Novosibirsk).

The PNET permitted data collection from a temporarily installed local seismic network around the site of the explosion for the purpose of confirming the number of individual explosions in a group explosion that had a yield over 150 kilotons.

In both cases, the monitors could install their own seismic equipment at the site for the period of the test and operate it according to the procedures specified in the protocols. While at the site, they could record seismic and universal time signals continuously from the time their equipment was installed until two hours after the test. For security purposes, the monitors had the right to install and operate tamper-detection equipment, keep the areas in which their seismic sensors were installed under constant observation, and confirm that there had been no interference with their seismic measurements and the recording of such measurements. The testing party had to facilitate these monitoring operations by providing necessary support.

To ensure that both parties would have access to the data developed (in case of an ambiguity), the verifying party was required to provide the testing party, upon arrival, with a description of the recording format and with the computer program, thus permitting it to read the data. Upon departure, the testing party was to be provided with a copy of all data recorded by all equipment, graphic representations of the seismic data from one minute prior to the test to thirty minutes afterwards, and the results of the calibration of all seismic equipment. Photography and other activities were to be coordinated and regulated. Designated personnel were required to arrive at the seismic stations at least ten days before the planned test and depart within two days after the test.

THE MONITORING SYSTEM OF THE CTBT

The International Monitoring System (IMS) of the Comprehensive Test Ban Treaty is designed to detect any nuclear explosion anywhere in the world. It does not have locally targeted on-site monitoring systems on the territory of each party like the TTBT/PNET, but rather is to be composed of a network of fifty primary and 120 auxiliary seismological monitoring stations designed to detect seismic activity and differentiate between naturally occurring seismic activity, such as earthquakes, and nuclear explosions. In addition to the seismic stations, the IMS also will have eighty radionuclide stations and sixteen radionuclide laboratories to identify any radioactive particles released during a nuclear explosion and sixty infrasound (acoustic) and eleven hydroacoustic stations that can pick up the sound of a nuclear explosion conducted in the atmosphere or underwater, respectively. The host state and location of each facility is contained in Annex 1 of the CTBT Verification Protocol.[9]

Information collected by the IMS will be transmitted to an International Data System (IDC) for processing. The IDC will produce integrated lists of data and provide states parties with a number of other services to help them monitor compliance with the CTBT. Ambiguous events will be subject to consultation and clarification procedures, and if this does not resolve the issue, states parties may request on-site inspections, which can employ drilling techniques at the suspect site.[10]

PORTAL AND PERIMETER CONTINUOUS MONITORING

Development of the PPCM Concepts

Portal and Perimeter Continuous Monitoring (PPCM) is the most complex of the verification tools implemented by modern on-site inspection regimes to date. The basic concepts and principles for PPCM were developed and agreed upon during negotiation of the INF Treaty and later accepted with only minor variations as part of the START inspection regime.

The concept of using continuous monitoring as an on-site inspection technique was first proposed by the United States during the negotiation of the INF Treaty as a way to help confirm the treaty's production ban on the Soviet SS-20 IRBM. Building on IAEA concepts, the United States initially envisaged a fully automated monitoring system. This was based on the presumption (accurate to that point) that the then Soviet Union would never accept the continuous stationing of U.S. inspectors on Soviet soil, especially at one of its most sensitive missile production facilities. Accordingly, early research by U.S. Department of Defense contractors[11] concentrated on the development of unattended monitoring regimes, which would rely on remote sensors and other technical monitoring equipment and be installed, maintained, and remotely monitored primarily by technicians. These initial research concepts were significantly revised in late 1985, before being presented at the negotiating table, once it became apparent in Geneva that the Soviets might indeed accept a portal monitoring team on Soviet soil.

A PPCM monitoring regime employing continuous on-site inspectors (portal monitors) eventually was accepted late in the INF negotiations. The break-through came in October 1987 (the treaty was signed December 8, 1987) after Soviet negotiators confirmed U.S. suspicions that the first stage of the SS-25 mobile missile—which was a strategic system and thus not banned by the INF Treaty—has a stage outwardly similar to, although not interchangeable with, the first stage of the banned SS-20. To help confirm that banned SS-20s were not being produced in the guise of legal SS-25s, the Soviet Union agreed to accept U.S. proposals for continuous monitoring of the portals and perimeter of the Votkinsk Machine Building Plant (VMBP)—the missile final assembly facility for both missile systems—which is located in the Udmurt Republic approximately 1,000 kilometers east of Moscow. On a reciprocal basis, the Soviets were permitted to station a similar monitoring team at Hercules (now Alliant) Plant #1 in West Valley (Magna), Utah, near Salt Lake City, which had produced the first stage of the banned Pershing II missile.

Later, the PPCM concept also was incorporated in the START Treaty to help track the sublimits on mobile ICBMs established by that agreement. PPCM was permitted at the missile production facilities for the canisterized Russian SS-25 (Votkinsk) and SS-24 (Pavlograd) and for the first stage of the U.S. Peacekeeper located at Thiokol Strategic Operations in Promontory, Utah. It is designed to help confirm that the major facilities producing (or, in the case of Thiokol, capable of producing) mobile ICBMs produce only those mobile ICBMs they are declared to produce and to account for each such ICBM produced.

To assist in confirming the numerical limits on mobile missiles, each missile must have a unique identifier—a nonrepeating, alpha-numeric production number —applied to it.[12] The unique identifier serves as a permanent license plate for each missile. The number had to be provided for all existing mobile ICBMs at entry into force (EIF) of the treaty and within five days after completion of production for all mobile missiles produced thereafter. It must be accessible for reading by inspectors during continuous monitoring operations and other specified inspections. The sole exception to this rule applies to mobile missiles deployed in silos where the number could not be read without first removing the missile from the silo—a complex and dangerous procedure.

Under the START Agreement, the United States can conduct START, as well as INF, continuous monitoring at Votkinsk, which is the missile final assembly plant for the SS-25 mobile ICBM, and establish a new START portal at Pavlograd in the Ukraine, the SS-24 final assembly facility. U.S. PPCM preparations began at Pavlograd in January 1995 but ended five months later following a bilateral agreement with the Ukraine to cease mobile missile production operations at that site. Subsequently, the PPCM equipment erected at Pavlograd was dismantled, removed from the Ukraine, and placed in storage at Rhein Main AFB in Frankfurt, Germany, the location of the U.S. On-Site Inspection Agency's European Operations. Storage preserved the option to rapidly re-deploy the equipment should SS-24 production operations be resumed in the Ukraine or the units be needed to support other future continuous monitoring operations in the FSU.

A special provision of the START Treaty—the Twenty Second Agreed Statement—provides for harmonizing the continuous monitoring provisions of the INF and START treaties at Votkinsk. The U.S. INF facility at Magna is not subject to continuous monitoring under START. However, the Russians have the option to establish a PPCM operation at Thiokol Corporation in Promontory, Utah, which was the first-stage assembly facility for the U.S. Peacekeeper missile. The United States had no facilities that were actually producing mobile missiles. Indeed, no United States missile production facility had even produced a mobile missile prototype. However, the United States agreed to permit portal monitoring at Thiokol on a reciprocal basis because eventual production of mobile ICBMs had been planned there.

Basic PPCM Concepts

The portal and perimeter monitoring in the INF and START treaties resolves the problem of how to monitor production at a vital missile production facility without permitting intrusive interior inspections of the plant that would reveal sensitive information on missile production techniques and equipment. PPCM achieves this result by requiring any missile, missile stage, and container large enough to contain a treaty-limited missile or stage to pass through a single exit at the plant (the portal) where it is subject to examination by inspectors (monitors) from the other side. To assist the monitoring process, the number of additional exits from the facility is limited, and any exit through which an object large enough to be treaty-limited could pass is subject to monitoring. The basic layout of the INF and START PPCM regimes thus consists of the portal, additional exits, and an inspectable perimeter.[13]

The portal is the sole area through which all objects, containers, launcher canisters, or vehicles that are large enough to contain, or to be, an item of continuous monitoring are allowed to leave the monitored facility. It can contain only one road and rail line. The monitoring country can install agreed monitoring equipment and construct, operate, and maintain at the portal three buildings for operations and team headquarters and one additional building for storage and supplies. The monitored plant can erect an environmental building there to shelter the items subject to viewing by the portal monitors from the elements.

Two additional monitored road exits at other locations are permitted, as well as four exits for plant personnel, which can be no wider than one meter. No rail exits other than the one at the portal are allowed. As with the portal, the monitoring country can install agreed monitoring equipment at the exits, while the inspected party can erect an environmental shelter there.[14]

The entire monitored facility is to be surrounded by a defined perimeter subject to patrol by the portal monitoring team. This perimeter is determined by the inspected party, delineated by a fence, and may not be changed without prior notification.[15] The host country is obligated to designate a perimeter continuous monitoring area around the entire perimeter within which the monitors have the right to install monitoring equipment and carry out their continuous monitoring activities. The portal monitors are permitted to carry out spot patrols of the entire perimeter area at any time of their choosing and must be promptly provided with a vehicle for that purpose. Any other means of exit that could be used clandestinely to remove a missile from the facility, such as by air or water transport, is prohibited.

The perimeters at Magna and Votkinsk are of two different variants. The inspectable facility in Utah is located within the confines of a broader missile production complex. The perimeter, therefore, is defined by a double fence around the portalled area, which allows the Russian portal monitors to ensure the integrity of the portalled site, but constrains them from wandering into other

Figure 8.2
Basic Portal Structure, Magna, Utah

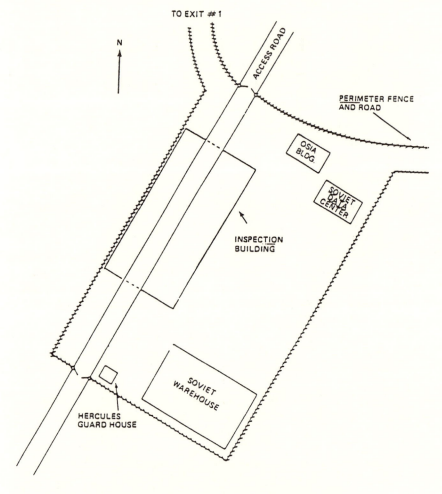

Source: Defense Nuclear Agency, Public Affairs Office, Washington, D.C.

Figure 8.3
Exit at Magna Portal Site

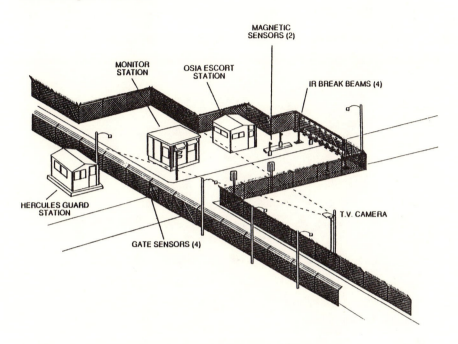

Source: **Defense Nuclear Agency, Public Affairs Office, Washington, D.C.**

plant areas not covered by treaty constraints. In Russia, the portalled facility is entirely surrounded by a mostly concrete slab wall, and U.S. portal monitors patrol the three-mile perimeter enclosing the whole missile plant.

Like other aspects of on-site inspection, there is an inherent tensions in any portal and perimeter continuous monitoring regime. The PPCM monitors (inspectors) must be allowed to carry out their treaty-authorized activity without undue interference. But the continuous presence of inspection personnel outside a vital military production facility also raises serious national security concerns that must be considered. These concerns are dealt with by carefully constructed procedures that regulate the activities both of the host country and of the continuous monitors and cover use of the monitoring equipment at the site. These procedures start with initial construction of the PPCM site and continue during the entire period of PPCM operation. Any change in the agreed procedures, or any ambiguity that should occur on their application, is documented for subsequent review by the parties, including possible discussion in the treaty implementation and compliance bodies.

Figure 8.4
Design of Perimeter Fence, Magna Portal Site

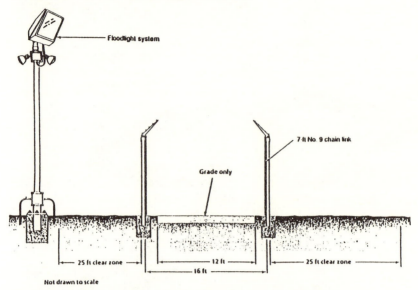

Source: **Defense Nuclear Agency, Public Affairs Office, Washington, D.C.**

Establishing and Ending a PPCM Operation

PPCM regimes have a defined beginning and end. Both the INF and START
PPCM regimes began thirty days after EIF, that is, on July 1, 1988, and
January 4, 1995, respectively. The INF Treaty permits portal monitoring to
remain in effect from a minimum of three years to the full thirteen-year life of
the treaty's verification regime (i.e., until May 30, 2001). Should Russia notify
the United States that final assembly of SS-25's has ceased, the United States
may continue INF monitoring for a year after such notification to confirm
cessation of production. The length of Russian monitoring at the Hercules (now
Alliant) Plant is linking to U.S. INF monitoring at Votkinsk; at the time U.S.
INF monitoring ceases at Votkinsk, the reciprocal Soviet monitoring at Magna
also must stop.

The START Treaty provides that the right to continuous monitoring extends
until May 31, 1995, or until one year after notification that the plant is no
longer assembling mobile ICBMs. However, if monitoring ceases, a facility then
becomes subject to data update and new facility inspections, if it is converted to
a facility subject to those types of inspection. In all other cases, it is subject to
suspect site inspections of the missile final assembly areas. START also provides
that a party may maintain its continuous monitoring activities even though the
other party ceases its activity.

Erecting the PPCM Site

The monitoring team may install and use only agreed structures and equipment at the PPCM site. Furthermore, installation drawings, manuals, and other documentation related to testing and installing the monitoring equipment intended for use at the site must be provided to the host country. For its part, the host country is obligated to provide the necessary logistical support to assist establishment of the PPCM site. It must provide utilities and basic construction materials, permit site surveys and preparations, assist transportation of all equipment to the site, and meet communications requirements. Temporary structures also must be provided pending completion of more permanent facilities. The inspecting party bears all the costs of this construction.

Initial visits may be necessary to survey and prepare the PPCM sites, familiarize the teams with the area, and begin logistical preparations. These are governed by treaty provisions or worked out on an ad hoc basis. The PPCM operations initiated to date have been based heavily on consideration of reciprocity, with a strong interest on both sides to develop practical, workable procedures.

The initial INF experience quickly demonstrated that setting up a PPCM site is a complex and time-consuming process, fraught with potential complications. The agreement to establish portal monitoring sites came very late in the INF negotiating "endgame," requiring crash efforts to construct the portals in preparation for the beginning of monitoring. As a result, both sides had to make do with temporary portal monitoring equipment until permanent equipment could be erected and brought online. Erection of the some permanent equipment was delayed by weather-related and other construction difficulties. In addition, the need to agree, in follow-up talks, on the procedures for the use, characteristics, operations, and transportation of the nondamaging imaging equipment used by the United States at Votkinsk resulted in a two-year delay after EIF in bringing this equipment into operation. As a result, preconstructed modular equipment was developed for START and the previously approved INF imaging equipment and procedures were applied to START requirements.

The Portal Monitoring Team

Portal monitoring teams are limited to thirty people. However, this number can be increased under special circumstances, such as during the initial engineering site survey and portal construction period, during routine replacement of monitoring team personnel, and for maintenance purposes. Monitors are drawn from a list (periodically updated) of 200 to 300 people submitted by each side. Portal monitoring personnel may be rejected for any reason within twenty days after their names are submitted. They also can be expelled later and removed from the list for cause, such as criminal indictment in the host country, conviction in a criminal case, previous expulsion, or violation of treaty conditions. Listed monitors are issued twenty-four month visas and other documentation within a month after being designated on the lists. Like other START inspectors, monitors are badged and wear civilian clothing during their in-country stay. This latter requirement also met national sensitivities: Neither side wanted highly visible uniformed military personnel of the other party patrolling its missile production plant sites.

The United States uses a combination of professional monitors and contract technicians at its portal sites, while the Russians use only professional monitors. This reflects a U.S. bias toward relying more heavily on monitoring technology requiring more maintenance and upkeep, while the Russians—more motivated by cost considerations—prefer to use people to perform basic operations. The U.S. portal at Votkinsk is manned by a contingent of four or five professional monitors headed by a site commander, typically an officer with the rank of lt. colonel or navy commander. This core team provides the official U.S. government presence at the portal, supervises monitoring operations, carries out all contacts with Russian officials, and certifies the monitoring data. It is supported by a team of over twenty contract personnel who install, operate, and maintain the technical monitoring equipment at the portal site and provide support services. The Russian portal team at Magna is composed entirely of military and other government personnel, headed by a site chief generally with the rank of colonel. Both portal teams rotate personnel on a regular basis.

Monitors and aircrew, like other inspectors, are accorded the diplomatic inviolability enjoyed by diplomatic agents. Living quarters, office premises, papers, and correspondence are inviolable but, for reasons of national security, the operations center and other inspection buildings occupied by the portal monitors at the PPCM site are inspectable. To guard against abuse of their diplomatic status, monitors are restricted from interfering in the host country's internal affairs or engaging in any activity for personal profit. The monitoring team chief has the right to waive a portal monitor's diplomatic immunity if this would "impede the course of justice," for example, in a criminal case involving a monitor, but such a waiver must be expressly authorized in each individual case.

For security reasons, the movement of INF portal monitors initially was restricted to a fifty-kilometer radius from the portal site. START liberalized these procedures by permitting free movement of monitors within a defined zone, except for restricted areas. However, prior permission is required for such travel, and the host country determines whether to provide an escort. Contacts with the local population are permitted and even encouraged but monitored by the host country for safety, political, and security reasons.

To permit close and continuing contacts with their governments on portal monitoring issues, two members of the monitoring team are permitted to travel between the portal and their embassy or consulate once a week, upon request. The traveling side bears the expense of such travel, while the host nation makes the necessary arrangements. Generally such travel is by air, but in the Russian Republic travel by train also has been permitted.

The travel of embassy personnel to the portal site also is restricted. Such travel is limited to personnel from the Embassy's treaty implementation unit—two members of which can travel two times per year to each site for two days each. During in-country travel, personal baggage, except for papers, is subject to examination to control the introduction of unauthorized (e.g. intelligence-collecting) equipment into the portal area. For similar reasons, the host country escorts can control electronic equipment purchased by monitors for their personal use, including securing such equipment in storage until departure of the monitor from the country. Portal monitoring teams establish their own rotation schedule but must give seven days notice prior to rotation and provide the number and names of personnel rotating into and out of the portal.

Housing and Communications

At Votkinsk, the U.S. portal team has both living and office quarters at the portal site. At Magna, the Russian living quarters are located approximately five miles from the portal site. Under the INF Treaty, the Soviets sought to house some of their personnel in the basement of the U.S. housing complex, citing the severe Soviet housing shortage. This arrangement was rejected by the United States as a violation of the diplomatic inviolability of living quarters and office premises and the issue eventually was dropped.[16] Reflecting this experience, START portal provisions explicitly ban use of inspector housing for other purposes.

The use of communications equipment by monitors at the sensitive portal also is regulated for security and plant safety reasons. Internal communications systems are permitted to link the portal sites, team headquarters, and other portal buildings and living quarters and to provide continuous contact with the host country escort team. Monitors patrolling the perimeter also are allowed to use their own two-way radio systems, but these are restricted in power level and to a single frequency, can have no other capability, and are subject to inspection by the escort team at any time. The portals also permit dedicated direct telephone and fax capability to the embassy and other diplomatic offices of the inspecting country.

The INF Treaty did not permit satellite communications between the portal site and the monitoring country's territory. However, after U.S. monitors encountered frequent communications problems attributable to the antiquated Russian communications system, this restriction was somewhat liberalized for START monitoring. START provisions permit the use of satellite communications equipment but relegate the use of such equipment to a back-up role. Monitors can use satellite communications only when a monitor and the host country escort conclude that a fax communication to the embassy via the dedicated phone line cannot be established within twenty minutes.

Portal Procedures

Both the INF and START Treaties use size criteria to determine whether an object, container, launch canister, or vehicle is inspectable. The inspected party must notify the portal monitors thirty minutes before moving any inspectable item through the portal. In addition, in the case of a START treaty-limited item, the applicable number and type must be identified and the monitor is accorded the right to read and record the unique identifier number.

Vehicles declared not to contain an inspectable item can be measured and weighed to determine if they are capable of containing an illegal missile or stage. In practice, however, weighing is not used. The United States was concerned during the Cold War that the Soviets could "spoof" the weight of railcar by removing weight elements after the rail car had entered the plant. This would make the combined weight of the exiting rail car and its missile cargo as it passed over rail scales, appear too light to require inspection. In addition, heavy snow cover, icing, and bitter cold at Votkinsk could complicate use of the weighing scales. Accordingly, the United States waived its right to weighing in exchange for the more reliable right to visually inspect the interior of all vehicles leaving the plant that are large enough to contain an SS-20.

If a vehicle is not large enough to contain a treaty inspectable item, it may pass without further inspection. If the vehicle is large enough and heavy enough to contain a treaty-inspectable item but declared not to contain one, it can be inspected in a manner that minimizes delay of the shipment. If there is a container or shrouded item in the vehicle large enough to hold a treaty-limited item, it is up to the host country officials to demonstrate to the satisfaction of portal monitors that it does not, in fact, contain such an item. This could be done, for example, by lifting a section of the shroud. Any vehicle leaving the facility at an exit other than the portal can be measured or examined to determine if it is large enough to contain an object of continuous monitoring. If so, the vehicle must proceed to the portal for normal processing.

Rail cars, like other vehicles, can be opened and internally inspected by monitors. In Votkinsk, however, an exception was granted for rail cars leaving the plant for the sole purpose of turning around. In such a case, the host country escort informs the monitoring team at least thirty minutes in advance that a rail car will be moved through the portal solely to reverse its direction. Two monitors then accompany the rail car from the time it arrives at the portal until it completes the turnaround procedure and returns to the plant. They are permitted to keep the rail car under observation at all times, no cargo may be removed, and the entire procedure must be completed without delay.

In the case of INF missiles, since Russian missiles are also shipped in enclosed canisters, the United States is permitted to open up to eight existing

Soviet missile canisters a year at random for interior viewing and measurement without removing the missile from its canister. To facilitate this process, the United States and Russia jointly cooperated in the development of a stage measuring device that allows measurements of the length and diameter of a missile within its canister. START provides for an annual quota of up to five opportunities, spread across all the facilities where mobile ICBMs are produced, to inspect containers or vehicles to confirm that no first stages of mobiles with nozzles attached leave the monitored facility.

Portal Equipment

Inspection operations by both sides at the portal site are monitored from a Data Collection Center (DCC) staffed around the clock. A console at the DCC allows monitors to automatically control traffic entering and exiting the portal and to acquire video data to substantiate any ambiguity. The field of view of surveillance cameras operated by the portal monitoring team is mutually agreed to permit effective monitoring of the portal, exits, and perimeter, while limiting observation of plant operations not subject to treaty provisions.

Equipment used at the portal is carefully regulated for security reasons. Only agreed equipment is permitted at the portal site, and its characteristics and use must be mutually agreed before it can be installed and operated. All structures and monitoring systems at the portal site are open to inspection by the host country escort team and equipment may not be changed without its prior agreement. Once in place, the host country is not permitted to interfere with installed equipment or to restrict the access of portal monitors to it.

Both sides are permitted to use similar monitoring equipment, but equipment layouts vary in practice. Only the United States uses nondamaging imaging equipment. In general, the Russians have opted for less complicated equipment than the United States uses. Portal equipment consists of a series of induction loops, sensors, traffic lights, and semaphore gates to alert monitors to traffic and to allow them to control it at the portals and exits; infrared (IR) break beam profilers are used to determine automatically whether the exiting vehicle is large enough to contain an object of continuous monitoring; and video cameras, with flood lights for clear night vision, are used for surveillance and documentation. The video cameras can take single-frame video images for use in inspection reports, if necessary. The Russians also have provided for installing a perimeter fence integrity system, which permits them to monitor changes in fence tension that might indicate a breach of the perimeter. Other equipment can be used at the portal sites, if mutually agreed.

Non-Damaging X-Ray Equipment and Procedures

Both the START and INF treaties permit the United States to X-ray the content of containers declared not to contain a treaty-regulated item. This is accomplished by using nondamaging imaging equipment under conditions that permit close regulation and supervision by the inspected party. Installing this equipment proved to be time consuming and expensive and its use has caused problems.

The X-raying concept was agreed to late in the INF negotiations to deal with the issue of how to verify that a canisterized SS-25 was not a banned SS-20 when both have similar first stages and both are canisterized during their life cycle and thus not easily inspectable. The Soviets would not agree to remove missiles from their canisters, since this is a complex and potentially dangerous activity requiring specialized equipment, but they did eventually agree to permit nondamaging imaging of the SS-25 canisters, subject to prior agreement on the characteristics and use of the X-ray equipment.

The system selected by the United States to do this imaging was the trademarked CARGOSCAN system, which X-rays a slice of the canister to ensure that it does not contain a treaty-related item either directly or within the shell of another missile. The CARGOSCAN is located on a rail spur at the portal site and is used only to image canisters large enough to contain an object of continuous monitoring. Since intrusive imaging of a missile can reveal critical information of its performance, protracted and difficult negotiations were required to agree upon the precise operating procedures for CARGOSCAN. Initial discussions began at the INF technical talks in spring 1988, and the final procedures were not agreed until early 1990—some two years later. Even then, the Soviets refused to permit imaging of the first three SS-25 missile canisters leaving the plant after the mutually agreed date for beginning CARGOSCAN operations on the grounds that essential security and safety concerns had not been resolved. These included storage of the magnetic tapes of the imaging, joint operating procedures, and safety measures. The U.S. portal monitoring team resorted to alternative inspection procedures, including opening the canisters to inspect the missiles, and found no violation. However, the Soviet actions in blocking application of the X-ray equipment created a verification crisis that required emergency meetings at Votkinsk of expert delegations on both sides to defuse. The United States also charged the Soviet Union with a violation of the INF Treaty for refusing to permit the nondamaging imaging to begin on schedule.[17] Subsequent problems have arisen in connection with imaging new missiles, resulting in further procedural negotiations.

The CARGOSCAN experience illustrates the difficulty of using highly intrusive equipment at continuous monitoring sites. The procedures for such equipment can be difficult to negotiate, the equipment can be costly and time consuming to develop and install, and its operation can be contentious. When proposing use of such highly intrusive technical monitoring equipment, these factors must be weighed carefully against the overall benefits of the monitoring gains achieved.

Transportation, Examination, and Documentation of Portal Equipment

Since continuous monitoring operations involve the installation of large and bulky pieces of equipment not customarily dealt with in other on-site inspections, special treaty provisions exist for transporting, examining, and documenting portal equipment. The INF Treaty had no provisions specifically covering these issues. Accordingly, they were worked out in the treaty's Special Verification Commission after EIF and codified in a separate Memorandum of Agreement (MOA) on Verification Provisions. In general, they differentiate portal flights from other inspection flights in a number of ways. They permit the heaviest military cargo aircraft of both sides to be used to transport continuous monitoring equipment and allow such flights to carry portal monitors rotating into or out of portal sites, as well as equipment. The flights may use a larger aircrew than normal inspection flights—twenty-five instead of ten—to accommo-date return crews and specialized personnel for loading and unloading. Less time (fifteen days vice twenty days) is allowed for rejecting listed portal aircrew members, but because of their specialized, often ad hoc composition, they receive only single-entry visas.

For reasons of national security, portal equipment, like other inspection equipment is subject to examination by the host country to ensure that it performs only treaty-related functions. It is carefully documented so that it can be closely controlled by both sides from the time it enters the country until it is installed. An inventory of such cargo must be provided through the embassy of the inspecting party at least ten days before the portal equipment and supplies are due to arrive at the POE. The inventory provides information on the weight and dimensions of each shipping unit, its contents, and the exact location at the portal site where each major item is to be installed or used. Black and white photographs or clear facsimile copies of the shipment are required, and shipping containers must be marked with appropriate freight markings and contain a complete packing list.

The equipment and supplies are inspectable at either the POE or the portal at the host country's choosing. If the examination is at the POE, aircrew members and portal inspectors witness the examination and resealing of the cargo. To keep the monitoring equipment from being altered by the host country, the portal team can keep the cargo under observation at all stages after it is unloaded—at the POE, at each transshipment point, and at the portal. At the portal, the shipment is reopened by the portal monitors in the presence of the host country escort, and the contents are checked against the joint inventory list. Installation, testing, and operation of the equipment at the site is carefully monitored by the escort team. If it is established that the equipment can perform functions unconnected with the treaty, the host country escort can halt its installation or—if already installed—demand that it be removed and taken out of the country.

Portal Experience to Date

In general, the portal concept has worked remarkably well. Relations between the monitors and host country at the portals in the United States and former Soviet Union have proceeded in a businesslike and professional manner. The special treaty provisions governing portal operations have weathered the test of time and have been found to work effectively. The portal monitoring process has led to the declaration of a number of treaty ambiguities, in addition to the CARGOSCAN issues noted previously, requiring extensive diplomatic efforts to resolve. The exits of two separate cargos from the Votkinsk portal in 1993 and 1994 caused the United States to declare ambiguities.[18] The first involved the exit from the facility on December 25, 1993, of a training model of the SS-X-27—a successor missile to the SS-25 ICBM. During the exit, Russian officials refused to allow U.S. inspectors to use the full-range of existing INF inspection procedures, causing the United States to declare an ambiguity. On July 18, 1994, a rail car exited Votkinsk, which contained an empty, canister-like cylinder whose length was inconsistent with several INF Treaty provisions.[19] The Russian Ministry of Foreign Affairs subsequently expressed regret over the incident and indicated that exit of the empty canister was a result of a misunderstanding at the plant.

An interim policy agreement was reached in 1994 to establish procedures for new missiles exiting Votkinsk. These included, in addition to the SS-X-27 ICBM, the "Start" and "Start-1" space launch vehicles which are derived from the SS-25 ICBM. The interim procedures allowed a limited number of missiles to exit the facility without being imaged by the CARGOSCAN system, but subjected them to all other inspection procedures. In mid-1995, the interim policy was extended and modified to permit CARGOSCAN imaging, while discussions of permanent procedures continued. In January 1997, an exhibition was conducted to demonstrate these procedures.

ALTERNATIVE PPCM CONCEPTS

The PPCM operations under the INF and START treaties have provided a rich base of experience that arms control specialists can draw on in connection with emerging arms control requirements. In addition, during the negotiation of those treaties, the United States developed a number of alternative portal technologies, including easily portable modular units and concepts for monitoring the entry as well as exit of treaty-limited items, which have possible application in other arms control areas.

The experience in erecting the INF portals prompted the development in the United States for possible START application of more readily transportable, easily erected, standardized modular units containing all necessary monitoring equipment that could be quickly installed at the site. These units were designed for phased installation. The Phase I system, which does not require permanent foundations or support, could be used on a temporary basis until more permanent, fixed monitoring equipment was installed at the site. It could be installed within twenty-four hours and contained all the basic sensors for the continuous monitoring process. The Phase II module consisted of a more robust, permanently installed monitoring system. The modular concept introduces an element of considerable flexibility. It permits the relatively rapid deployment of PPCM monitoring systems that are tailored in advance to their geographic environments and any unusual site characteristics and that can be quickly moved to, and put into operation at, the site.

In addition to modular units, new PPCM-applicable equipment has been developed to provide monitors with greater flexibility in monitoring traffic. Such equipment can detect and monitor traffic entering, exiting, or both entering and exiting a site in contrast to current equipment, which focuses on vehicles leaving a facility. The equipment also consists of a broader range of commercially available sensors, such as video cameras with motion detectors, bistatic radar, seismic sensors, and fence tension detectors. Other equipment also could be readily adapted to detect or distinguish the characteristics of controlled items such as improved radiographic imaging systems, radiation detectors, easily transportable weighing systems, linear measurement tools, remote viewing devices, and acoustic resonance sensors to name a few.

These developments could be easily applied, if required, to any PPCM concepts connected with emerging verification requirements, such as those related to the chemical weapons destruction, to the demilitarization of nuclear weapons, and to protection of highly sensitive military components removed from eliminated or converted weapons systems, such as advanced guidance systems. In addition, the existing INF and START portal operations could be used to monitor adjunct continuous monitoring operations located nearby connected with other arms control agreements. They also could serve as the model for future systems designed to monitor a number of portalled sites (corrals) simultaneously by using remote reporting and control capabilities linked into a single system and monitored from a centralized location.

Potential CWC Applications

The Chemical Weapons Convention (CWC) Verification Annex provisions for verifying the destruction of chemical weapons[20] calls for monitoring the "integrity of the destruction process and of the facility as a whole" with access to the facility by the inspection team "during the entire active phase." Since significant chemical weapons destruction facilities could be located near the current portals (e.g., at Toele in Utah and Kambarka in Russia) it may be possible to help verify destruction through permanently installed continuous monitoring systems built as adjunct operations to the existing portals. This would simplify the logistics and minimize the inspection expenses associated with monitoring the chemical weapons destruction process.

A possible system, installed simultaneously with construction of a chemical weapons destruction facility, would use tailored monitoring equipment surrounding a site monitored by a small continent of on-site personnel drawn from the central portal operation and rotated on a regular basis. The monitors would use modular units, similar to those developed for START, for both operational centers and housing. Standard PPCM procedures would be used to inspect vehicles or items entering or leaving the CWC destruction facility. To facilitate the use of small adjunct teams, the destruction site could operate on a normal work-day (eight to twelve hour) basis. The monitoring team would not actively monitor the site during periods of shutdown but would rely on remote video cameras and other monitoring technology to ensure integrity of the site. To enhance the reliability of monitoring technology during inactive facility periods, tamper proof equipment, tamper indicators and data authentication devices would be used. Repair and maintenance of the technical monitoring equipment would be performed by technicians located at the central PPCM location.

Nuclear Warhead Control and Accountability

The use of PPCM regimes also has been discussed in connection with proposals to verify the destruction of nuclear warheads. The entire process would have to be sufficiently controlled to confirm that the nuclear material from warheads being dismantled comes from those warheads (and not some other source) and to supervise the destruction or storage of the fissile materials removed from the weapons. A verification system for such a purpose could use concepts developed both in connection with PPCM monitoring and in IAEA material control and accountability procedures. It would require an intrusive inspection process that did not expose the technical details of nuclear warhead design which, for national security reasons, must be carefully protected.

Such monitoring might involve nuclear warhead dismantlement at portalled facilities suitably equipped with sensors to confirm that all personnel and materials entering or leaving the facility do so only through agreed access points under observation and control of inspectors. Accountability for fissile material (plutonium and highly enriched uranium) extracted from dismantled warheads could be achieved by applying IAEA safeguards after warhead elimination to confirm that the amount of such material is equivalent to the number of warheads transferred and eliminated.

The PPCM operation would be designed to confirm the number of warheads entering the facility, verify that such warheads remain inside the destruction facility and are not surreptitiously removed, and ensure that any fissile material leaving the facility does so only in a specified manner and under IAEA safeguard provisions. It would require, at a minimum, sensitive perimeter monitoring detectors with the capacity to detect even minute amounts of fissile material leaving the site.

Physical Security Monitoring

PPCM also could be used in connection with possible future proliferation control agreements, for example, one designed to tightly control sensitive military components from dismantled missiles, such as warheads, guidance systems, or other high technology elements. Such components could be subject to physical security and accountability by storing them at small portalled facilities, located at or near dismantlement sites, which are subject to continuous monitoring either directly or through remotely monitored emplaced sensors.

One such remote monitoring concept is a so-called corral monitoring system. This is a computerized system designed to detect and document accountable items that enter or depart one or several "corralled" sites, that is, sites at which the portal and perimeters are continuously technically monitored by permanently placed sensors and video cameras, but at which there is no physical presence of inspectors.[21] Such a system would employ field elements to collect data at entry and exit points and perimeter boundaries and communicate it to a centrally located data center for incorporation into a master data base. The data obtained would have to be able to differentiate an accountable item from its background, archive the data, and transmit it to other desired locations. All such data would be subjected to tamper protection, authentication and validation and have back-up power systems. Any ambiguous or suspicious activity at any of the "corrals" would be documented and immediately investigated by a centrally located group of monitors who would positioned to deploy rapidly to the site.

NOTES

1. Myron B. Kratzer, *International Nuclear Safeguards: Promise and Performance* (Washington, D.C.: The Atlantic Council, April 1994) pp. 28–30, presents an excellent description of containment and surveillance to which the author is heavily indebted.

2. IAEA Internet Factsheet, *International Safeguards and the Peaceful Uses of Nuclear Energy* (Vienna: IAEA, No date) p. 2.

3. Kratzer, *International Nuclear Safeguards*. p. 29.

4. Ibid. p.31.

5. For a comprehensive discussion of methods of evading a monitoring network see, U.S. Congress, Office of Technology Assessment, *Seismic Verification of Nuclear Testing Treaties*, OTA-ISC-361 (Washington, D.C.: U.S. Government Printing Office, May 1988), pp. 95–112.

6. Ibid. p. 18.

7. The implementing provisions on hydrodynamic yield measurement are contained in Section V of both the TTBT Protocol and PNET Protocol.

8. Provisions for implementing the seismic yield measurement method are contained in Sections VI of both the TTBT and PNET protocols.

9. "CTB Treaty Executive Summary," *Arms Control Today* (August 1996): 17–18.

10. A more comprehensive description of the OSI activity permitted under the CTBT is contained in chapter 11.

11. The PPCM concept was principally developed by Sandia National Laboratory in Albuquerque, New Mexico, under a variety of DoD contracts, and the first portal monitoring test site was established at Kirkland Air Force Base.

12. START Article IX, paragraph 4, establishes the unique identifier regime. Annex 6 to the treaty's Protocol on Inspections and Continuous Monitoring sets out the procedures related to unique identifiers.

13. Basic portal monitoring provisions are contained in Article XI, paragraph 6, of the INF Treaty and Section IX of its Inspection Protocol. For START, the relevant provisions are in Article XI, paragraph 14, and in Section XVI of the Protocol on Inspections and Continuous Monitoring Provisions.

14. The floor space of the environmental shelters are limited in the treaty.

15. Changes to the perimeter and perimeter continuous monitoring area are regulated. The START Treaty (Inspection Protocol, Section XVI, paragraph 7), for example, requires that changes to the perimeter must be prenotified, including the date on which such work is to commence. An annotated site diagram indicating the proposed changes in the perimeter continuous monitoring area must be provided through diplomatic channels, and both the boundary and procedures for relocating the perimeter and perimeter equipment must be mutually agreed upon before work begins so that there is no interruption of continuous monitoring activity.

16. The United States threatened to deny the Soviet portal team at Magna permission to move from its temporary quarters to its permanent housing complex until the Votkinsk housing issue was settled, leading the Soviets to drop the issue.

17. An official account of this early CARGOSCAN incident and the U.S. finding of a violation is contained in the *Unclassified Report on Soviet Noncompliance with Arms Control Agreement* (Washington, D.C.: Arms Control and Disarmament Agency) submitted by the president to Congress on February 15, 1991.

18. Both of these compliance issues are discussed in the 1994 and 1995 U.S. Arms Control and Disarmament Agency, *Threat Control Through Arms Control: Annual Report to Congress* (Washington, D.C: ACDA, July 13, 1995, and July 26, 1996, respectively).

19. The exit was inconsistent with the INF Agreed Minute of May 12, 1988, and the Votkinsk Agreed Statement to the INF Treaty of December 8, 1988.

20. Chemical Weapons Convention Verification Annex Part IV (A).

21. A description of the equipment and working of a possible corral system are contained in U.S. Defense Nuclear Agency, *Corral Monitoring System: Summary Description*, brochure provided at the 4th Annual Conference on Controlling Arms, Philadelphia, Pennsylvania, June 1995 (Washington, D.C.: DNA, June 1995).

Part IV

Implementing On-Site Inspection

Chapter 9

The Role of National Military Structures

The formidable array of on-site inspection provisions now contained in arms control treaties has required adjustments in existing bureaucracies and the creation of some new structures at both the national and multinational level to ensure proper implementation and compliance. As a rule, the major responsibilities for handling on-site inspections are centered in a relatively few bodies, although many departments, agencies, and offices throughout the government may have specialized operational roles. Since the thrust of most arms control treaties is the elimination, limitation, or banning of military weapons systems or activities, national defense establishments generally have assumed the bulk of responsibility for ensuring arms control implementation and compliance, including on-site inspection activities.

In the United States, the Department of Defense (DoD) ensures most arms control implementation and compliance. A centralized structure has been established within the Department of Defense to ensure proper oversight, while the operational responsibilities for carrying out on-site inspections and other arms control obligations are widely dispersed throughout the department. The Joint Chiefs of Staff and each of the military services—the Army, Air Force, Navy and Marines—implement specific on-site inspection obligations within their respective areas of responsibility. Other DoD components, such as the Defense Special Weapons Agency (formerly the Defense Nuclear Agency), the Advanced Research Projects Agency, and the Air Force Technical Applications Center also have specialized verification research and monitoring and implementation responsibilities.

An entirely new body—the On-Site Inspection Agency (OSIA)—was established within DoD in January 1988 to handle the unprecedented on-site inspection and escort responsibilities contained in the Intermediate-Range Nuclear Forces (INF) Treaty. OSIA's on-site inspection responsibilities subsequently have been extended to all arms control agreements with on-site inspection (OSI) regimes and to a number of related on-site inspection activities. Current DoD reform plans call for some further restructuring, leading to the formation by 1999 of a Threat Reduction and Treaty Compliance Agency, incorporating OSIA.

A number of other U.S. Government departments and agencies also have responsibilities for ensuring that U.S. on-site inspection commitments are met. These include the National Security Council, the Departments of State, Energy, and Commerce, the Federal Bureau of Investigation (FBI) and the intelligence community. The important responsibilities of the former Arms Control and Disarmament Agency (ACDA)—a separate agency established by the Kennedy administration to act as an independent voice on arms control issues—were integrated into the U.S. Department of State in 1997, as part of a major foreign affairs restructuring effort. Two specialized bodies of particular importance for on-site inspections also are located in the State Department. These are the Nuclear Risk Reduction Center (NRRC)—a centralized body created to process inspection-related notifications—and the U.S. National Authority—a new body established to serve as the central coordinating point for collecting and transmitting data required by the Chemical Weapons Convention (CWC).

This chapter focuses primarily on the role of the U.S. Defense Department bodies in implementing on-site inspection activities, while also touching on the related national defense ministry structures set up in the former Soviet Union (FSU), a large European country (Germany), and a small European country (Romania). The major on-site inspection responsibilities of other components of the U.S. Executive Branch are described in chapter 10. Chapter 11 discusses the structures and operations of the principal multinational bodies established to implement on-site inspections.

THE DoD ARMS CONTROL IMPLEMENTATION STRUCTURE

Roles and Missions Within DoD

The U.S. Department of Defense has had an established structure for implementing arms control agreements for over two decades. With the entry into force (EIF) of the Anti-Ballistic Missile (ABM) Treaty in 1972, the director of Defense Research and Engineering was assigned responsibility for overseeing DoD compliance with that treaty and with the Interim Agreement of the Strategic Arms Limitation Treaty (SALT I). Since then, DoD has periodically redefined the arms control roles and missions of its various components to accord with the provisions of each new arms control agreement as it has come on line. The current responsibilities within DoD for arms control implementation and compliance are defined in DoD Directive 2060.1, dated July 31, 1992, which delineates the responsibilities of various DoD policy and implementation components.

Centralized Oversight Responsibilities

Arms control policy in DoD, including that related to arms control implementation and compliance, is set by the Under Secretary of Defense for Policy (USD/P). That office represents DoD in discussions with the National Security Council, the Department of State, and other elements of the administration and has the lead DoD role in international negotiations and discussions with representatives of foreign governments. Within DoD, it provides advice and guidance on all arms control policy issues, including responses to questions of U.S. compliance raised by other treaty signatories. The Joint Chiefs of Staff (JCS) also has a central role in providing advice and in formulating and coordinating positions and procedures with the military services and with the major commands on arms control implementation and compliance issues affecting those elements.

The office of the Under Secretary of Defense for Acquisition and Technology (USD/A&T) has overall oversight for arms control implementation planning and execution. That office must ensure that all DoD activities comply fully with DoD obligations under all arms control treaties and associated agreements to which the United States is a party. Within USD(A&T), action responsibilities are essentially divided between two bodies. The Assistant to the Secretary of Defense for Nuclear, Chemical and Biological Defense Programs handles issues related to nuclear, chemical, and biological arms control, including the Comprehensive Test Ban Treaty, the Chemical Weapons Convention and the Biological Weapons Convention. The Director of Strategic and Tactical Systems, through its Office of Arms Control Implementation and Compliance (USD A&T/ACI&C), is responsible for issues related to the ABM Treaty, the INF Treaty, the strategic arms reduction treaties (START I and II), the Treaty on Conventional Armed Forces in Europe (CFE), and the Open Skies Treaty.

These offices provide centralized oversight over all implementation and compliance issues, including those involving on-site inspections. They must ensure that all Defense Department components—including the military services—meet their treaty obligations. This oversight extends across a broad range of implementation planning and execution responsibilities. These include the development of DoD plans for implementing arms control eliminations, inspections, notifications, and other obligations; coordination of arms control budgeting and of the relations between DoD components and defense contractors impacted by arms control agreement; and the provision of overall guidance on operational arms control implementation and compliance issues. USD(A&T) also provides direction and oversight of DoD research and development activities to ensure compliance with arms control commitments and provides technical experts to support arms control negotiations, international meetings, and discussions within the U.S. government on implementation and compliance issues.

Figure 9.1
DoD Compliance Process for Each Treaty

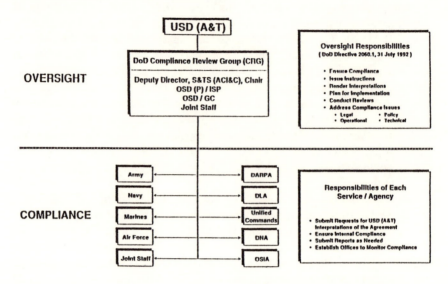

Source: **Office of Arms Control Compliance and Implementation, U.S. Department of Defense, Washington, D.C.**

Decentralized Execution

Within the parameters of this centralized direction, it is the responsibility of the individual DoD components—primarily the military services—to ensure that all affected military facilities understand their obligations and are operationally prepared to host on-site inspections and comply with the other provisions of existing and emerging arms control agreements. To do this, each component develops its own detailed compliance and implementation planning documents and respective supporting budget. Once approved, these plans are carried out by each component using its existing operational structure. Centralized direction and guidance thus is coupled with the decentralized execution of individual responsibilities by the DoD components best qualified to carry out each function.

To assist internal coordination, each affected DoD component is required periodically to review and report on its implementation and compliance activities. Any compliance question that may arise must be raised in the appropriate DoD arms control compliance body for resolution. Communications with the outlying military commands on implementation and compliance issues, including specifics of arms control procedures, is coordinated by the Joint Chiefs of Staff.

Figure 9.2
U.S. Department of Defense Arms Control Implementation and Compliance Structure

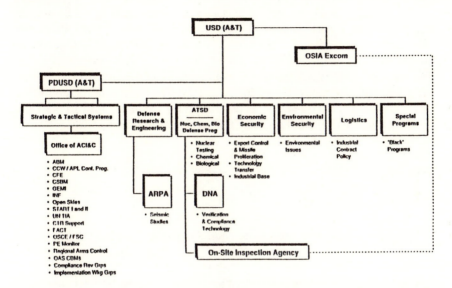

Source: **Office of Arms Control Compliance and Implementation, U.S. Department of Defense, Washington, D.C.**

Implementation and Compliance Working Groups

Implementation Working Groups (IWGs) have been established within DoD for each arms control agreement to assist coordination between all affected components. These groups are chaired by USD(A&T) directors and used to monitor and coordinate activities involving arms control issues, which can include any operational, administrative, financial, and logistic matter connected with the implementation of an arms control regime.

Questions of compliance involving either planned or ongoing DoD activities are handled by a Compliance Review Group (CRG) for the treaty concerned, which is also chaired by a USD(A&T) director. The CRGs can address a broad range of matters, including guidance on compliance issues; on the relationship of arms control agreements to DoD acquisition, testing, and operation of weapons systems and supporting activities; and on operational on-site inspection, escort, and other implementation activities.

The CRGs and IWGs are composed of representatives from all policy and operational bodies affected by a specific agreement. They are the central coordinating point within DoD for the clearance and execution of arms control and implementation guidance and for dealing with individual issues as they arise. However, they do not provide legal interpretations on arms control agreements or issues, which are responsibility of the DoD General Counsel.

The primary DoD Agency responsible for implementing U.S. on-site inspection and escort responsibilities—the OSIA—also comes under the administrative authority of USD(A&T). Because of OSIA's paramount role in the execution of on-site inspection and escort activities, DoD has established a separate body—the OSIA Executive Committee (EXCOM)—to provide oversight and policy and technical guidance to that agency. The major DoD organizations with responsibility for on-site inspection, including the Joint Chiefs of Staff and the Under Secretary for Policy, have representatives on the EXCOM.

THE U.S. ON-SITE INSPECTION AGENCY

Establishment of OSIA

When the first of the modern arms control agreements with a comprehensive on-site inspection regime—the INF Treaty—was signed in December 1987, a structure to implement these new obligations did not exist. After examining various options, the United States created OSIA to carry out its new arms control inspection and escort provisions, while the Soviet Union assigned them to an already existing body—its Nuclear Risk Reduction Center.[1]

OSIA was established by a National Security Decision Directive (NSDD-296) signed by President Reagan on January 15, 1988. This directive was issued over a month after the INF Treaty was signed and within a few months of the initially projected dates for beginning inspections.[2] The delay in issuing the directive reflected uncertainty, until late in the INF negotiating "end game," about the final scope of the treaty's on-site inspection regime.[3] In addition, there was some initial indecision within the U.S. government on how the new agency should be staffed and where it should be located within the Executive Department. Specifically, decisions needed to be made on whether the new agency should use military or civilian inspection and escort personnel and whether it should be an adjunct of the Arms Control and Disarmament Agency, the State Department, or the Department of Defense—all of which had legitimate claims to oversight of the new organization.[4] In addition, the Federal Bureau of Investigation, with its responsibility for domestic security issues, had an interest in the counter-intelligence aspects of arms control inspections that needed to be accommodated in the new agency.

In the end, the White House decided to give the new inspection agency a hybrid structure responsive to the concerns of all of these organizations.

Accordingly, NSDD 296 designates OSIA as an independent agency of the Department of Defense, but provides for management representation by the other organizations with direct on-site inspection-related responsibilities.[5] OSIA's director is appointed by the secretary of defense, with the concurrence of the secretary of state and the president, and its most senior management personnel are drawn from the three other U.S. government agencies with major responsibilities for on site inspection implementation—ACDA, the State Department, and the FBI. Within DoD, the EXCOM was established to ensure proper oversight on both policy and operational implementation and compliance issues.

NSDD-296 also carefully delineates OSIA's role to protect White House prerogatives for making the ultimate decisions on whether an inspected country is, or is not, in violations of its arms control commitments. The directive limits OSIA to operational, not policy making, activities by defining its purpose as managing the conduct of inspections and coordinating the operational activities connected with them, such as the acquisition, training, equipment, maintenance, and management of the inspection-related personnel and other resources required to carry out its mission. It thus makes clear that OSIA's basic role is to *monitor* —not make judgments on—arms control compliance. OSIA inspection and monitoring reports are but one element in a broader evaluation of compliance. They are integrated with other information collected by the intelligence community from national technical means (NTM) and all other intelligence sources to provide a total picture of compliance. The ultimate judgment on whether a country is complying with its arms control commitments then is made by an established interagency verification policy body under oversight of the National Security Council.

Should this broader evaluation process establish that a treaty violation has occurred, the National Security Council formulates the recommended response options for the president based on the significance of the violation for U.S. national security interests. Such options could range from raising the issue at the diplomatic level or discussing it in an established arms control compliance body to withdrawal from the treaty concerned and the initiation of political or military countermeasures, depending on the seriousness of the violation.

Expanding Responsibilities

Since its founding, OSIA's defined mission has remained fundamentally the same, but its responsibilities have been steadily expanded to cover the on-site inspection responsibilities of subsequent arms control agreements and some ad hoc functions involving on-site presence.[6] Expansion of its basic mandate began in May 1990 when OSIA was directed by President George Bush to begin planning to support the inspection and escort provisions of the projected CFE and START treaties, the two nuclear test agreements—the Threshold Test Ban Treaty (TTBT) and Peaceful Nuclear Explosions Treaty (PNET)—and the various chemical weapons agreements, including the CWC. These were subsequently followed up by operational directives to implement the inspection and escort responsibilities of these and other arms control agreements as they came into force.

In addition, in June 1991, OSIA was tasked by the National Security Council with carrying out inspection and escort functions under the Vienna Documents, and in July 1991, it was made the Defense Department's Executive Agent for supporting the inspections conducted by the United Nations Special Commission on Iraq (UNSCOM). After the signing of the Open Skies Treaty in March 1992, it was given additional responsibilities in that area. In February 1996, the secretary of defense directed OSIA to support multilateral inspection activities in Bosnia and Herzegovina under the auspices of the Organization for Security and Cooperation in Europe (OSCE).[7]

Because of it worldwide infrastructure, logistic and linguistic capabilities, operational working relationships with military forces in other countries, and experience in operating in remote areas, OSIA also has been called upon to perform a variety of ad hoc inspection-related activities. Following the collapse of the Soviet Union, the agency assisted U.S. humanitarian efforts to deliver food and medical supplies throughout the former Soviet republics until private charitable organizations could assume all of these responsibilities.[8] OSIA also participated in a secret nonproliferation-related operation in late 1994 to remove weapons-grade highly enriched uranium from Kazakstan to the United States; provided on-site operational and training support to the U.S. forces in Korea; and supported the Cooperative Threat Reduction (CTR) programs in the former Soviet Union with linguistic, auditing, examination, and other support.[9]

Commensurate with the rapid expansions of treaty on-site inspection provisions, OSIA also has assumed responsibilities for coordinating inspection and escort activities with other arms control treaty partners, with regional organizations such as NATO and the OSCE, and with broader multinational organizations, including the United Nations.

Figure 9.3
OSIA Mission History

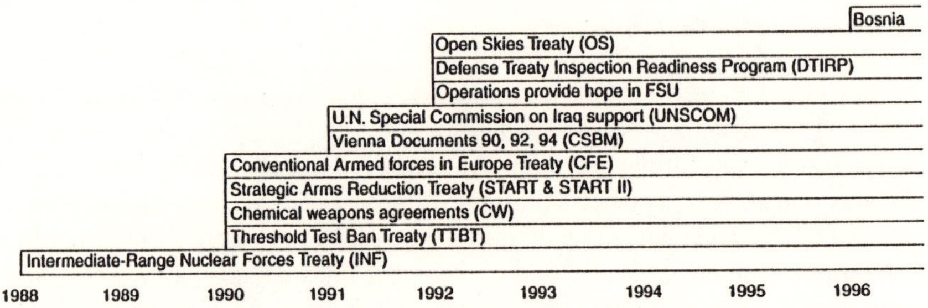

1988	1989	1990	1991	1992	1993	1994	1995	1996

- Bosnia
- Open Skies Treaty (OS)
- Defense Treaty Inspection Readiness Program (DTIRP)
- Operations provide hope in FSU
- U.N. Special Commission on Iraq support (UNSCOM)
- Vienna Documents 90, 92, 94 (CSBM)
- Conventional Armed forces in Europe Treaty (CFE)
- Strategic Arms Reduction Treaty (START & START II)
- Chemical weapons agreements (CW)
- Threshold Test Ban Treaty (TTBT)
- Intermediate-Range Nuclear Forces Treaty (INF)

Source: **U.S. On-Site Inspection Agency, Washington, D.C.**

Organization and Infrastructure

From the outset, OSIA's organizational structure has been determined by two major considerations: It is first and foremost an operational agency, and its operations are global. The agency was originally organized around its core responsibilities for inspection, portal monitoring, and escort operations, and although its size and responsibilities have steadily expanded, the majority of its personnel remained assigned to those operational areas. The core operational units are assisted by a support staff to handle administrative and logistics operations and technical staff which performs specialized functions such as legal, congressional and public affairs. To deal with the mounting health and safety concerns connected with inspection of an increasing range of hazardous sites involving nuclear, chemical, biological and conventional weapons, OSIA has established a Safety and Occupational Health Office.

Figure 9.4
Basic OSIA Organization

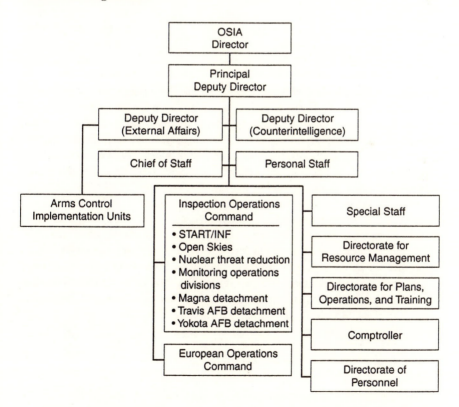

Source: U.S. On-Site Inspection Agency.

OSIA's organizational structure also mirrors its responsibilities to respond rapidly to inspection requirements across the globe. Currently the agency is composed of the following main elements.

Headquarters and Field Offices

OSIA headquarters contains the agency's director, deputy directors, and other top management personnel, including the chiefs of the operational and support directorates. During its founding, OSIA was temporarily headquartered in the Coast Guard Building located at Buzzard's Point near Fort McNair in the District of Columbia,[10] and the Agency operated separate field offices to support the INF treaty points of entry (POEs) at Dulles International Airport near Washington D.C, and at Travis Air Force Base (AFB) near San Francisco. In spring 1989, OSIA moved its headquarters to its present Dulles Airport site, combining it with its Dulles field office.

Gateway Sites

In addition to its U.S. operations, OSIA initially established a "gateway" site at Frankfurt AFB in then West Germany to assist inspection and escort operations in Eastern and Western Europe and in the western part of the Soviet Union and at the U.S. air base in Yokota, Japan, to assist similar operations in the Soviet Far East. The gateway at Yokota has remained a relatively modest operation. However, as OSIA took on new inspection responsibilities, the Frankfurt gateway developed into a major separate administrative unit composed of approximately 150 people, now called European Operations. This important subunit is charged with supporting the INF Treaty, the CFE Treaty—implementation of which is focused on the area from the Atlantic to the Ural Mountains—and the Vienna Document, which also has a predominantly European focus. It also serves as the principal logistics point for supporting the U.S. portal monitoring operations in the former Soviet Union. As part of its overall responsibility as the major coordinating point on inspection and escort issues requiring close working relationships with NATO, the OSCE, and the individual European countries, OSIA's European Operations also provides inspection support to the OSCE in Bosnia under the Dayton Accords.

The Arms Control Implementation Units

OSIA personnel staff Arms Control Implementation Units (ACIUs) located at a number of U.S. embassies in the former Soviet Union. The first ACIU was established in Moscow to support the INF Treaty. Following the break-up of the Soviet Union, separate ACIUs also were set up in Minsk (Belarus), Kiev (Ukraine), and Almaty (Kazakstan). In addition, to support INF inspection aircraft from Yokota, an auxiliary support unit was established at Ulan Ude in Russia, near Lake Baikal. The ACIU and Ulan Ude personnel meet incoming aircraft carrying U.S. inspectors, assist the aircrews with their flight-related activities, and support U.S. inspection teams during POE processing. Embassy ACIU personnel also act as the principal contact point for inspection teams carrying out inspections at sites in the host country and initiate actions on any on-site inspection issue raised with the embassy by an inspection team chief. They also conduct discussions with foreign ministry and inspection agency officials in the capitals on ongoing operational inspection and escort issues.

The Portal Sites

As indicated earlier, OSIA personnel also make up the core staff of the portal and perimeter continuous monitoring (PPCM) operations at Votkinsk in Russia. A separate OSIA Escort Detachment directs the U.S. escort responsibilities for the portaled missile plant at West Valley (Magna), Utah, near Salt Lake City. That detachment also has jurisdiction for PPCM matters related to START portal monitoring at Thiokol Strategic Operations in Promontory, Utah, although Russia had decided not to exercise its right to conduct continuous monitoring at that site.

Projected Chemical Weapons Agreements and Open Skies Sites

In connection with its responsibilities under chemical weapons (CW) agreements, OSIA also plans to have operational units at Toele, Utah, a major repository of U.S. chemical weapons stocks, and at Johnston Island, located approximately 750 miles from Hawaii, the principal site for the destruction of U.S. chemical weapons. Agency plans also call for a unit at Mildenhall, England, to assist Open Skies overflights.

The Defense Treaty Inspection Readiness Program

In addition to its inspection, monitoring, and escort responsibilities, OSIA also is the executive agency for administering a program within the DoD to assist both DoD components and defense contractor facilities to prepare for arms control inspections. In 1990, the Deputy Under Secretary of Defense for Security Policy established the Defense Contractor Inspection Readiness Program (DCIRP) to help defense contractors understand START inspection requirements

Figure 9.5
OSIA Locations

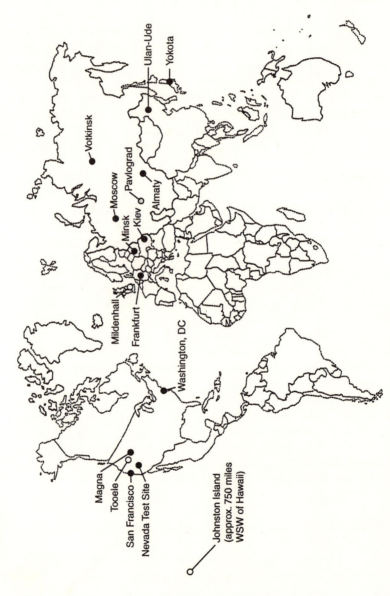

●— Former portal monitoring site (January – June 1995).
○— Sites not yet activated under provisions of arms control treaties.

Source: U.S. On-Site Inspection Agency, Washington, D.C.

that could affect their facilities and develop measures to protect sensitive classified and business proprietary information during such inspections. The DCIRP brought together representatives from various U.S. government security and intelligence agencies in order to develop a centrally coordinated assessment of the security threat posed to an affected facility by arms control inspections. In fall 1991, DCIRP underwent several administrative and functional changes. The program was reorganized, transferred to the Assistant Secretary of Defense for Command, Control, Communications and Intelligence, and renamed the Defense Treaty Inspection Readiness Program (DTIRP). Moreover, its mission was expanded beyond the DoD contractor community to cover inspectable sites in general and broadened beyond START to apply to all arms control treaties. In June 1992 the OSIA was designated as the executive agency for DTIRP with responsibility for planning and executing its mission. Memoranda of Agreement were developed with the various intelligence and security agencies involved in the program to clarify the respective roles and missions of all participants.

The DTIRP has developed an industry outreach program to increase awareness within the defense contractor community of arms control agreements and their potential impacts on industry. It also provides training; carries out preinspection or previsit assessments of facility vulnerabilities; assists in the identification of sensitive programs, operations, and technologies and of their vulnerability during inspections or visits; and develops uniform and cost effective countermeasures. To protect both national security and business confidentiality concerns, the results of DTIRP assessments of individual defense industries are closely held within the U.S. government, being provided only to the facility concerned and its responsible DoD component.

OSIA Operational Procedures

In addition to implementing arms control treaty provisions and assisting technical discussions in various fora to develop other mutually agreed operational procedures, OSIA has developed its own internal operational inspection and escort procedures. Some of these were drawn from military practice or the experience of earlier on-site inspection agencies, such as the International Atomic Energy Agency (IAEA), while others are unique. By and large, the core operational procedures developed by OSIA to implement the initial INF Treaty remain fundamental elements of its operations today and, indeed, have been widely copied by subsequent national and international on-site inspection bodies.

These core operational concepts include the predominant (but by no means exclusive) use of military personnel drawn from all military services as inspection and escort personnel; the careful selection of team chiefs; the concept of tailored inspection teams; the institution of formal training courses; widespread use of mock inspections to test procedures and train personnel; the use of "gateway sites" to assist inspections and escort responsibilities overseas;

the use of well-structured pre-inspection briefings and post inspection debriefings to ensure focused inspections and reporting; and a tendency to favor the use of relatively simple, durable, and easily portable inspection equipment for field inspections whenever possible.

OSIA Staffing Patterns

OSIA is staffed by both permanent and temporary duty personnel, although use of the latter has been steadily declining in recent years. Its permanent staff is made up both of military and civilian technical experts and support personnel. Its inspection and escort teams are composed both of male and female personnel, generally between twenty and forty years of age led by more senior team chiefs. Commensurate with its steadily expanding responsibilities, OSIA's staff had grown from an initial cadre of forty people in February 1988 to some 850 people by mid-1996. Military personnel are drawn from all of the military services. The U.S. Army and Air Force each provide just over a quarter of the agency's personnel, while the Navy and Marines provide about 11 percent. Somewhat over a third (37 percent) of OSIA's personnel are civilian employees. OSIA's joint service make-up is mirrored in other national on-site inspection agencies. For example, the British on-site inspection agency—the Joint Arms

Figure 9.6
OSIA Staffing Profile: July 31, 1995

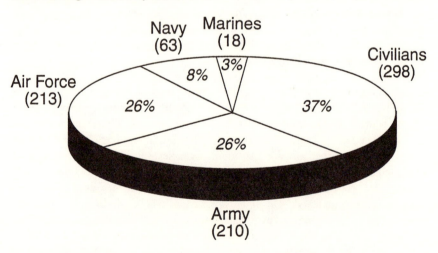

Source: **U.S. On-Site Inspection Agency, Washington, D.C.**

Control Implementation Group—is a tri-service organization which currently has a staff of thirty-two Army, thirty-three Royal Air Force, five Royal Navy, five Royal Marines, and nine civil servants.[11]

Permanently assigned OSIA personnel are augmented by a cadre of trained temporary-duty inspection and escort personnel, primarily from DoD, but also from other U.S. government agencies, who provide support as required to meet the ebb and flow of inspection and escort activities.[12] These activities tend to peak, for example, during baseline periods as new agreements come on line, slowing somewhat once this intensive inspection period is past. During official activities, OSIA inspection and escort teams wear OSIA outer garments over civilian clothing, while Russian teams typically wear civilian suits.

Carefully Selected Team Chiefs

OSIA team chiefs, as a rule, are experienced military officers, generally with the rank of lt. colonel or navy commander or above. They are selected with particular attention to maturity and judgment, since the team chief plays a critical role in the success (or failure) of the inspection. The team chief must have a firm understanding of treaty provisions and possess the ability to tactfully, but firmly, handle difficult issues as they arise in the field. He or she also sets the tone for the rest of the team and signs the final report, which provides the official account of the inspection. The use of senior military officers for these positions generally ensures prior knowledge of the military weapons systems being inspected or destroyed and of the organization and operations of the predominantly military facilities being inspected. As a rule, other national inspection agencies also rely predominantly on senior military officers of lt. colonel/colonel or equivalent rank to head their inspection and escort teams.

Tailored Inspection Teams

OSIA does not rely on a single cadre of inspectors to cover the full spectrum of arms control treaties but, instead, has constructed teams with specialized expertise for each treaty. While certain treaties, such as the INF and START treaties, both of which deal with nuclear, predominantly missile-related, delivery systems, lend themselves to interchangeable use of the same inspectors, other agreements, such as CFE and the CWC, require a quite different range of military knowledge and inspection skills. To ensure that it can meet the broad range of skills required by the various treaties, OSIA recruits its military and civilian personnel on the basis of skills categories that have been previously identified and delineated. Personnel meeting these skills categories then are drawn from the military or civilian government organizations possessing that skill base. For example, OSIA personnel for CWC support are recruited primarily from the U.S. Army, which has primary responsibility for the maintenance and destruction of U.S. chemical weapons; while personnel for Open Skies support are recruited predominantly from the Air Force. Recruitment on the basis of a previously identified skill base also is standard procedure for other on-site inspection agencies, both national and international.

Formal Training Courses

Because of the complexity of modern arms control agreements, OSIA has maintained a formal training program since its inception to familiarize personnel with treaty provisions, inspection and escort procedures, and the use of inspection equipment. While these courses initially were taught predominantly by outside personnel, OSIA's training program currently relies heavily on team chiefs and other OSIA personnel as instructors. Placing a potential teaching burden on agency personnel provides an additional incentive for them to deepen their understanding of treaty provisions. In addition, it facilitates the infusion of practical experience and "lessons learned" into the training programs.

The training of linguists poses a special problem. Linguists usually are recruited from the military services on the basis of tested language competencies. But, no matter how extensive their language skill base, linguists usually must be given some supplemental training to ensure they properly understand and can accurately translate the sometimes highly specialized or arcane treaty terminology during the course of their dual role as linguist-inspector.

The sheer complexity of modern arms control treaties requires all national and international inspection agencies to operate formal training programs or at a minimum, to have their inspectors participate in programs offered by other nations. In connection with CFE inspections, NATO has instituted a training program at Oberammergau, Germany, which now is attended by inspection personnel from all CFE countries—East and West. This program has proved to be a highly effective means of introducing uniformity into CFE inspection practices. It also has served to promote a common understanding by all parties of CFE Treaty terminology and provisions, enhance cooperation, and ensure smoother implementation of inspection and escort operations in the field. Inspector and inspector assistant candidate for the CWC must successfully undertake comprehensive training programs before final approval.[13]

Mock Inspections

Prior to implementation of the unprecedented on-site inspection and escort obligations of the INF treaty, OSIA initiated mock (practice) arms control inspections at all U.S. inspectable sites as means of training personnel and preparing sites. These inspections proved to be so valuable that mock inspections were incorporated as an essential element in the preparations for all subsequent agreements. Indeed, during the lengthy period between signing of the START Treaty and its entry into force, five separate rounds of mock inspections were held at DoD facilities not only for preparatory and training purposes, but also to retain a high readiness status during the hiatus.

Mock inspections serve multiple purposes. They help develop a unified national approach to the inspection process among the diverse facilities subject to inspection.[14] They are a valuable tool for training inspectors and escorts. They permit field testing of the individual readiness plans prepared by inspectable sites and provide operational training for site personnel subject to inspections. Mock inspections also allow field testing of inspection equipment, such as field-operated chemical and biological weapons detection equipment, in realistic conditions. In addition, they are frequently used by DoD planners to develop operational material and procedures for implementing treaty provisions which are only vaguely defined in treaty documents. For example, they have been used by the DoD to develop basic inspection handbooks and to work out possible approaches for implementing unusual procedures, such as START special access visits.

Because of their broad utility, virtually all national and international inspection agencies use mock inspections for training purposes and final preparations for treaty inspections. Like OSIA, the Russians conducted full-scale mock inspections, including unannounced spot inspections, to prepare inspection and site personnel for INF implementation.[15] As additional examples, during the period between the CFE Treaty's signature in November 1990 and its entry into force in July 1992, the United States, Germany, France, and Great Britain conducted a series of mock inspections, *inter alia* to provide each national inspection agency with practice in implementing treaty notification, communication, and information requirements.[16] On an individual country basis, in preparation for the CFE Treaty, German inspectors conducted or participated in over 200 mock inspections. The French carried out a three-phase training program for the CFE Treaty, which involved national mock inspections, bilateral mock inspections with NATO allies, and, finally, mock inspections with Russia, Belarus, Hungary, Romania, and the Czech Republic. Recently, mock inspections were used to prepare for OSCE inspection activities in Bosnia under the Dayton Agreement.

The Use of Gateway Sites

Since the INF Treaty required inspections in Eastern Europe and throughout the entire landmass of the former Soviet Union, OSIA developed the concept of first sending inspection teams to the Frankfurt and Yokota gateway sites before deploying them on inspection missions. Forward deployment of inspectors and the scheduling of briefings at the gateway sites enabled inspection teams to arrive relatively fresh even at remote sites in the Soviet Union and helped them to carry out more focused inspections. It also enhanced the simultaneous use of multiple inspection teams during baseline or other inspections and permitted more effective debriefings at the conclusion of the inspection.

Moreover, the gateway concept allowed the permanent stationing of OSIA escort teams in Europe to assist Soviet and other inspections of U.S. bases in Europe and facilitated essential liaison between OSIA and European defense establishments and inspection agencies. The gateway concept subsequently has been used by the United Nations to support UNSCOM inspections in Iraq. UNSCOM inspectors are forward deployed to a field office in Bahrain which is used as an assembly and training point prior to deployment of the inspection teams into Iraq.

Inspector Briefing and Debriefing

OSIA inspectors receive detailed briefings on inspection sites prior to departure and are debriefed upon their return. The predeparture briefings integrate information received from national technical means and other intelligence sources as well as from previous inspections and are designed to impart as clear a focus as possible to each inspection. In cases where there is a great variety of different types and models of treaty-limited equipment to inspect, such as during CFE inspections of conventional weapons, inspectors also are provided with portable reference materials that can be used at the site to assist the inspection process. Inspection teams are routinely debriefed immediately upon their return from each inspection. The information from these debriefings complements the material contained in the official inspection report and assists understanding of any implementation or operational issues that have arisen during an inspection and that could require follow-up or resolution in other channels.

OTHER U.S. DEFENSE DEPARTMENT AGENCIES

Two other DoD offices and agencies with important roles for on-site inspection should be briefly noted at this point. The Defense Special Weapons Agency (formerly the Defense Nuclear Agency) develops and manages an integrated research, development, technology and equipment (RDT&E) and acquisition program to support DoD agencies and the operational commands on arms control verification issues. Much of this research and acquisition activity is aimed at increasing the effectiveness and efficiency of on-site inspections in the field through the development of better verification equipment, technologies, and procedures. The agency also assists administration of Nunn Lugar Act funds to help the successor states to the former Soviet Union meet their treaty commitments on the destruction of strategic offensive arms and chemical weapons for which OSIA has carried some auditing and other functions. Another key agency—the Air Force Technical Applications Center—has responsibility for operating and maintaining the global network of nuclear event detection sensors used to monitor compliance with the Limited Test Ban Treaty, TTBT and PNET, and plays a primary role in installing and managing the U.S. monitoring systems for the global ban on testing under the Comprehensive Test Ban Treaty. While not directly involved in on-site inspections, its monitoring systems could trigger such activity.

OTHER NATIONAL ON-SITE INSPECTION AGENCIES

By January 1996, national on-site inspection agencies had been established in thirty-five countries to implement arms control treaties. Like OSIA, virtually all national on-site inspection agencies are located in the defense agency (Ministry of Defense) of the country concerned and use a mix of military and civilian personnel for inspection activities. In addition, most use senior military officers as team chiefs.

As a rule, national on-site inspection agencies carry out six basic functions. They obtain and verify treaty-related military data; maintain an around-the-clock communications center; select, train, and deploy inspection and escort teams; assist national military sites, when requested, to respond to inspection requirements under the treaties; and coordinate information, including inspection schedules, with other treaty nations.

Table 9.1
Countries with On-Site Inspection Agencies

• Armenia	• Germany	• Portugal
• Azerbaijan	• Greece	• Romania
• Belarus	• Hungary	• Russian Federation
• Belgium	• Italy	• Slovak Republic
• Bulgaria	• Kazakstan	• Spain
• Canada	• Luxembourg	• Turkey
• Czech Republic	• Moldova	• Ukraine
• Denmark	• Netherlands	• United Kingdom
• France	• Norway	• United States
• Georgia	• Poland	

Source: **U.S. On-Site Inspection Agency, Washington, D.C.**

Inspection Agencies in the Former Soviet Union

After the United States, Russia has the largest national on-site inspection agency. As the repository of much of the military equipment of the former Soviet Union, Russia is required to devote more resources, receive more inspections, and reduce more weapons under the complex of modern arms control agreements than any other country. However, the Russian and U.S. on-site inspection agencies differ in one major respect. In Russia, both on-site inspection and notification responsibilities have been combined in a single body—the Russian National Risk Reduction Center (NRRC)—while these two functions are handled by separate organizations in the United States.

In the Soviet Union, the NRRC was created at the end of 1987 as an independent directorate of the Soviet General Staff and, in contrast to the U.S. NRRC, located in the Ministry of Defense. When the INF Treaty was signed in December 1987, the Moscow NRRC was also assigned responsibility for conducting Soviet on-site inspection and escort activities, combining the arms control notification, inspection, and escort functions in a single body.[17]

The Russian NRRC is part of the Chief Directorate of International Military Cooperation of the Russian General Staff. In carrying out its global implementation and compliance responsibilities, the NRRC coordinates closely with a host of other Russian Federation ministries and departments including the Ministry of Foreign Affairs, the State Committee on Defense Industries, the State Customs Committee, and the Ministries of Transportation, Communications, Finance, and Railways. It also is the central coordination point on inspection issues between Russia and the national arms control implementation organizations in the other FSU countries and works closely with OSIA's Moscow Arms Control Implementation Unit on operational arms control issues.

Figure 9.7
Russian Implementation Structure for Arms Control Treaties

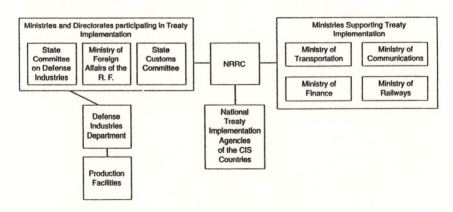

Source: **Lt. Gen. V. A. Romanov, Briefing to OSIA, Washington D.C., July 1995**

The Russian NRRC consists of an operations division, a foreign inspections division, a domestic inspections (escort) division, a support division, and an operations center group, supported by specialized subgroups for translation and information, and administration.[18] Like OSIA, this basic organizational and personnel structure has evolved as the Russian NRRC has assumed responsibility for the implementation and compliance of new arms control agreements, including for the INF, START, CFE, and Open Skies treaties and the Vienna Document. Its notification responsibilities extend beyond these agreements to include the TTBT, PNET and Wyoming Agreement, CWC, Ballistic Launch Agreement, major strategic exercises, and a series of other agreements. To provide an idea of the scope of its combined activity, the Russian NRRC through June 1995 had forwarded nearly 8,000 treaty-related messages and received over 11,600 notifications. Russian inspection teams also had conducted 728 inspections abroad and served as escorts for 1,033 domestic inspections.[19]

In Russia, operational responsibility for the implementation of arms control treaties is assumed by treaty implementation support offices within each branch of the armed forces. In coordination with these offices, the Russian NRRC has responsibility for conducting foreign and domestic inspections; selecting and training inspectors and escorts; carrying out Open Skies planning and training;

Figure 9.8
Russian Ministry of Defense On-Site Inspection Implementation Structure

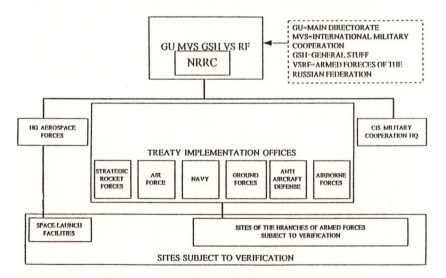

Source: **Lt. Gen. V. A. Romanov, Briefing to OSIA, Washington, D.C., July 1995**

planning and training; organizing logistic support for inspection and escort activities; and handling all notifications and interpreter support for, and general administration of, inspection-related activity.

Following the break-up of the Soviet Union, a number of other countries of the former Soviet Union, which were parties to arms control agreements—principally the Ukraine, Belarus, and Kazakstan—established separate arms control implementation structures generally modeled on those in Russia.

In the Ukraine, the National Committee on Disarmament, which is located in the Ministry of Foreign Affairs and reports to the president of the Ukraine, has overall policy responsibility for implementing arms control agreements. The Committee has set up a special directorate for harmonizing interdepartmental issues; conducting treaty negotiations; providing oversight of treaty implementation; and handling the collection, processing, and preparation of treaty data and reports.

Like other national inspection agencies, however, on-site inspection operational responsibilities are carried out by a body located in the Ministry of Defense—the Verification Center for the Armed Forces of Ukraine. The center is organized into four departments, which conduct inspection and escort missions for the treaties to which the Ukraine is a party and deal with various related administrative, planning, and organizational matters. Subordinate to the Verification Center are special treaty implementation support centers located at POEs in Kiev, Odessa, and Lvov.[20]

Belarus established a similar body—the National Agency for Control and Inspection (NACI)—in its Ministry of Defense in June 1992. The NACI has responsibility for implementing seven arms control agreements, coordinating cooperative programs with the United States to assist arms control implementation financed under the Nunn-Lugar Act and monitoring the withdrawal of Russian strategic nuclear forces from Belarus.[21]

The Kazakstan Center for Monitoring Arms Reductions and Supporting Inspection Activities, likewise located in the Ministry of Defense, has a staff of thirty-two military and seven civilian employees in two main divisions: an Arms Reduction Department and an Inspection Activities Department. The center has worked closely with the Russian and Ukrainian verification centers and with the NATO school in Oberammergau on inspector training related to Kazakstan's responsibilities under the INF, START, and CFE treaties, the Vienna Document, and the Nunn-Lugar Cooperative Threat Reduction Program.[22]

Other National Inspection Agencies

Verification agencies also have been set up in the European nations that are CFE signatories. For purposes of illustration, a larger and smaller European national inspection agency are briefly described below.

The German Federal Armed Forces Verification Center

The largest of the Western European inspection agencies is the German Federal Armed Forces Verification Center (Zentrum fuer Verifikationsaufgaben der Bundeswehr, or ZVBw). It has perhaps the most far reaching national arms control inspection responsibilities outside the United States and Russia. Since reunification, the ZVBw has integrated responsibility for all CFE reductions in both East and West Germany. This includes over 900 CFE objects of verification (inspectable sites)—more than any other NATO country.

The ZVBw is a joint service organization located in the Ministry of Defense. It is based at Geilenkirchen, near Aachen, and consists of a headquarters element, a communications center, an inspection and escort staff, language section, and a training unit. Until January 1994 when its mission there ceased, the ZVBw also had a branch office at Stausberg, near Berlin, to escort foreign inspection teams to CFE Treaty reduction sites.

The ZVBw is composed of over 500 military officers, noncommissioned officers (NCOs), and civilians responsible for implementing the inspection provisions of the CFE Treaty, Vienna Document, Open Skies Treaty, and the INF Treaty.[23] Like OSIA, all German team chiefs are professional military officers, generally colonels, forty to fifty years old and with fifteen to twenty-five years of military service. The ZVBw cooperates closely with the verification agencies of the other NATO countries. When the CFE Treaty entered into force, it became part of an informal network with its U.S., British, and French counterparts—known as the G-4—to exchange operational information on inspection and escort team activities and on other operational matters and assist in standardizing operations and improving coordination between those countries.[24] It also has trained Eastern European inspectors, runs a language program for CFE inspectors, and has taken the lead within the multinational NATO Verification Coordinating Committee in advocating the participation of inspectors from cooperating partner nations on CFE treaty inspection teams.

Romania's Arms Control Directorate

Romania's Arms Control Directorate is a typical example of a smaller, more narrowly focused European national inspection agency. The directorate is primarily responsible for implementing Romania's CFE Treaty and CFE-1A Final Act obligations, although Romania has also concluded some bilateral and regional agreements involving additional confidence-building measures, including an Open Skies agreement with Hungary. The directorate is located in the Ministry of National Defense and has a total complement of forty-eight people (thirty-one officers, six NCOs, and eleven civilians). Its structure, main responsibilities and personnel distribution are illustrated in Figure 9.9.[25]

The smaller European on-site inspection agencies have had to rely heavily on the larger countries for training purposes and other support. For example, to augment its training programs and reduce transportation and other costs, Romania has made full use of participation in multinational teams and combined its inspection activities with other CFE signatories. During the period from 1992 through mid-1996, 111 Romania inspectors were included in multinational teams of other states, and 59 inspectors from other states were included in its multinational inspection teams. Romania also has receiving important support from NATO and from the inspection agencies in Germany, the United Kingdom, Italy, and Belgium on language and other training programs.

Figure 9.9
Romanian Arms Control Directorate

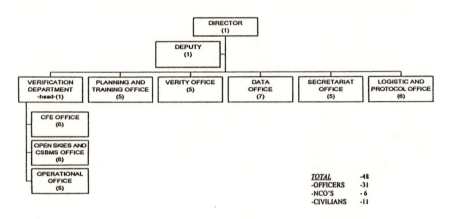

Source: **B. Gen. Cordeneaunu, Romanian Ministry of Defense, 5th DNA Conference on Controlling Arms, Norfolk, Virginia, June 1996**

NOTES

1. The operation of the NRRCs is discussed in chapter 10.

2. At the time the INF Treaty was signed (December 8, 1987), it was projected that inspection and escort activities could begin as early as March 1988. However, the INF Treaty was ratified by the Senate only on May 27, 1988, and the instruments of ratification were exchanged on June 1, 1988, at which time the Treaty entered into force and baseline inspections began.

3. A more complete explanation is contained in George Rueckert, *Global Double Zero: the INF Treaty from it Origins to Implementation* (Westport, CT: Greenwood Press, 1993) pp. 113–114; and in Rueckert, "Managing On-Site Inspections: Initial Experience and Future Challenges," in *Verification: the Key to Arms Control in the 1990s*, John Tower, James Brown and William Check, eds (Washington, D.C.: Brassey's, 1992) pp.

155-156.

4. The State Department had responsibility for foreign affairs; the Arms Control and Disarmament Agency had statutory responsibility for implementing arms control provisions; and the Department of Defense had responsibility for eliminating weapons systems and for the military facilities and sites to be inspected.

5. DoD was given the lead not only because it controlled the requisite weapons systems and inspection sites, but also because it was considered the only agency at the time with the necessary budgetary, logistical, and staffing capacity to rapidly implement the INF Treaty's inspection and escort responsibilities.

6. For a more complete overview of OSIA's expanding mission, see Joseph Harahan, "New Director Inherits Agency with a Brief History, But a Proud and Important One," *On-Site Insights* (August 1995): 6-8.

7. Tim Downey, "European Operations Concludes First Inspections Inside Bosnia," *On-Site Insights* (April 1996): 1-2.

8. OSIA provided assistance under this project, termed Project Hope, from February 1992 until September 1994.

9. Tim Downey, "Cooperative Threat Reduction: Agency Plays Important Role", *On-Site Insights* (July 1996): pp.1, 4-6; and Lt Col Michael Culpepper, "Audits and Examinations: Keeping the Other Guy Honest," *On-Site Insights* (February 1996): 10-11.

10. Founding members of OSIA are still known respectfully as "Old Buzzards."

11. Joseph Harahan, "Great Britain's Joint Arms Control Implementation Group—JACIG," *On-Site Insights* (August 1996): p. 8.

12. While all team chiefs for the initial INF inspections, held just over six months after the INF Treaty was signed, were permanent OSIA personnel, 70 percent of the other inspection team personnel were then temporary duty personnel. Currently only a small fraction of OSIA personnel are temporary duty personnel.

13. For a comprehensive treatment of the CWC training scheme, see Provisional Technical Secretariat of the Preparatory Commission for the Organization for the Prohibition of Chemical Weapons, Information Series 7, *Training of Inspectors for the OPCW* (The Hague, Netherlands: November 1996).

14. This was particularly the case with the INF Treaty where, with no prior experience in such inspections, individual military site preparations varied widely, often expressing the personal whims of the site commanders, particularly on how Soviet inspection team personnel was to be handled. The mock inspections served to iron out these differences and introduce more uniformity.

15. Joseph Harahan, "The Russian Federation's Nuclear Risk Reduction Center," *On-Site Insights* (November/December 1995): 13

16. Joseph Harahan, "Origin and Development of the G-4: United States, Germany, Great Britain and France," *On-Site Insights* (September 1996): 9.

17. For a brief discussion of the Russian NRRC, see Joseph Harahan, "Russian Federation's Nuclear Risk Reduction Center," *On-Site Insights* (November/December 1995): 12-13.

18. Untitled presentation by General-Lieutenant Viacheslav A. Romanov, director of the Russian NRRC, during a visit of the verification agency heads of the Russian Federation, Belarus, and Ukraine to the U.S. On-Site Inspection Agency on July 31, 1995.

19. Ibid.

20. Joseph Harahan, "Verification Center of the Armed Forces of Ukraine," *On-Site Insights* (February 1996): pp. 4,28.

21. Joseph Harahan, "The Belarus Republic National Agency for Control and Inspection," *On-Site Insights* (September 1995): 8–9.

22. Joseph Harahan, "The Kazakstan Center for Monitoring Arms Reductions and Supporting Inspection Activities," *On-Site Insights* (June 1996): 6–7.

23. Dr. Wilhelm-Nikolai Germann, "Lessons Learned in Controlling Arms" (paper presented at U.S. Defense Nuclear Agency, 4th International Conference on Controlling Arms, Philadelphia, Pennsylvania, June 1995).

24. Joseph Harahan, "Origin and Development of the G-4," pp. 8–9.

25. B. Gen. Nicolae Corduneaunu "Main Lessons Learned from the Implementation of the CFE Treaty and the CFE-1A Final Act" paper presented to U.S. Defense Nuclear Agency, 5th International Conference on Controlling Arms, Norfolk, Virginia, June 3–6, 1996.

Chapter 10

Other National Inspection Structures

While the great bulk of on-site inspection implementation and compliance responsibilities in the United States fall to the Department of Defense (DoD) and its agencies, a number of other Executive Branch bodies also have important political and operational roles. These include the National Security Council, the U.S. Department of State, the Arms Control and Disarmament Agency (whose functions are to be integrated into the State Department by October 1998), the Departments of Energy and Commerce, the intelligence community, and the Federal Bureau of Investigation (FBI). In addition to its broader arms control responsibilities, two specialized implementation bodies are located in the State Department to perform specific on-site inspection functions. These are the U.S. Nuclear Risk Reduction Center—the central point for the receipt and transmission of arms control notifications—and the U.S. National Authority, which is responsible for assembling and transmitting the U.S. data vital to functioning of the on-site inspection regime of the Chemical Weapons Convention (CWC).

NON-DEFENSE AGENCIES WITH OSI RESPONSIBILITIES

The National Security Council

The National Security Council (NSC), established by the National Security Act of 1947, advises the president on the integration of domestic, foreign, and military policies related to national security. It has three bodies overseeing any policy issues that may arise in connection with on-site inspection activity: a Principals Committee, a Deputies Committee, and Interagency Working Groups (IWGs). The Principals Committee, composed of Cabinet officials and others by invitation, is the highest interagency forum for consideration of national security issues. It typically deals only with issues of the highest national importance, such as a U.S. response to a serious arms control violation. The Deputies Committee is the highest level sub-Cabinet interagency forum. It reviews and monitors the work of the IWGs and is made up of the deputy-level officials most directly concerned with the specific issues at hand. Within the NSC, two special assistants with arms control responsibilities—one for Defense Policy and Arms Control; the other for Nonproliferation and Export Control—head up the IWGs, which include representatives at the assistant secretary level from each of the executive departments or agencies involved with a specific matter.

The U.S. Department of State

The U.S. Department of State, as the lead U.S. foreign affairs agency, plays the principal role in the formulation of overall arms control policy. Within that department, the Under Secretary of State for Arms Control and International Security Policy oversees arms control policy development and application. That office is supported chiefly by the Bureaus of Political-Military Affairs (PM) and Intelligence and Research, with other regional and functional bureaus participating as appropriate. Within PM, a number of separate offices handle the full range of arms control policy issues, including issues of arms control compliance and implementation. The Under Secretary of State for Political Affairs is responsible for regional activities, including regional nonproliferation issues, while the Office of European and Canadian Affairs handles issues related to the Open Skies Treaty and the Organization for Security and Cooperation in Europe, in coordination with PM.

In addition to these bodies, the State Department houses a specialized implementation body—the Nuclear Risk Reduction Center—that processes all arms control notifications, including those essential for on-site inspections.
The State Department also will administer the U.S. National Authority which handles U.S. contacts with the International Organization for the Prohibition of Chemical Weapons (OPCW) and other CWC signatories on data and other issues essential to the CWC's on-site inspection process.

The Arms Control and Disarmament Agency

The Arms Control and Disarmament Agency (ACDA) was created by President John F. Kennedy in 1961 as an independent government agency to deal solely with arms control, nonproliferation, and disarmament policies. Its director was given a Cabinet role to ensure that his or her voice on arms control issues would be communicated directly to the president, rather than through another department.

Under initiatives instituted in spring 1997, ACDA will be fully integrated into the Department of State by October 1998 by merging both agencies' related arms control and nonproliferation functions. The ACDA Director will become the Under Secretary of State for Arms Control and International Security Affairs and also assume the title of Senior Advisor to the President and Secretary of State, thus preserving ACDA's unique advocacy role with the White House on arms control issues. Several new bureaus will be created under his jurisdiction which will be designed to eliminate any duplication between the current functions of ACDA and the State Department's Bureau of Political Military Affairs, while preserving the essential responsibilities of ACDA.

ACDA has provided the legal advisors to arms control negotiations in its area of jurisdiction. As part of its broad mandate, ACDA helps manage arms control negotiations, conducts and coordinates arms control research, participates in verifying compliance with existing agreements, and produces and disseminates arms control information to the public. This latter function has involved the dissemination of information on CWC inspections to affected U.S. private industry groups.

ACDA's areas of concern extend to all arms control agreements. It has either led or been a member of the U.S. delegations to all arms control negotiations. The agency leads the U.S. delegations to the U.N. Conference on Disarmament —the principal venue for negotiation of the Chemical Weapons Convention, the Comprehensive Test Ban Agreement, and other arms control measures—and chairs the Washington policy support ("backstopping") groups for that body. It provides the leadership for specialized arms control conferences and various follow-up negotiations, such as the 1995 conference on extension of the Nuclear Test Ban Treaty, the meetings and conferences on the Biological Weapons Convention (BWC), the Chemical Weapons Convention Preparatory Commission, and similar discussions, many of which deal with on-site inspection measures and procedures. ACDA also provides the leadership, some staff and general administrative support for the implementation and compliance bodies set up by the various treaties, such as the Special Verification Commission of the Intermediate Nuclear Forces (INF) Treaty and the Joint Compliance and Inspection Commission of the Strategic Arms Reduction Treaty (START).[1]

In two other areas of major concern for the implementation of on-site inspection regimes, ACDA provides the principal deputy director of the On-Site Inspection Agency (OSIA) and drafts, with interagency coordination, the annual reports to Congress that assess the record of the various arms control signatories (including the United States) on adherence to, and compliance with, arms control agreements.

The Departments of Energy and Commerce

In coordination with the State Department, the Department of Energy (DOE) provides technical advice and support to arms control negotiations involving energy resources and technologies, including nuclear weapons reduction, testing, nonproliferation, and control issues. Within DOE, the Office of Arms Control and Nonproliferation is responsible for the development of DOE's policy, plans, and procedures related to arms control and nonproliferation. These include export controls, technology transfer controls, and international nuclear safeguards. It manages various nuclear safeguards research and development (R&D) programs and physical security issues. It also coordinates the policy requirements for DOE's research on verification and monitoring technologies for arms control treaties and agreements, much of which is carried out in the U.S. National Laboratories.

The Department of Commerce's Bureau of Export Administration (BXA) is its principal office involved with arms control. Its primary focus is on the formulation and implementation of export control policies, including assistance to Russia and other newly emerging countries on the development of export control systems. However, BXA also is involved in developing procedures, under the CWC and BWC, to protect confidential business information during on-site inspections involving those agreements and for gathering industry data required by them.

The Intelligence Community and FBI

The intelligence community (IC) is composed of all elements in the Executive Branch that conduct the U.S. national foreign intelligence effort.[2] The efforts of the IC on arms control issues, including support for treaty negotiations and for treaty inspections and monitoring, is coordinated by the Arms Control Intelligence Staff (ACIS). The Director of Central Intelligence (DCI), who serves as the primary advisor to the president and National Security Council on intelligence issues, directs the analytical and collection tasking of the IC elements on arms control compliance issues.

The Federal Bureau of Investigation conducts and coordinates, within the United States and at U.S. facilities in Europe, the various counterintelligence activities that may be necessary to protect sensitive information during arms control inspections and monitoring.

THE U.S. NUCLEAR RISK REDUCTION AGENCY

Establishment of the NRRCs

A significant problem of modern on-site inspection regimes is how to process and control the enormous data requirements, including the transmission and receipt of the thousands of individual notifications now required by arms control agreements. For the United States and Russia, the two countries with the most extensive arms control obligations, a centralized body—the Nuclear Risk

Reduction Center (NRRC)—has been established in each country to handle data and inspection notifications.

The NRRCs had their origins in ideas originally expressed by senators Sam Nunn and John Warner, who sought to reduce the risk of nuclear accident, miscalculation or misunderstanding between the United States and the Soviet Union by establishing a high speed communications link for the exchange of messages relating to confidence-building measures and arms control accords. Studies of NRRC responsibilities and operations were started at the 1985 summit between President Reagan and General Secretary Gorbachev, and negotiations on setting up the NRRCs began at the Reykjavik Summit a year later.

The NRRCs were formally established by a U.S.-Soviet agreement signed on September 15, 1987, several months before the INF Treaty was signed. They became operational on April 1, 1988. The U.S. NRRC is located in the U.S. Department of State. As noted early, the Soviet NRRC, by way of contrast, is located in the Ministry of Defense and also handles on-site inspection and escort responsibilities.

Initially, the NRRCs transmitted the notifications called for in the 1971 "Accidents Measures" Agreement and the 1972 Agreement on the Prevention of Incidents On and Over the High Seas, but their functions quickly expanded to include the notifications required by the INF Treaty and the Strategic Ballistic Missile Launch Notification Agreements. Subsequently, the NRRCs have been designated the central transmission point for the notifications required by each new arms control agreements as they have entered into force. After the break-up of the Soviet Union in 1991, Russia assumed the NRRC responsibilities of the former Soviet Union (FSU) for bilateral agreements. Separate government-to-government communications links (GGCLs) were established in the ministries of defense of the other FSU nuclear successor states—Ukraine, Belarus, and Kazakstan—to administer arms control notification requirements.

Like OSIA, the NRRCs are operational, not policy-making, bodies. Despite the name, they do not handle crisis management, process "hot line" communications, which are regulated by a separate agreement, nor compete with traditional diplomatic or other policy channels in resolving implementation, compliance, or negotiating matters.

Operations of the U.S. NRRC

The U.S. NRRC is the central U.S. body for the receipt and transmission of treaty-related data in connection with the arms control and security-building agreements to which the United States is a party. In addition to its initial bilateral arms control responsibilities, it has been designated by the National Security Council to serve as the U.S node of the multinational communications network now operated by the Organization for Security and Cooperation in Europe (OSCE). Most of the fifty-three participants in the OSCE are linked to a central communications network, which exchanges notifications under the terms of the CFE, Open Skies Treaty, Confidence and Security-Building Measures provisions of the Vienna Document 1994, and the Global Exchange of Military Information (GEMI) Agreement. During 1995, the U.S. NRRC handled over 16,000 messages in connection with this broad range of responsibilities.

The U.S. NRRC is staffed around the clock by State Department foreign service officers and civil service personnel, who are trained to operate the center's data automation systems, and supported by technical communications specialists. Watch officers are qualified in the various OSCE foreign languages (French, German, Spanish, Russian, and Italian). Reflecting the importance of the often time-sensitive INF and START notifications, a watch officer with a knowledge of Russian is always on duty. To provide clarity and assist rapid processing, only previously negotiated and agreed formats are used to transmit the information required under each treaty. These formats contain a standardized language and structure that is readily understood and translated.

The NRRC uses several different arms control communications networks to carry out its functions. It is linked into *the Compliance Monitoring and Tracking Systems* (CMTS)—an interagency network with secure communications maintained by DoD—which is used to generate the U.S. notifications required by arms control treaties. The CMTS transmits such notifications to the NRRC for final processing and transmission to the addressees abroad. The NRRC is directly connected with each of the CMTS's three subsystems, which include: the START Central Data System (SCDS), which handles START notifications; the Data Management and Notification System (DMNS), which supports CFE, confidence- and security-building measure (CSBM), and Open Skies notifications; and a separate system supporting the INF notification regime.

When drafts of outgoing U.S. notifications are received from these systems by the NRRC, the notifications are first screened by NRRC operational and supervisory personnel prior to transmission to ensure they contain no errors, are in the correct format, and comply with treaty requirements. The outgoing notifications then are transmitted in English with careful attention to their urgency and to other transmission "windows" specified by the drafting agency.

The United States has a bilateral communications system with each of the four FSU successor states. The U.S. and Russian NRRCS are linked by dual satellite communications systems (one U.S., one Russian) providing redundant, virtually 100 percent reliable, high-speed computer communications and scanned document (fax) transfers. The three other FSU nuclear successor states (Ukraine, Belarus, Kazakstan) currently are linked by single satellites. Messages on all of these bilateral systems are encrypted to maintain confidentiality on impending inspections and other treaty-related data. For similar reasons, no voice communications are used to transmit data or notifications. This also ensures accuracy and avoids any possibility of misunderstanding of a communication that could result in a possible compliance issue.

The U.S. NRRC also operates the U.S. node of the *OSCE Communications Network* linking the participating states. The network operates through a central mail server (CMS) located in The Hague and maintained by the Dutch Foreign Ministry. The NRRC link with the less sensitive CMS is unclassified and via a dedicated commercial line.

Incoming notifications most often are received by the U.S. NRRC in Russian or another foreign language, translated into English by its personnel, and forwarded to action officers on a prioritized basis according to their time and operational urgency. If a notification contains routine data, the NRCC disseminates the information through electronic transmission directly to all involved U.S. government addresses. If the notification announces a short-notice or other time urgent inspection, it is passed immediately by telephone to the affected DoD communications centers, each of which then undertakes onward transmission of the notification to components within their jurisdiction, including all possible inspection sites. Verbal notifications are followed up as soon as possible by an electronic "hard copy" to ensure accuracy. Key operational nodes linked to the NRRC, such as the OSIA Communication Center, also provide action officers in DoD and at field units with other critical information throughout the inspection, such as the arrival and departure of inspection teams. Sequential inspections are announced by using the same notification procedures as for normal incoming inspections.

CWC NATIONAL AUTHORITIES

Because of its sweeping nature, the Chemical Weapons Convention will require close monitoring by each country of its chemical industry to provide data necessary to ensure compliance. Chemical weapons (CW) production differs from nuclear weapons and much other military production in that it does not require a large, specialized and costly industrial base. Chemical warfare agents can be made with commercial equipment generally available to any country. In addition, many of the chemicals used to make CW agents are "dual use" chemicals which have many legitimate commercial uses, including the production of pesticides, pharmaceutical, plastics and paints.

The CWC has a "general-purpose criterion," which bans any toxic chemical agent, regardless of origin, that interferes with life processes and does not have legitimate civil applications in the quantities in which it is produced. This extends treaty application to all conceivable CW agents, including the production of future novel chemicals not listed in the treaty. The CWC also bans certain intermediate compounds or precursors that can be converted to CW agents in one or a few steps, as well as the military use of biological toxins. As indicated earlier, these chemical compounds are listed in three schedules related to their legitimate commercial and industrial uses and structured so that the most hazardous compounds are subject to the most stringent controls. Each schedule has its own set of reporting requirements and inspections.

To facilitate monitoring of the chemical industry, The CWC obligates each state party to take the domestic, legal, and administrative measures necessary to ensure that industrial facilities operating on their territory are in compliance with treaty provisions. A specific application of this requirement is the obligation of each state party to designate or establish a "National Authority" (or, at a minimum, a central coordination office for CWC implementation) to serve as a liaison between its domestic industry and the OPCW and with other state parties, collect data from its chemical industry and ensure proper functioning of the inspection regime.[3]

Scope and Functions of the National Authority

The scope and functions of the National Authority differ from country to country depending on whether the state possesses chemical weapons and chemical weapons production facilities, the potential of its industry to produce such weapons, and the general size and nature of its chemical industry. Thus, the data collection responsibilities of the National Authority will be particularly extensive for the United States, which has a large stockpile of chemical weapons as well as a large and economically important chemical industry consisting of some 20,000 chemical manufacturing plants with about a third of the world's total chemical production capacity. The data responsibilities of the National Authorities in Russia, with the world's largest stockpile of chemical weapons and a substantial chemical industry, and in the other highly industrialized countries, such as Germany, Japan, Britain, and France, also are demanding.

The National Authority is responsible for transmitting to the OPCW both the initial data[4] and the annual declarations[5] from all affected government and private industry facilities, working in close coordination with other interested agencies. In the United States, these include the Department of Commerce, the central contact point with industry, and, within the Department of Defense, the U.S. Army, which serves as executive agent for the U.S. chemical weapons stockpile. In collecting the necessary CWC data, each treaty signatory must identify all facilities affected by the CWC, including producers, processors, consumers, importers and exporters; ensure that these facilities are aware of their obligations under the treaty; develop procedures, including declaration forms, to assist in supplying the required data; and coordinate with industry trade associations and individual companies to ensure smooth implementation. In particular, each country must ascertain national trade in scheduled chemicals and imports and exports of these chemicals and determine the number of plants liable to inspection by the OPCW. The National Authority must then collect this essential data in a manner that does not sacrifice either state security or confidential business information (CBI) and transmit it to the OPCW in a timely fashion. Chemical industry data, once provided to the OPCW by the National

Authority, is verified in part by the on-site inspections carried out by the OPCW Technical Inspectorate.

The treaty responsibility of each signatory to collect and transmit the data required by the CWC is complicated by several factors. Few countries maintain comprehensive data on the range of chemicals produced in their chemical industry or the number of chemical plants and plant sites involved in chemical production. Thus, extensive cooperation with industry associations and a focused government effort to educate industry is essential to ensure compliance. In addition, governments are ultimately responsible for the treaty compliance of all of the companies located on their territory, including foreign-owned branches and subsidiaries, raising potentially troublesome issues in countries like the United States, which have a great many such companies. Moreover, the data needed for CWC verification in some key countries, including the United States, differs both quantitatively and qualitatively from that collected for other management and regulatory purposes. It may, therefore, require augmentation of existing corporate reporting systems. Finally, the need to report data within a shorter time frame than is typical of domestic reporting may require the development, by both industry and government, of new accounting subroutines to improve the speed as well as accuracy of data collection and analysis.

Beyond the transmission of critical data and general coordination functions with other treaty signatories, the precise operation of the National Authority varies from country to country. The United States with major arms control responsibilities in other areas has a National Authority with an interagency composition for overall direction and oversight, while still relying primarily on the extensive arms control infrastructure already in place for many implementation responsibilities. Other countries with lesser arms control responsibilities may rely directly on their National Authority for full implementation of the agreement.

The U.S. National Authority

In addition to ratification of the Chemical Weapons Treaty, the U.S. Congress promulgates implementing legislation to provide a legal basis for the U.S. National Authority to carry out its responsibilities. Implementing legislation is needed to meet the CWC requirement that each state party prohibit all individuals and legal entities within its territory, regardless of their nationality, and all of its citizens outside its territory from engaging in activities that are prohibited under the convention. Such legislation helps ensure chemical industry compliance with CWC declaration requirements, in cases not already adequately covered under other sections of U.S. law, such as privileges and immunities for members of the international inspection teams and export controls. It also provides a basis for protecting confidential business information, such as data on finances, sales and marketing (other than shipments), pricing, personnel, research, and patents. It establishes criminal provisions related to chemical weapons, such as outlawing their possession, development, and use, and the transfer of prohibited chemicals to states that are not party to the CWC; authorizes the collection of data from the chemical industry required by the CWC; and outlaws both the failure to provide such information and the disclosure of such information to unauthorized personnel. Legislation also regulates the conduct of the international inspections required by the CWC, including the provisions regarding notice, sampling, and safety, and establishes legal mechanisms to ensure U.S. compliance, such as procedures for obtaining any legal warrants that may be necessary to ensure inspection and for dealing with any legal claims than may result from an inspection.

U.S. implementing legislation designates the U.S. Department of State as the U.S. National Authority and requires it to implement the CWC in coordination with an interagency group designated by the president and consisting of the U.S. Departments of Defense, Commerce and Energy, the Attorney General, and such other agencies as may be advisable. It coordinates decision making on CWC implementation issues, such as requests for challenge inspections in the United States or against other states, for CWC-related information and cooperation or for protective and technical assistance. It also coordinates issues related to CWC inspections at U.S. facilities and provides advice on treaty obligations and compliance issues.

The National Authority handles the administrative and logistical aspects of transmitting CWC data and serves as the point of contact with the OPCW, other parties to the convention, and other government and international organizations and entities on CWC matters. The U.S. agencies charged with collecting, validating, and formatting data provide this data to the National Authority for transmission to the OPCW in the form of U.S. national declarations and annual reports, with due regard for protecting its confidentiality. For example, within the Department of Defense, the U.S. Army prepares the declarations on military chemical weapons activities and takes actions connected with the required destruction of the U.S. chemical weapons stockpiles and former CW production facilities. DoD also manages the CW protective activities permitted by the CWC. OSIA meets, escorts and processes the CWC inspection teams at the POE; handles logistical arrangements; and provides in-country escorts. The Department of Commerce keeps the business community informed of OPCW requirements and activities and oversees its compliance with CWC obligations, including the collection of data from business entities, coordination of export licensing for dual-use chemicals, and administration and enforcement of the trade restriction provisions of the CWC. The Department of Justice (Attorney General) handles legal issues and enforcement actions. Other agencies have similar specialized obligations within their areas of jurisdiction.

NOTES

1. For a comprehensive overview of the status of major arms control agreements and initiatives, see the U.S. Arms Control and Disarmament Agency's annual reports to Congress entitled *Threat Control through Arms Control* (Washington, D.C., ACDA Public Affairs).

2. These include staff elements of the director of Central Intelligence; the Central Intelligence Agency; the National Security Agency; the Defense Intelligence Agency; the Department of Defense offices responsible for collection of specialized national foreign intelligence through reconnaissance programs; the Bureau of Intelligence and Research of the State Department; and the intelligence elements of the military services, the Federal Bureau of Investigation, and the departments of Treasury and Energy.

3. CWC Article VII, paragraph 4 states that "in order to fulfill its obligations under (the CWC), each State Party shall designate or establish a National Authority to serve as the national focal point for effective liaison with the (OPCW) and other States Parties"

4. Required under Articles III, IV, V, and VI of the CWC.

5. Required under CWC Articles IV, V, and VI.

Chapter 11

Multinational Structures

The disintegration of the Soviet Union has led to the multinationalization of several previously bilateral U.S.-U.S.S.R. arms control agreements, including the Intermediate-Range Nuclear Forces (INF) and Strategic Arms Reduction (START I) treaties.[1] In addition, the oldest global multinational on-site inspection body—the International Atomic Energy Agency (IAEA)—has significantly expanded the scope and intrusiveness of its inspections in recent years as a result of experience in Iraq and North Korea and the new international readiness to accept tougher on-site inspection regimes; a new multinational on-site inspection agency has been created in The Hague to implement the global Chemical Weapons Convention (CWC); and another will be set up in Vienna to implement the Comprehensive Test Ban Treaty (CTBT).

All of the organizations to implement treaties with global scope have similar basic structures—generally modeled on the IAEA prototype—although the terminology used for, and the specific functions of, the various bodies differs somewhat for each treaty. In addition, both the CWC and CTBT provide for the establishment of national authorities in each member country to serve as a national contact point with the multinational organization and assist in the development and transmission of treaty-related national data.

On a regional basis, the United Nations has created a specialized on-site inspection body—the U.N. Special Commission on Iraq (UNSCOM)—to monitor implementation of the U. N. Security Council resolutions requiring Iraq to destroy its weapons of mass destruction. NATO also has established a separate body, the Verification Coordinating Committee, to handle inspection-related activities for the regional Treaty on Conventional Forces in Europe (CFE). This chapter looks briefly at the structure and basic functions of these global and regional multinational on-site inspection bodies.

THE INTERNATIONAL ATOMIC ENERGY AGENCY

The IAEA Statute

The IAEA Statute, which entered into force on July 29, 1957, provides for a close link between the United Nations and the IAEA, but establishes the IAEA as an autonomous and independent organization. It calls for the IAEA to "conduct its activities in accordance with the purposes and principles of the United Nations" and to "submit reports on its activities annually to the General Assembly of the United Nations and, when appropriate, to the Security Council"[2] The Agency also has engaged in jointly funded and staffed activities with a number of U.N. specialized agencies and programs. However, the IAEA, which is headquartered in Vienna, is not a specialized agency of the United Nations, such as the World Health Organization. Members of the United Nations are not automatically members of the IAEA. To become a member of the IAEA, a state must specifically adopt the Statute of the IAEA and apply to, and be accepted by, the IAEA General Conference as a member upon the recommendation of the Board of Governors. Moreover, the IAEA is funded by direct assessment of its members, rather than through the budget of the United Nations or any of its organs.

The IAEA has a multiple mandate: to facilitate the peaceful use of nuclear energy, promote nuclear facility safety, and provide safeguards against the diversion of nuclear materials and equipment from civilian to military purposes. The safeguard provisions—Article III of the statute—authorize the agency to "establish and administer safeguards designed to ensure that special fissionable and other materials, services, equipment, facilities and information made available by the Agency or under its supervision or control are not used in such a way as to further any military purpose." It authorizes the agency to apply such safeguards at the "request of the parties, to any bilateral or multilateral arrangement, or at the request of a State, to any of that State's activities in the field of atomic energy." The statute also contains the principal provisions to be included in implementing every IAEA safeguards agreement—design review, materials accounting records and reports, confidentiality of the information obtained, and independent verification by means of on-site inspections.

When the centerpiece of the nuclear nonproliferation regime—the Nuclear Nonproliferation Treaty—was signed in 1968, the IAEA safeguards system became its principal means of verification. While on-site inspections are only a part of the safeguards regime, the international acceptance of such inspections was unprecedented for its time and it has provided the basis for the IAEA to play a continuing—and expanding—role in international arms control.

Organization of the IAEA

As the first of the multinational inspection agencies, the IAEA pioneered and set the model for subsequent global arms control organizations. Its organization consists of three main elements: (1) a General Conference of all members, which is the highest decision-making body; (2) an executive organ, the Board of Governors; and (3) the Secretariat, headed by the director general, which carries out the safeguards regime and performs other activities, such as technical assistance to member states.

The General Conference

The General Conference is made up of all member states and meets each September, normally in Vienna. Each conference elects its president and other officers. The conference hears, and considers for approval, the director general's annual report on the agency's activities and the IAEA budget for the forthcoming year; approves the IAEA reports to the United Nations; elects those members to the Board of Governors that are its statutory responsibility; and engages in general debate on agency programs. It also approves the appointment of the director general and applications for IAEA membership.

The conference has authority to make decisions on matters referred to it by the board or "to propose matters for consideration by the Board and to request from the Board reports on any matters relating to the functions of the Agency." This latter authority has been frequently invoked and the relatively limited influence that the conference has on IAEA policy and operations stems from resolutions passed under this provision. The true value of the conference lies not in its limited formal powers, but in its role as a forum where those not represented on the Board of Governors can express their views and exchange information. At the same time, the conference's role as a forum has sometimes served to introduce extraneous political issues into agency deliberations.

The Board of Governors

The Board of Governors was designed to be the most important body of the agency. The statute assigns more functions and authority to it than was usual, at the time, for the policy-making bodies of other international organizations. The board formulates the annual budget, which the General Conference can only approve *in toto*, reject, or send back to the board.[3] The Board also appoints the director general, with the approval of the General Conference; recommends to the General Conference applicants for membership; authorizes the director general to enter into specific agreements for projects and safeguards; approves the designation of staff members to serve as safeguards inspectors and the issuance of safety codes and standards; reviews the implementation of the safeguards and other programs; and submits an annual report to the General Conference covering the agency's activities.

The composition of the Board of Governors was the subject of much debate during the drafting of the IAEA Statute. Its make-up represents a compromise between those countries that have advanced nuclear technology or deposits of uranium ore and those that have neither of these assets. The thirty-five member board is composed of thirteen members representing the countries "most advanced in the technology of atomic energy including the production of source material" designated by the outgoing board and twenty-two members elected by the General Conference with due regard for an equitable geographic distribution.

The Secretariat

The operational staff of the IAEA, commonly referred to as the Secretariat, is headed by a director general (DG) who is appointed to a four-year term by the Board of Governors with the approval of the General Conference. There are five deputy director generals, one each for the departments of Administration, Technical Cooperation, Nuclear Energy and Safety, Research and Isotopes, and Safeguards.[4] Appointment of the deputy director generals—normally for a five-year term subject to extension—is the subject of consultations by the DG with interested member states and finally with the Board of Governors in closed session, that is, with only members of the Board of Governors present.

Each department is made up of divisions which are further divided into sections. Division directors and section heads have a special status. Other staff personnel are classified as professional, general service, or maintenance and operating personnel. In addition, the agency employs personnel, usually with qualifications similar to those for positions in the professional category, under Special Service Agreements or other arrangements for short-term assignments. These include "cost-free" experts—individuals provided by member states for specific functions or tasks at the request of the IAEA, whose salary and allowances are covered by the providing state. The Department of Safeguards has a number of such experts—often from the United States—who normally serve one or more years.

All agency personnel are international civil servants who owe their allegiance to the IAEA. In contrast to inspectors of the national on-site inspection agencies, they are prohibited from acting as representatives of, or in support of, their countries' interests. However, like all arms control inspectors, they are accorded the diplomatic privileges and immunities necessary to carry out their functions. In recruiting and promotions, the IAEA takes into account geographic considerations, in addition to professional qualifications, technical competence, and the contributions to the agency's budget of member states. The majority of staff thus comes from the industrialized nations, although in recent years, a serious effort has been made to increase representation on the staff from developing countries.

The Department of Safeguards

The Department of Safeguards—the on-site inspection agency of the IAEA—is responsible for the application of the safeguards regimes under the agreements to which the IAEA is a party. The department establishes safeguards approaches and ensures that safeguards are implemented in an effective and efficient manner. Its staff assists in the preparation of the annual Safeguards Implementation Report to the IAEA Board of Governors; develops new safeguards implementation and evaluation criteria; and prepares management, personnel, and financial policies.

There are six divisions within the Department of Safeguards. Three Operations Divisions—simply titled A, B, and C—carry out the IAEA's independent on-site inspection verification activities. The remaining three divisions, referred to as "support" divisions, provide the equipment, information services, planning and analysis assistance, and other support required by the operations divisions.

The three Operations Divisions have equal status and responsibility for applying safeguards in the countries under their jurisdiction. Their structure reflects both functional and geographic considerations. In general, Operations A covers the Far East, South East Asia, and the Middle East; Operations B covers North and South America, Africa, Central and Northern Europe, and the non-Common Market countries of western Europe; and Operations C covers Western Europe (EURATOM countries) and the former Eastern Bloc nations.

To carry out their verification activities, the IAEA Operations Divisions must schedule and plan inspections; carry them out; evaluate the results; perform follow-up activities, if needed; and prepare a final report. In addition, Operations Division personnel negotiate with individual governments or regional multinational organizations the legal documents that provide the fundamental basis for the specific implementation of safeguards in each country and at each facility. In 1995, 2,285 safeguards inspections were performed at 548 facilities and other locations worldwide; 2,638 surveillance films and 3,807 video tapes were reviewed; and 23,877 affixed seals were verified by agency inspectors.[5]

Three support divisions assist the Operations Divisions to fulfill their inspection responsibilities. The largest support division is the Division of Safeguards Information Treatment (SGIT), which is responsible for processing, storage, retrieval, and analyses of the safeguards information reported by the member states or collected by inspectors. The Division of Development and Technical Support (SGDE) is responsible for development, testing, procurement, shipping, maintenance, and management of inspection equipment, for the development and documentation of technical procedures and for technical training. The Division of Concepts and Planning (SGCP) handles strategic planning and the development and standardization of safeguards concepts, approaches, procedures, and practices.

Broadening IAEA Inspection Responsibilities

The IAEA Statute[6] sets limits on safeguards inspections. The statute's on-site inspection provisions are stated in broad terms in Article XII (paragraph A), which authorizes the agency

to send into the territory of the recipient State or States inspectors, designated by the Agency after consultation with the State or States concerned, who shall have access at all times to all places and data and to any person who by reason of his occupation deals with materials, equipment or facilities which are required to be safeguarded, as necessary to account for source and special fissionable materials and to determine whether there is compliance with the undertaking against use in furtherance of any military purpose and with any other conditions prescribed in the agreement between the Agency and the State or States concerned.[7]

A basic feature of safeguards is that verification can take place only on the basis of an agreement with the state in which inspection is to occur. Thus, the statute addresses only the matter of governments complying with the undertakings or obligations set forth in these formal agreements with the agency. The IAEA is not a supranational organization with powers to impose its inspections on any state. The IAEA safeguards system was designed to verify that *declared* nuclear material was not being diverted from declared nuclear uses, not to provide assurance that no *undeclared* nuclear material or installations exist. Moreover, the assurances provided by the IAEA's safeguards system relates to the *correctness* of the information provided by member states, not its *completeness*.[8]

In addition, the seemingly broad right of access by Agency inspectors in Article XII is limited to places, data, and persons "as necessary to account for materials and to determine compliance with conditions prescribed in the agreement." Accordingly, inspectors cannot roam freely within the inspected state nor have they been assigned any intelligence-gathering function. Moreover, the "as necessary" limitation is subject to the provisions in agency documents that define the frequencies of routine inspections or the intensity of routine inspection effort for various quantities of fissionable materials of various types.

Following the defeat of Iraq in the 1991 Persian Gulf War, the U.N. Security Council assigned new inspection responsibilities to the IAEA Inspection Directorate, which go significantly beyond those contained in the IAEA Statute. The U.N. Security Council Resolution 687 of April 3, 1991, contains a cease fire arrangement that mandates the destruction, removal, or rendering harmless of Iraq's unconventional weapons capabilities. This includes the elimination, under international supervision, of Iraq's nuclear, chemical, and biological weapons and ballistic missiles with ranges over 150 kilometers, together with the related items and facilities. It also calls for measures to ensure acquisition and production are not resumed.

To implement these restriction, Resolution 687 charged two bodies, the IAEA and a newly formed U.N. inspection agency—the U.N. Special Commission on Iraq (UNSCOM)—with determining and neutralizing Iraq's programs for weapons of mass destruction.[9] The IAEA was given the task of neutralizing the nuclear component, with UNSCOM assistance. UNSCOM was assigned responsibility for dismantling Iraq's remaining biological, chemical, and ballistic missile programs. Two additional U.N. Security Council (UNSC) Resolutions further broaden IAEA and UNSCOM inspection rights. UNSC Res. 707, approved in August 1991, establishes the right of the inspection teams to conduct fixed wing and helicopter flights throughout Iraq "for all relevant purposes including inspection, surveillance, aerial surveys, transportation and logistics." It also requires "full, final, and complete disclosure" of Iraq's programs to develop weapons of mass destruction and ballistic missiles. UNSC Res.715 of October 1991 establishes a program of "on-going monitoring and verification" to prevent reacquisition of these weapons systems.[10]

To implement its on-site inspection responsibilities under UNSC Res 687, IAEA set up an "action team" using IAEA's inspection and technical expertise, including its laboratories and network of international contacts.[11] IAEA on-site inspections in Iraq began in May 1991. Despite Iraqi intransigence regarding submission of procurement data, these inspections resulted in the development of a detailed picture of the Iraqi nuclear weapons program, both in scope and technical detail. Among other things, they revealed that Iraq had pursued at least three different paths toward acquiring key materials for nuclear weapons.[12] This picture was further validated by analyses of thousands of samples taken in Iraq by inspection teams, by the content of hundreds of secret Iraqi documents confiscated by inspectors, and by intelligence information. The new information on the extent of the Iraqi nuclear weapons program uncovered by the IAEA inspections in Iraq revealed serious shortcomings of the IAEA safeguards system.

Strengthening the Safeguards Regime

The inspections in Iraq led simultaneously to recognition of the need to strengthen the IAEA safeguards regime and to a renewed willingness of nations to support such a process. During 1992 and 1993, the IAEA Board of Governors supported measures for strengthening the agency's safeguards regime, especially by increasing the ability of the safeguards system to detect the existence of, and gain access to, undeclared nuclear activities. In particular, it moved to ensure that the IAEA's safeguards regime would cover both the correctness and completeness of declarations by states and extend to both declared and undeclared facilities. In December 1993, the Board of Governors formally endorsed "Programme 93+2" to design, develop, and test a set of comprehensive measures to accomplish these objectives.[13]

The thrust of the proposals generated under Programme 93+2 is to make the IAEA safeguards regime more effective by giving the IAEA greater access to relevant information and sites and making it more efficient in the use of available resources (staff, equipment, and money) to achieve its objectives. The Programme is divided into Part 1 measures that can be undertaken using existing legal authority and Part 2 measures that will require complementary legal authority for implementation in member states.[14] The new proposals—which build upon the existing safeguards regime—fall within three broad categories: (1) measures to strengthen the IAEA's access to information, thus making safeguards more effective; (2) measures to increase physical access to sites and make such access more effective; and (3) measures to further streamline the functioning and administration of safeguards.[15]

In June 1995, the IAEA's Board of Governors approved several Part 1 measures. These included the continued development of new safeguards measurement and surveillance system technology; measures to increase agency cooperation with member states to enhance the efficiency of inspections, joint inspections, and support activity and to establish direct communications between inspectors in the field and IAEA Headquarters; the use of environmental monitoring at nuclear facilities to which IAEA has access to detect possible undeclared nuclear activities at and around such facilities; improved analysis procedures covering all information available to the agency; and increased use of unannounced inspections to detect possible undeclared nuclear activities at declared facilities.

Part 2 measures under consideration by the board in 1995 included expanding declarations to provide broader information on states' nuclear activities; increased physical access by inspectors to locations related to the nuclear fuel cycle, but not containing nuclear fuel; and the taking and analysis of environmental samples to verify the absence of nuclear activities and material at such locations.

THE ORGANIZATION FOR THE PROHIBITION OF CHEMICAL WEAPONS

The Chemical Weapons Convention creates a new international on-site inspection agency—the Organization for the Prohibition of Chemical Weapons (OPCW)—in The Hague, The Netherlands, to administer the treaty. The OPCW is charged with achieving the objectives and purpose of CWC, ensuring the implementation of its provisions, including those concerning international verification and compliance, and providing a forum for consultation and cooperation among states parties. All signatories of the treaty are members of the OPCW, but a member state may be deprived of its vote if it has failed to pay its financial contributions for two years, and its rights and privileges may be restricted or suspended if it fails to fulfill an Executive Council request to redress a compliance problem.

Preparatory Activities

When the CWC was opened for signature on January 13, 1993, in Paris, the signatory states established a Preparatory Commission (PrepCom) to prepare detailed operational procedures and to establish the permanent infrastructure of the organization. During its first Plenary Session, convened in the Hague by the Secretary General of the United Nations on February 8, 1993, the PrepCom established a Provisional Technical Secretariat (PTS) as its executive arm. When the CWC entered into force in April 1997, the PrepCom was superseded by the Council of States Parties and the OPCW Technical Secretariat.

The PrepCom established the basic infrastructure of the OPCW, recruited the core staff and developed detailed procedures for implementing the CWC. The latter included the formats required for different types of declarations, guidelines for inspection procedures, the contents of inspector training courses, equipment requirements, time frames during inspections, criteria and methods of destruction of chemical weapons and facilities, analytical support, and technical cooperation and assistance. The PrepCom also established policies related to inspection confidentiality, health and safety, media relations, and visa issues.

Structure of the OPCW

The OPCW has a three-tiered organization, similar to that of the IAEA. It consists of a Conference of State Parties, an Executive Council, and a Technical Secretariat.[16]

The Conference of States Parties

The Conference of States Parties, the highest body of the OPCW, is composed of all members of the CWC. Each member state has one representative, who can be accompanied by alternates and advisors, and one vote. The conference meets in regular annual sessions, but special sessions may be convened by the Executive Council or by a state party supported by one-third of the members of the organization to address serious problems in implementing the treaty. The CWC also has provisions for review conferences to be held at regular five-year intervals to review operation of the convention.

As the principal organ of the OPCW, the conference can deal with any issue within the scope of the CWC, including the powers of the other organs. It oversees implementation of the CWC and reviews compliance. Votes on issues of procedure are by simple majority. On matters of substance, however, the work of the Conference is approved by consensus. If consensus on an issue cannot be reached at the end of twenty-four hours, the conference decides the matter by a vote but, in this case, a two-thirds majority of members present and voting is required for a decision.

The Executive Council

The Executive Council is responsible to the Conference of States Parties and has the day-to-day responsibility for supervising the activities of the OPCW. The council has forty-one members, with each member state, in accordance with the principal of rotation, having the right to serve on it. Its primary functions are to promote effective implementation of the CWC and compliance with its provisions.

Representatives to the council are elected for two-year terms on the basis of geopolitical and general industrial criteria, which take into consideration geographic factors and the variations among regions in the extent and nature of their chemical industry and in their political and security interests. The composition of the Executive Council is allocated as follows: Africa: nine seats of which three are allocated to states with the most significant chemical industry; Asia: nine seats of which four are allocated to states with the most significant chemical industry; Latin American and the Caribbean: seven seats of which three are allocated to states with the most significant chemical industry; Eastern Europe: five seats of which one is allocated to the state with the most significant chemical industry; Western Europe and other States (including the United States and Canada): ten seats of which five are allocated to states with the most significant chemical industry. In addition to the above, one seat rotates between the Asian region and the Latin American and Caribbean region.

The Technical Secretariat

The Technical Secretariat, similar to the IAEA's secretariat, has the primary responsibility for carrying out the verification activities mandated by the CWC. It also provides assistance if chemical weapons are used, supports the conference and the Executive Council and communicates on behalf of the OPCW. The Technical Secretariat is headed by a director-general who is appointed for a term of four years, renewable once only. A Scientific Advisory Board, established by the director general, contains independent experts who provide specialized advice in areas of science and technology of particular importance for the CWC.

Only citizens of parties to the CWC may serve as the director-general, inspectors, or as other members of the professional and clerical staff of the Technical Inspectorate. Like IAEA inspectors, they are international civil servants, have diplomatic privileges and immunities, may not seek or receive instructions from any government or from any other source external to the OPCW, and must refrain from any activities that could reflect adversely on their positions as international officials.

Inspector Composition and Training

The OPCW has over 200 inspectors. Inspectors must have at least a BS-level university degree or its equivalent in science or engineering and six years of professional experience in fields such as process chemistry, process engineering, material resources planning, or other skills necessary to the inspection process. A good working knowledge of English is required (but has been sometimes been difficult to achieve in practice), and fluency is sought in one of the official organization languages (Arabic, Chinese, English, French, Russian, and Spanish) or in other important languages such as German and Japanese. The age ceiling for inspectors is set at fifty-two years of age for inspectors of chemical weapons-related facilities and fifty-six years of age for inspections of chemical industry-related facilities.

Since inspectors must be capable of executing sensitive and complicated missions, careful training is critical to success of the verification mission. International inspectors are recruited on the basis of the relevant technical skills they possess and given twenty weeks of additional training relevant to on-site inspections. The general training scheme consists of three training modules: (1) a basic course to acquaint inspectors with the CWC, the OPCW, inspections, the chemical industry, and protection against and destruction of chemical weapons; (2) specialized courses to develop and improve essential skills; and (3) on-site inspection training. Training is conducted at a number of locations offered by member states, including chemical weapons production, storage, and destruction facilities and at chemical plants producing Schedule 1, 2, and 3 chemicals.

Inspector Activities

OPCW inspection teams vary in size depending on the type of facility to be inspected. In addition, the teams for various types of inspection are composed of inspectors, tailored to the specific requirements of each type of inspection. Thus, an inspection team of about fourteen specialists would normally be employed to inspect a chemical weapons destruction facility and the team would be composed of both chemical and conventional munitions specialists, chemical technologists, analytical chemists, and medical specialists. An inspection team for a chemical industry-related facility would consist of about eight specialists, and would include chemical production technologists, industrial chemists, chemical production specialists, and analytical chemists. In practice, the initial inspection teams sent to the United States to inspect military facilities were smaller than these projections. The teams have tended to be extremely conscious of the need to protect security information and meticulous in carrying out their duties. Language fluency, however, has been a problem.

THE COMPREHENSIVE NUCLEAR TEST BAN TREATY

Article I of the Comprehensive Test Ban Treaty prohibits all states parties from conducting "any nuclear weapons test explosion or any other nuclear explosion." On the basis of the negotiating record, this is understood to include all nuclear explosions with a yield greater than zero.[17] To implement this total ban and provide a forum for consultation and cooperation, the CTBT provides for establishment of a new international organization—the Comprehensive Nuclear Test-Ban Treaty Organization—to be located in Vienna.[18] Since the treaty will not enter into force until 180 days after forty-four states deposit their instruments of ratification with the U.N. Secretary General, a preparatory commission, similar to that for the OPCW, will develop detailed implementation provisions not contained in the treaty text in the period prior to entry into force (EIF).

Organizational Structure

The organization of the CTBT closely matches that of the IAEA and OPCW. Like those organizations, it consists of three main bodies: a Conference of the States Parties, an Executive Council, and a Technical Secretariat.

The Conference of States Parties

The Conference of States Parties is the overall governing body of the CTBT.[19] It will handle treaty-related policy issues and oversee the treaty's implementation, including the activities of the other treaty bodies. Among its specific functions will be the adoption of key implementation, programmatic, and budget reports; election and appointment of the leadership of the other organs; review of scientific and technological developments that could affect operation of the treaty; and institution of any measures necessary to ensure compliance and deal with any contravention of the treaty. It also will approve all actions of the Preparatory Commission and all agreements and arrangements negotiated by the Technical Secretariat with signatory states, other states, and international organizations.

Each member state will have one representative on the conference, who can be accompanied by alternates and advisers, and who will have one vote. The conference will meet in Vienna in regular annual sessions, unless otherwise decided. A special session can be convened by the conference, Executive Council, or upon request of any member state supported by a majority of the other states parties to deal with urgent issues. The conference will adopt its own rules of procedure and, at the beginning of each session, elect its president and other officers. Voting is similar to that in the OPCW. Procedural issues will be decided by majority vote, while substantive issues will be decided by consensus.[20] If no consensus can be reached within twenty-four hours, a decision will then be made by a two-thirds majority vote of members.

The Executive Council

The Executive Council, which will meet regularly and act as the treaty's principal decision-making body, will consist of fifty-one members.[21] As the executive organ of the organization, the council will act as the principal implementation and compliance policy body, oversee the work of the Technical Secretariat, and submit the major reports. It also will consider concerns about possible noncompliance, consult with the parties concerned, and request measures to redress the situation. To ensure equitable geographic distribution, the council will be made up of ten member states from Africa; seven from Eastern Europe; nine from Latin America and the Caribbean; seven from the Middle East and South Asia; ten from North America and Western Europe; and eight from Southeast Asia, the Pacific, and the Far East. The states in each of these geographic regions are listed in Annex 1 to the treaty.

The members of the council will be elected by the Conference. To ensure that the countries with the strongest vested interest in the CTBT are adequately represented on the Council, at least one-third of the seats allotted to each region will be filled on the basis of such treaty-related nuclear capabilities as the number of monitoring facilities states contribute to the International Monitoring System. Each member state eventually will have the right to serve on the Council; one seat allocated to each region will be assigned on an alphabetical basis, with the remaining seats determined by rotation or elections.

The Technical Secretariat

As in the previous models, the Technical Secretariat will be the primary body responsible for implementing the treaty's verification procedures.[22] It will supervise the operation of the International Monitoring System (IMS) and receive, process, analyze, and report on the system's data. It also will manage the International Data Center (IDC) and perform the procedural tasks related to conducting on-site inspections.

The purpose of the IMS is to detect and identify any nuclear explosions. It is the outgrowth of years of study and deliberation by the U.N. Committee on Disarmament going back to 1976.[23] The IMS will comprise facilities for seismological, radionuclide, hydroacoustic, and infrasound monitoring and the respective means of communication and be supported by the International Data Center. All monitoring facilities will be owned and operated by the states hosting or otherwise taking responsibility for them. The costs for operating the IMS are divided between each member state and the organization and delineated in the treaty text. The treaty also provides for the establishment of separate cooperative arrangements with the organization to make available supplementary data from national monitoring stations that are not formally part of the IMS.

Information collected by the IMS will be transmitted to the IDC for data storage and processing. Because the IMS will generate an enormous amount of raw data, the IDC will regularly provide member states with a number of services to help them monitor compliance. In this regard, it will produce integrated lists of all signals picked up by the IMS, as well as standard event lists and bulletins. The center also will generate standard screened event bulletins that filter out those events that appear to be of a non-nuclear nature. Both raw and processed data will be made available to all member states.

On-Site Inspection Procedures

The CTBT permits any member state to request an on-site inspection anywhere for the sole purpose of clarifying whether a nuclear explosion of any kind has been carried out in contravention of Article I and to gather facts to assist in identifying a possible violator. The request can be based on information developed by the IMS or national technical means, or both, but must be within the scope of the treaty. The request for an inspection is presented simultaneously to the Executive Council and to the director-general of the Technical Secretariat to permit immediate processing. The council is required to begin consideration of the request immediately upon receiving it. The director-general must acknowledge receipt of an on-site inspection (OSI) request within two hours, communicate it to the inspectable party within six hours, and begin preparations for the inspection without delay. The director general also is required to make immediate efforts with the inspectable party to clarify and resolve the concern. The party receiving such a request for a clarification must respond within seventy-two hours.

The director-general then will transmit to the Executive Council, prior to any decision on the OSI, all pertinent facts related to the possible inspection, including information from the IMS, from any member state, from the response to the request for clarification, and from within the Technical Secretariat. Unless it is withdrawn, the Executive Council must take a decision on the OSI request within ninety-six hours of its receipt. Thirty (of fifty-one) votes are required for approval.

Once approved, an on-site inspection must be conducted without delay. The inspection team must arrive at the point of entry (POE) no later than six days after receipt of the request, providing at least twenty-four hours prior notification to the inspected party. During the course of the inspection, the inspection team may submit to the council, through the director-general, a proposal to begin drilling for the purpose of verification. Approval of such a proposal requires a majority of the council. The duration of an on-site inspection under the CTBT is limited to sixty days, but the inspection may be extended by a maximum of seventy additional days, if the inspection team determines it needs more time and the council approves. As an interim measure, the inspection team must provide the council with a progress inspection report within twenty-five days after approval of the OSI. Submission of the report does not affect the inspection process, which may continue unless the council decides within seventy-two hours of receiving the report to terminate the inspection.

If the council rejects an on-site inspection request, or terminates an OSI already underway, because it is considered to be of a frivolous or abusive nature, it may impose punitive measures on the requesting state. These could involve financial compensation for the preparations made by the Technical Secretariat and/or temporary suspension of the party's right to request an inspection and serve on the council.

The country identified in the inspection request must permit an inspection. However, it does not have to accept several simultaneous inspections on its territory or places under its jurisdiction or control. It must make every reasonable effort to demonstrate compliance or enable the inspectors to fulfill their mandate but has the right to take measures to protect its national security interests and confidential business information not related to the inspection. Inspectors are required to carry out their functions in the least intrusive manner possible, consistent with the efficient and timely accomplishment of their mandate. Operationally, this means inspectors must begin with the least intrusive inspection procedures, then proceed to more intrusive procedures only if this is necessary to collect enough information to clarify the compliance concern. Inspectors also must confine their search for information and data to that required for the inspection and minimize interference with normal operations at the site. The country that requested the OSI may send an observer, subject to agreement of the inspected county.

Like other treaties, the inspection report must be factual (not judgmental). It is to describe the inspection activities, findings, cooperation of the inspected party including access granted, and other details of the inspection. If inspectors have differing observations, these may be attached to the inspection report. The draft report then is provided to the inspected country, which has forty-eight hours to append its comments and explanations and to identify any information and data that, in its view, are not related to the inspection and should not be circulated outside the Technical Secretariat. The inspection report must be promptly provided to the requesting party and all other member states, along with the results of sample analyses and relevant IMS or other information. Based on a review of the report and other material, the Executive Council then addresses compliance concerns and any further action that may be necessary.

REGIONAL ON-SITE INSPECTION BODIES

In addition to the global verification bodies, several multinational verification agencies have been set up at the regional level to carry out or assist on-site inspection activity. Principal among these are the U. N. Special Commission, created to carry out the U.N. non-nuclear related inspections in Iraq, and the NATO Verification Coordinating Committee to coordinate CFE inspection activity in the area from the Atlantic to the Urals.

The U. N. Special Commission on Iraq

On April 18, 1991, after Iraq had formally accepted the provisions of UNSC Resolution 687, the U.N. Secretary General submitted to the Security Council a report recommending establishment of a new organization—the United Nations Special Commission—to implement the non-nuclear provisions of resolution 687 and to assist IAEA in the nuclear areas. UNSCOM was given a multiple mandate. It was charged with carrying out immediate on-site inspections of Iraq's biological, chemical, and missile capabilities; taking possession of and destroying, removing, or rendering harmless all chemical and biological weapons, stocks of agents, and related subsystems, components, RDT&E support, and manufacturing facilities; supervising destruction of all Iraqi ballistic missiles with ranges greater than 150 kilometers, including parts, repair, and production facilities; and monitoring and verifying Iraq's agreement not to use, develop, produce, or acquire any of these items. Although these missions originally were viewed as consecutive phases, in practice they have overlapped extensively.[24]   UNSCOM's mandate also included providing assistance to IAEA's on-site inspections of nuclear activities and designating for inspection any additional site needed to fulfill the UNSCOM or IAEA mandate.

UNSCOM Composition and Organization

UNSCOM consists of twenty-one members representing different countries. It is headed by an executive chairman who reports to the U.N. Security Council. Its staff is provided by member states, the U.N. Secretariat—in particular the

Office of Disarmament Affairs—and the World Health Organization. The United States has several key positions on the UNSCOM staff, including that of deputy executive chairman and director for operations. UNSCOM inspectors are selected on the basis of their technical qualifications and expertise and are drawn from as many member states as possible within the range of available capabilities and experience.[25]

UNSCOM is organized into groups responsible for eliminating Iraq's weapons of mass destruction. These include a Nuclear Group, Chemical-Biological Group, Ballistic Missile Group, and Long-Term Compliance Monitoring Group. It also has an Information Assessment Unit (IAU), which provides analytical support to all of these groups.[26] The IAU was established within six months after the initial inspections began to serve as a data collection and assessment center and develop mission planning. Prior to its creation, the UNSCOM on-site inspection activity in Iraq was based on information provided by the concerned governments, particularly by the United States, Great Britain, and France. However, this information was sometimes dated, and UNSCOM needed the capability to better evaluate and integrate it with information gained from its on-site inspection activity on the ground.

Following UNSCOM's establishment, an office was set up in the U.N. Secretariat at United Nations Headquarters in New York, with a field office in Bahrain and a Monitoring and Verification Center in Baghdad (BVC). Inspection operations are planned and managed from New York; the Bahrain office serves as a forward-based assembly, acclimatization, and training point for inspection teams; and the Baghdad office provides communications and logistical support to teams in the field. The Baghdad office contains a medical clinic, offices, working areas for inspectors, laboratories for conducting chemical and biological analyses, and an operations center. The operations center maintains radio contact with the inspection teams when they are in the country and monitors dozens of dual-capable factories throughout Iraq with closed-circuit video cameras. Of the approximately 150 UNSCOM staff personnel, about a third are located in New York, half in Baghdad, and the remainder in Bahrain.

To support UNSCOM, the United States established a Special Commission Support Office in the U.S. Department of State, which chairs an interagency group of other interested U.S. government agencies, including the Arms Control and Disarmament Agency (ACDA), the On-Site Inspection Agency (OSIA), The Department of Defense (DoD), the Joint Chiefs of Staff (JCS) and the Central Intelligence Agency.[27] In July 1991, OSIA was made the executive agent for DoD support to UNSCOM and given a charter spelling out its roles and responsibilities, which include managing UNSCOM requests to the United States for inspection team personnel, monitoring equipment, and logistical support. In coordination with the U.S. Special Commission Support office and DoD policy and operational components, OSIA has helped procure and provide personnel, services, facilities, supplies, equipment, and other support to UNSCOM, including assistance in the conduct of U-2 aerial inspections overflights. As of mid-1995, OSIA had coordinated over 160 UNSCOM requests for support involving expenditures in excess of $50 million. OSIA inspectors also have served temporary tours of duty in Iraq involving the full range of UNSCOM inspection responsibilities.

Initial Development of UNSCOM Procedures

UNSC Res. 687 requires Iraq to "unconditionally accept the destruction, removal or rendering harmless" of its weapons of mass destruction (WMD). However, the resolution does not specify the rights of UNSCOM and the IAEA in carrying out this mandate. These are contained in a separate set of detailed inspection provisions that make up the most intrusive and far-reaching on-site inspection regime implemented to date.[28] They permit UNSCOM and the IAEA to conduct on-site inspections in Iraq without prior notice, at both declared and undeclared facilities, with full access to the facilities, and no right of refusal of the inspections. Inspectors may request and retain data and documents, take photographs, conduct interviews, install remote-controlled monitoring equipment, perform aerial reconnaissance, and collect samples for laboratory analysis. Moreover, UNSC Res. 687 requires Iraq to "respond fully, completely and promptly" to requests or questions by the inspectors.

Initial UNSCOM inspection procedures were largely improvised, and there was no clear, detailed definition of the division of labor between UNSCOM and the IAEA. This resulted in some early conceptual, organizational, operational, and communications problems. There was some early jurisdictional tension between the UNSCOM and IAEA inspectors. In addition, many basic operational procedures, such as assembling inspection teams; transporting them to and around Iraq; preparing and analyzing the results of the on-site inspections; and destroying weapons, stockpiles, and facilities, were developed largely by trial and error.[29]

Among the early operational problems was the tendency of individual team members to use their own national chemical weapons detection, sampling, decontamination, and analysis equipment. This equipment varied in efficiency and standards and created problems on teams with mixed nationalities. This experience led to an early conclusion that, if international teams are to be used, equipment issues must be decided early and time allowed for training inspectors in their use. In addition, the widespread destruction of Iraq's national and international communications system during the Persian Gulf War put a premium on the development of effective inspector-provided communications equipment. The use of satellite systems using secure communications equipment provided reliable, confidential communications, but indigenous power sources were vulnerable to interruption, and portable generators thus were found to be essential. Moreover, UNSCOM inspectors initially used Iraqi-provided ground transportation. This was soon found to be unsatisfactory, especially for suspect site inspections, since it gave the Iraqis both advance warning and excessive control of the inspection process. As a result, UNSCOM soon developed its own inspector-controlled transportation.

Current Inspection Team Operations

UNSCOM inspectors are drawn from supporting countries[30] and serve for two or more weeks. Inspection teams range from as few as three members to more than fifty in special cases. They are composed of both technical experts in a particular field of weapons development and production and support personnel. The latter include an operations officer, photographer, report coordinator, Arabic-English interpreter, and one or more translators for documentary material. UNSCOM inspectors must have a working knowledge of English, but in practice, the quality of their language varies and this has sometimes complicated the inspection process and report writing.

UNSCOM personnel are international civil servants, have diplomatic privileges and immunities, inspect under a blue U.N. certification in lieu of a passport, and may neither seek nor accept instructions from any government authority outside the United Nations.[31] Mission planning is carried out by an analytical staff at New York Headquarters based on all available information sources, including intelligence reports received from member states. Each inspection team is given a specific task. The team then is forward deployed to Manama, Bahrain, for orientation and briefing prior to traveling to Baghdad. In Baghdad, inspection teams work out of UNSCOM's Monitoring and Verification Center.

Prior to an inspection, UNSCOM team chiefs meet with Iraqi officials from the Iraqi National Monitoring Directorate (NMD), which coordinates internal Iraqi government activities related to the U.N. inspections. The team chief presents the team's credentials, explains the purpose of the mission and requests Iraqi cooperation. During the inspection process, the inspection team travels to sites in and around Baghdad by bus or Land Rover and to more distant facilities by helicopter. The team is accompanied by Iraqi government escorts (generally referred to as "minders") who often videotape walk-throughs, meetings, and interviews. Upon completion of the inspection mission, the team chief meets with NMD officials to clarify outstanding issues, after which the inspection team returns to Bahrain (not Baghdad) for debriefing and final report writing to ensure enhanced confidentiality.[32] The IAEA nuclear inspection teams have prepared their inspection reports both in Bahrain and Vienna.

In carrying out its responsibilities, UNSCOM relies on a broad range of verification measures. In addition to on-site inspections, these include aerial overflights, the emplacement and operation of unattended ground sensors (mainly cameras) and the examination of documentation. The aerial inspections have been carried out both at high altitude, using a U.S. U-2 reconnaissance aircraft and at lower levels, using German and Chilean helicopters. As of December 1, 1995, more than 270 U-2 missions and 600 helicopter inspection flights had been completed over Iraq.[33]

Like the IAEA inspections, the extensive and highly intrusive UNSCOM inspections have provided a great deal of information on Iraq's weapons programs. In conjunction with data from other sources, this inspection information has helped to reveal the extent of Iraq's hidden chemical, biological, and missile programs. The inspections, however, have not uncovered undeclared missiles or active continuing chemical or biological weapons production programs. The main accomplishment has been in uncovering documentary and other evidence, despite Iraqi efforts to frustrate targeted inspection activity, that confirm that Iraq had hidden the real extent of its biological, chemical, and missile programs and had provided the United Nations with misleading and incomplete declarations about them.

NATO's Verification Coordinating Committee (VCC)

The inspection provisions of the Treaty on Conventional Forces in Europe created the need to establish some method of coordinating the on-site inspection rights and obligations of the individual signatories to avoid inspection duplications and overlaps. The treaty stipulates, for example, that no country is obliged to accept more than two declared site inspections on its territory at the same time. But, without some internal coordination, it would have been extremely difficult, especially during baseline and residual level validation periods, not to have had more than two NATO teams conducting inspections simultaneously in the same country. The NATO allies also felt the need for a coordinated approach to other types of information exchanges. In addition, they wanted to implement inspection and escort activities in a uniform manner to reduce potential confusion or compliance problems that might arise should each country develop and use its own procedures.

To deal with these issues, NATO established the Verification Coordinating Committee (VCC) in 1990 to serve as a vehicle for coordination on CFE inspection and confidence-building issues. The VCC has a unique composition within NATO in that it combines both NATO's political and military structures, thus accurately reflecting the dual political-military nature of arms control verification. Each NATO country has two representatives on the VCC. There are no formal restrictions on the choice of these representatives but, as a general rule, each nation has selected one member representing its Ministry of Foreign Affairs and the other representing its Ministry of Defense. The VCC's support staff has a similar dual structure, consisting of fifteen civilian and fifteen military personnel drawn from eight NATO countries.[34]

The VCC has a broad range of coordinating activities related to CFE on-site inspections, including apportionment of inspection quotas to the NATO countries, transfers of any unused quotas among them, coordination of declared site inspections, assessments of compliance and non-compliance, the provision of guidance on training courses, and the development and use of common NATO data bases.

Multinational Teaming

A central feature of the VCC's coordination efforts has been the creation of multinational on-site inspection teams. Inspectors from the various Allied countries have been rotated to maximize inspection experience among the various countries, especially the smaller nations.

As a reflection of the commitments in the CFE Preamble to strive to replace military confrontation with a new pattern of security relations based on peaceful cooperation, the VCC conducted multinational trial inspections following treaty signature to train inspectors and implement uniform procedures. In early 1993, an invitation also was extended to members of the former Warsaw Pact to participate in NATO inspection teams and attend NATO training courses. Furthermore, in 1994 these countries were provided access to the NATO verification data base (called VERITY).

This increasing multinational coordination and cooperation has helped to expand the climate of confidence and transparency among CFE participants, assist the development of common standards for interpretation of treaty provisions, and reduce duplications of inspection efforts and costs. NATO also has accepted invitations from former Warsaw Pact countries for joint inspections, shared inspection quota allocation information, and carried out other cooperative inspection activity. This enhanced cooperation has not required any changes in the terms of treaty, and care has been taken not to violate the integrity of any treaty provisions. Participation is strictly voluntary, and all participants are treated equally.

The multinational coordination and cooperation in the VCC has assisted the exchange of information on inspection results, permitted better assessment of inspection activity deviating from the ordinary, and allowed each NATO country to benefit from inspections carried out by other countries. Multinational teams also have provided additional inspection opportunities for each country, particularly broadening the inspection experience of the smaller CFE signatories. Significantly, multinational teams, including those with mixed bloc composition, have been found to function harmoniously and without serious problems.

Although its role is more limited, the VCC also has assisted cooperation under the Vienna Document on activities related to confidence- and security-building inspections and information exchanges, including evaluation visits to military facilities. This activity is gradually orienting the VCC toward implementation of arms control agreements, which transcend the initial bloc-to-bloc orientation of the CFE Treaty.

The VERITY Data Base

To centralize the handling of CFE data, the VCC has established the computerized VERITY data base, which provides rapid access to all key information on treaty implementation, including the annual information exchanges, current force structure data, and inspection reports. A separate data base to cover the Bosnian inspections under the Dayton Accords also has been established. The VERITY data base is open to all CFE signatories and is linked with other data bases set up by the Organization for Security and Cooperation in Europe (OSCE). VERITY uses English and standardized communications structures that are consistent with those used by the NATO and OSCE networks. It operates around the clock and information in the data base is immediately open to all CFE countries. As of mid-1996, VERITY had some 120 users and had become the collective data base for all CFE signatories.

NOTES

1. START II, signed in January 1993, remains a bilateral U.S.-Russian treaty.

2. Article III, section B.

3. Although the conference has the power to return the budget to the board with recommendations for change, it has never used this authority.

4. During the late 1970s, the title of the chief of the safeguards inspectorate was changed from inspector general to deputy director general for safeguards.

5. Fact Sheet, *"International Safeguards and the Peaceful Uses of Nuclear Energy"* (Vienna: IAEA, 1996) p. 2.

6. Article III, section A, paragraph 5.

7. Article XII, section A.

8. Richard Hooper, "Strengthening IAEA Safeguards in an Era of Nuclear Cooperation," *Arms Control Today* (November 1995): 15.

9. For a more comprehensive treatment, see Maurizio Zifferero, "Iraq and UN Security Council Resolution 687: The Role of the IAEA and Lessons to be Learned," in *New Horizons and Challenges in Arms Control and Verification*, ed. James Brown, (Amsterdam: VU University Press) pp. 221–227.

10.   Long-term monitoring of Iraq involves routine inspection procedures and techniques as well as others, such as the use of sophisticated sensors; periodic monitoring of Iraq's principal bodies of water to examine signatures of prohibited activities; and unannounced visits of resident inspectors to plants, factories, and research centers.

11. Zifferero, "Iraq and U.N. Security Council," p. 221.

12. Ibid. p. 223.

13. The designation "93+2" denotes the time frame within which the work was to be carried out; the IAEA Secretariat was to provide the board with its assessment within two years—prior to the April 1995 NPT review conference.

14. A summary of the main elements of the program are contained in U.S. Arms Control and Disarmament Agency, *Threat Control Through Arms Control 1995*, Annual Report to Congress (Washington, D.C.: ACDA, July 1996), p. 6.

15. A comprehensive description of Program 93+2 is to found in Hooper, "Strengthening IAEA Safeguards," pp.14–18.

16. The organization of the CWC is set out in Article VIII, which is divided in five sections. The first section established the Organization for the Prohibition of Chemical Weapons and its three constituent organs.

17. "CTB Treaty Executive Summary," *Arms Control Today* (August 1996): 17

18. The organizational structure of the CTBT is set out in Article II.

19. CTBT Article II, section B.

20. If an issue arises as to whether a question is one of substance or not, the question must be treated as one of substance unless otherwise decided by a two-thirds majority (Article II, section B, paragraph 22.).

21. CTBT Article II, section C.

22. The organization and functions of the Technical Secretariat are contained in Article II, section D.

23. In 1976, a group of scientists attached to the Conference on Disarmament, led by Sweden, decided that it was time to establish an international project for exchanging scientific data to monitor a future CTBT. The United States initially objected to a verification role for the new organization on the grounds that verification was a national prerogative.

24. United Nations, *United Nations Focus: UNSCOM*, UN Information Pamphlet on United Nations Special Commission (New York: UN Secretariat, no date), p. 1.

25. Ibid. p. 2.

26. A good assessment of UNSCOM operations is contained in Edward J. Lacey, "The UNSCOM Experience: Implications for U.S. Arms Control Policy," *Arms Control Today* (August 1996): 9–14.

27. The Support Office is located within the Office of Regional Nonproliferation in the State Department's Bureau of Political-Military Affairs. It coordinates efforts with other relevant State Department offices including the Bureau of Intelligence and Research and the Bureau of Near Eastern Affairs.

28. The U.N. inspection provisions, communicated to Baghdad on May 6, 1991, in an exchange of letters between the U.N. secretary general and the Iraqi foreign minister, were initially rejected by the Iraqis, but the letter exchange was executed on May 14, 1991, after heavy pressure from the Security Council, including the implied threat of renewed military action.

29. Jonathan Tucker, "Monitoring and Verification in a Noncooperative Environment: Lessons from the UN Experience in Iraq," *Nonproliferation Review* (Spring-Summer 1996): 2.

30. Primarily Australia, Canada, France, Germany, New Zealand, Russia, Sweden, Switzerland, the United Kingdom, and the United States.

31. Tucker, "Monitoring and Verification," p. 2.

32. Ibid. pp. 2–3.

33. Lacey, "UNSCOM Experience," p. 10.

34. Information on the VCC is drawn primarily from a presentation "Lessons Learned from Coordinating Conventional Arms Control Implementation and Verification" by Necil Nedimoglu, head of the Verification and Implementation Coordinating Section,

Chapter 12

Issues of On-Site Inspection

The modern on-site inspection (OSI) regimes developed since the conclusion of the Intermediate Nuclear Forces (INF) Treaty have added new elements to the verification structures of arms control agreements, significantly increasing their effectiveness. By permitting the on-site presence of trained inspectors and the use of specialized verification equipment to help verify compliance with the provisions of an agreement, they increase the chance that illegal activity will be discovered and complicate and significantly raise the costs of cheating. They also contribute in a major way to military openness and transparency in the areas where they are applied, reducing the possibilities of misunderstanding and mistakes in interpreting military actions. In addition, the verification regimes containing OSI establish important internationally recognized norms that provide a stronger legal and political basis for a concerted response by an individual country or collectively by the international community should violations be found.

At bottom, however, OSI regimes are only an investigative tool. They are not—and do not purport to be—watertight assurances of compliance. Even the most carefully constructed OSI regimes can be "spoofed" by a country determined on cheating and prepared to expend the necessary resources to carry out covert activity. OSI regimes, therefore are not, and should not be viewed as, a panacea for ensuring full and complete compliance with bilateral, regional, or global arms control agreements.

All OSI regimes entail a varied mix of benefits, costs, and risks—all of which must be considered in evaluating their desirability and relative effectiveness. As arms control agreements with ever more intrusive verification regimes come online, there is a need to carefully balance the contributions of each regime with its real and potential costs. Such a balanced assessment becomes particularly essential when evaluating the benefits of implementing, funding, and supporting additional OSI activities at both the national and multinational level against competing economic and political costs.

THE BENEFITS OF OSI

Synergies between OSI and NTM

For highly developed countries like the United States, OSI is not a replacement for national technical means of verification (NTM), which has been the traditional means of verifying arms control agreements: rather it is a complement. Indeed, as we have shown, most OSI regimes not only recognize NTM as a fundamental element of arms control verification, but include special provisions to enhance its effectiveness in areas of special concern.

NTM has far-ranging capabilities and has made an enormous contribution to the verification of arms control in areas that are readily monitorable from space or suspectable to the other, often highly sophisticated, intelligence-gathering technologies developed in recent years. But only relatively few countries have such systems and even sophisticated NTM systems can be degraded by weather and intentional obfuscation by the other side. Moreover, they are expensive to erect and operate. Relying solely on them for an ever-increasing range of treaty-monitoring tasks would require either erecting more such systems or diverting the current systems from other strategic missions. There are also intrinsic problems in the sharing of NTM data that are not present with OSI information. The sharing of intelligence data with a broad number of allies and especially with multinational agencies, such as the United Nations—which may be necessary to develop a unified international response to an arms control violator—risks revealing sensitive sources and/or technological capabilities.[1] In addition, reliance on NTM data alone as the basis for international action, especially in a multinational forum, could lead to challenges that the data is fabricated or skewed since U.S. NTM capabilities, in particular, are far superior to those of other nations and may not be independently verifiable by other nations or sources.

The use of OSI, as a complement to NTM, can create a highly effective synergistic effect. OSI provides more easily shareable "ground truth" information, particularly in areas that may not be readily susceptible to NTM monitoring. OSI permits inspectors to look inside structures, examine military equipment or suspect items at close hand, apply specialized monitoring equipment directly to suspect military equipment at a site or facility, take environmental swipes or samples, and conduct interviews or record searches. Elaborate cover-ups against the possibility of an on-site inspection also might add to the risk of detection by NTM or other intelligence assets.

Moreover, the intelligence information developed by NTM can "cue" and focus inspections, greatly increasing the effectiveness of inspection teams once they arrive at declared or undeclared sites. This has proved to be particularly helpful in Iraq, where some supporting countries have provided intelligence information to assist inspectors, including satellite photographs, line drawings derived from overhead imagery, defector reports, and information on "signatures" or indicators of illicit weapons activity.[2] When coordinated with short-notice inspections, NTM also can observe whether certain OSI provisions are being implemented, for example, whether the required pre-inspection movement restrictions are being applied.

The Benefits of Various Types of Inspection

As we have seen, many individual types of inspection have been developed to perform specific tasks, each of which can help evaluate a piece of a puzzle that determines whether a country is complying with its treaty obligations.

The requirements levied by modern treaties with OSI provisions to provide comprehensive data on all military systems covered by the treaty and notifications, which assist in accounting for, and tracking, that data, add importantly to transparency, openness, and increased confidence building. The detailed information they provide on the equipment and facilities of all parties to the treaty provides a credible foundation for carrying out treaty obligations and monitoring compliance. The subsequent confirmation that data in baseline inspections and the continuous tracking of it during other types of OSI increases the difficulty and expense of cheating by making it harder to use existing bases and facilities to conduct illegal activities.

The data base and required notifications also make future anomalies or suspicious activities more visible. The very prospect of confirmatory inspections provides an incentive to both sides to provide an accurate exchange of data on treaty activities, and inspections help to identify and isolate any irregularities in the data that has been provided. Moreover, by forcing a potential evader to use other new or reconfigured facilities, to make special preparations, and to take steps out of the ordinary to carry out illegal activity, OSI heightens the chance of detection by NTM or other monitoring means.

Elimination and conversion inspections can provide certainty that destruction of treaty-limited items is actually being carried out and that this is in accordance with treaty provisions. Observation of the destruction process ensures that all parties to the agreement are faithfully complying with a treaty's commitments to destroy or reduce certain weapons systems and that real (not dummy) military equipment is being destroyed. They also confirm that the items being eliminated are destroyed in a manner that prevents their viable reconstruction and that allowable conversions are carried out in a manner that genuinely precludes use of the equipment for its original military purposes.

OSI regimes to detect illegal activities at the sites and facilities declared in the data base have generally focused on short-notice inspections with tight timelines to ensure that military sites and infrastructure are not being used for illegal purposes. Short timelines could force an evader to rush a clean-up, making missteps, such as the leaving behind of some tell-tale evidence, more likely. Inspection procedures that provide for broad access to a site and enable an inspection team to carry out its responsibilities in a relatively unfettered manner also serve to increase the chances that some unintended sign of an illegal activity will be detected. These procedures thus also contribute significantly to increasing the risk of detection.

Suspect site inspections, particularly challenge inspections and intrusive on-site visits, which can be directed at any site or facility where suspect activity is occurring, are particularly aimed at raising the risks of detection. Should such inspections come as a surprise, they could force a rapid clean-up, raising the probability that some residue (especially in the case of a biological weapons (BW) or chemical weapons (CW) facility) could be overlooked or that the hasty removal of equipment and incriminating records or other cover-up activity would be detected by NTM. The likelihood of such mistakes may be highest in Third World countries, which have fewer trained technicians, poorer communications and less developed industrial and technological bases. Specialized types of on-site monitoring also can help confirm compliance with specific requirements of individual treaties. Portal and perimeter continues monitoring (PPCM), for example, can help confirm that illegal weapons are not leaving declared production sites, while nuclear test monitoring in the country concerned or by an international network backed by on-site inspections wherever anomalies are detected can raise confidence that banned nuclear tests are not occurring.

The detection equipment used in on-site inspections and monitoring also can increase the likelihood that violations will be discovered and thus have a deterrent effect. Radiation detection devices are particularly important in detecting nuclear warhead violations. The development of robust, portable, highly sensitive instruments to analyze air, soil, or effluent samples makes it possible to detect extremely small trace residues in the case of CW and BW agreements. The right of inspectors to remove samples for more extensive off-site analysis also adds to the probability of detection. The deployment of a wide array of complementary monitoring technologies by inspectors provides synergies in the detection of violations. Continuing robust research on equipment that can be used by inspectors holds promises for yet further improvements in the likelihood that violations of arms control agreements will be detected during an on-site inspection.

Other Benefits of OSI

In addition to the verification benefits of specific types of inspection and of the use of inspection equipment, there are a number of political and military benefits of on-site inspection. The cooperative aspects of OSI regimes provide a valuable means for a country to publicly demonstrate its faithful implementation of treaty provisions. OSI can served as a political barometer. It can signal political consensus with international norms, thus facilitating improved political relations. On the other hand, reluctance to agree to OSI can demonstrate political deterioration, thus providing an additional warning element of a possible treaty violation or of a shift in the status quo. A repeated refusal by a party to an agreement to permit inspections or efforts to block their effective implementation could provide a sign of cheating or a warning of preparations to break out of an agreement and resume banned activities. While the increment of such a warning over NTM might be low, OSI could help reduce elements of ambiguity or increase the value of information gained by other means.

OSI also can be an important confidence-building step between governments. Full compliance by a country with its on-site inspection obligations helps to confirm that the country is abiding by its treaty obligations, thus increasing confidence in its military intentions. In addition, since both inspectors and escorts in national on-site inspection agencies are, to a large extent, military personnel, OSI is an important method of increasing military-to-military contacts and familiarity. On-site inspection activity, which, depending on the type of inspection, can last from a few days to continuous presence on the soil of the inspected party, can make an important contribution to acquainting all parties of an OSI regime with the military personnel, equipment, facilities, operations, and procedures of the other signatories. Figures 12.1, for example, which lists the START inspectable sites in the United States, illustrates the extent to which countries of the former Soviet Union (FSU) have access to key U.S. military facilities under that arms control agreement alone. The United States has similar access to strategic facilities in Russia and other FSU nuclear successor countries. Such access to key military facilities can do much to improve confidence that critical military arms limitations and reductions are being fully implemented, while the enhanced familiarity with the structures and operations of the military facilities of the other side at specific facilities can help inspectors focus their inspection activity on those areas where it will be most productive.

THE RISKS OF OSI

While OSI has many benefits, it also contains significant risks. There is mutual agreement between both proponents and opponents of arms control that, with determination, cheating can occur under even the most stringent OSI regimes. Unless this is clearly understood, OSI can instill in the general public a false sense of confidence in the reliability of arms control agreements.

Potential Cheating Scenarios

OSI can only confirm that illegal activities are not underway at a given site at the time of inspection. Taken alone, it does not necessarily provide conclusive

Figure 12.1
START Inspectable Sites in the United States

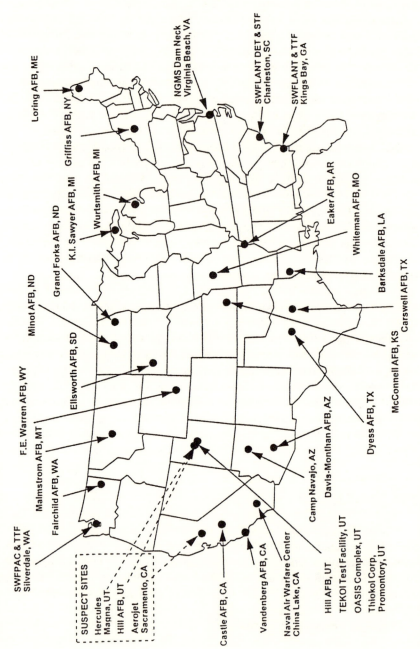

Source: DynMeridian Corporation, Alexandria, Virginia.

evidence that a country is in compliance. While each type of OSI is designed to accomplish a specific purpose, the effectiveness of that type of inspection in deterring cheating must be carefully evaluated against potential cheating scenarios. These would include such factors as the potential ease with which sites not listed as being inspectable in the treaty data base could be reconfigured to produce, service, or house treaty-limited items or illegal equipment or activities; how readily illegal activities or sites could be disguised; how much effort would be needed to avoid detection (for example, by clean-up) if an attempt were made to misuse an inspectable site; and the extent to which dual-use items, with both prohibited and permitted applications, are controlled or limited. Even the INF and Strategic Arms Reduction Treaty (START) continuous monitoring regimes can only confirm that prohibited missiles are not leaving a production facility. Since they do not permit inspectors to conduct inspections of the interior of the plant, they cannot provide conclusive evidence that illegal missiles are not being stored within the facility (although to be certified effective, stored missiles would need to be tested periodically at test-ranges, an activity subject to detection by NTM). Moreover, even the most comprehensive inspection regime cannot ensure that illegal activity (especially involving chemical or biological weapons) is not occurring at a secret site in a rogue country, especially one with a closed or repressive society, possessing a sophisticated industrial base, or having a large or difficult landmass not conducive to inspection activity.

In the end, the deterrent effect of OSI regimes depends on the calculations that might lead a country's leaders to violate an agreement, on the country's decision-making process, and on the perception of the response that might ensue in the event of detection. While strict OSI procedures greatly raise the risk of detection, if a rogue country believes that the benefits of violating its arms control commitments are overriding, it may be undeterred even by the fear that something may go wrong.

Exploitation of Unclear Language

Clear, carefully worded inspection language and well-constructed procedures also are essential to ensuring effective implementation, since ambiguities about what is, and is not, permitted, could heighten the prospects of successful cheating. In some cases, limited cheating for small gains also might stem less from high level decisions than from the actions of political or military officials, possibly driven by an unwillingness to cut their own programs or accept new constraints.

If language is unclear, there also can be legitimate differences of opinion among treaty signatories on what the treaty allows, permitting some countries to pursue activities that the other country believes are prohibited. In such cases, it is often necessary to undertake tedious research of the arms control negotiation record to determine the interpretation by various countries of the language at the time it was accepted at the negotiating table or, if this is unclear, to resolve the issue in a treaty's implementation and compliance body. The length and complexity of modern treaties containing on-site inspection regimes, with their legalistic language, multiple definitions, and precise counting and type rules, testifies to the care taken by negotiators to limit such ambiguities.

Deliberate Deception

Arms control inspections have proved their effectiveness by turning up many "ambiguities," providing evidence that a country was not complying with one or another provision of an agreement. Most often, these violations have occurred through oversight or a lack of proper training. Most have been resolvable by discussions on the spot between inspectors and host country escorts or during discussions in arms control implementation and compliance bodies or in diplomatic channels.

Nonetheless, there is a general assumption among students of arms control (borne out by experience to date) that on-site inspections are unlikely, by themselves, to reveal a "smoking gun" violation that provides unequivocal evidence of a deliberate arms control violation. It is assumed that a determined cheater will always find ways to delay or abort an undesired inspection, obfuscate evidence or otherwise escape detection. The experience of UNSCOM and IAEA inspectors in Iraq under the U. N. mandate following the Persian Gulf War demonstrates the range of measures available to a country, that is unhappy with an inspection regime, to frustrate inspection activity. UNSCOM and IAEA inspectors have uncovered countless records and other evidence demonstrating that Iraq's declarations about the extent of its programs on weapons of mass destruction and their missile delivery systems have been misleading and inaccurate. However, the inspectors have not found illegal production activity during the course of an inspection, despite their unequivocal right to conduct "anywhere, anytime" inspections with an unprecedented degree of access. This is widely suspected of being due less to Iraqi compliance than its ability to continue to hide such activity.

It is clear that, in reaction to IAEA and UNSCOM inspections, Iraq has employed a wide range of deception and denial tactics, including the following identified by an arms control scholar with personal experience as an UNSCOM inspector:[3] a pattern of misleading and incomplete declarations; efforts at confrontation and intimidation of inspectors; development of counterintelligence, surveillance, and infiltration measures to ferret out inspection plans in advance; systematic destruction, removal, or dispersal of evidence to conceal the purpose of key facilities; efforts to impede or delay inspection team arrival and buy time to remove evidence of activities; and employment of other deception and denial techniques based on a close monitoring of the inspection methods of U.N.

agencies and Western intelligence services. The latter have included suppressing the tell-tale signatures of facilities associated with the production of weapons of mass destruction; duplicating and dispersing weapons development and production activities at a large number of sites; efforts to confuse outside observers by using multiple and shifting code names for the same program or site; the development of byzantine procurement networks to conceal acquisition of sensitive technologies from abroad; and the exploitation of misconceptions by Western analysts based on their assumption that the Iraqis would proceed in certain weapons development programs in the same way an advanced industrial nation would do so ("mirror imaging"). Iraq also is suspected of hiding suspect materials and activities in official "palaces" that off limits to inspectors.

Other Potential Costs of OSI

In addition to potential risks of evasion, there are a number of further potential costs of OSI. These include the financial burdens of inspection, the potential for losses of sensitive national security or confidential business information, and the potential constitutional or legal issues that OSI raises.

The Financial Costs of OSI

There are currently no figures available that calculate the worldwide management and other financial costs of the national and multinational structures that have been erected to implement the OSI regimes established since the late 1980s. The fragmentary data that does exist is generally on the cost of arms control implementation as a whole, without specific breakouts for OSI activities.

Moreover, arms control budgets generally significantly understate the costs of treaty implementation and compliance. For example, they often do not cover the costs of military personnel diverted from other tasks to perform arms control-related activities or other indirect inspection-related costs assumed by military facilities. Nor do they cover all inspection-related costs assumed by defense contractor facilities or other private companies impacted by arms control inspections. Some costs to industry, such as those for maintaining portal monitoring systems and carrying out some treaty-required inspection activity at U.S. Department of Defense (DoD) contractor facilities, currently are reimbursed by the cognizant military services. However, the costs for complying with other inspection requirements, such as preparing for inspections under the Chemical Weapons Convention, could impose significant financial burdens on private industries for which there likely will be no government reimbursement. These include the direct financial costs of preparing the facilities for inspections; the salaries of the personnel needed to plan for, prepare, and host inspections; purchases of safety garments and equipment; and such potential costs as plant shut downs, lost production, and lessened efficiency during inspection periods. Such costs most likely will have to be assumed by the inspected facilities as a normal cost of doing business.

Nonetheless, by any calculations, arms control costs are still a relatively low portion of the overall costs of national security. The proposed budget for arms control activities for the U.S. Department of Defense in Fiscal Year (FY) 1997, for example, is $282 million, including implementation planning costs associated with the Chemical Weapons Convention and the Comprehensive Test Ban Treaty. This budget is about $16 million more than was requested in FY 96, but minuscule in comparison with the overall FY 97 DoD budget of $243.4 billion.

The total budget of the On-Site Inspection Agency (OSIA) for FY 97 is $112 million. This includes the costs for coordinating and conducting on-site inspections and continuous monitoring overseas, escorting foreign inspection teams, and coordinating continuous monitoring activities at U.S. facilities, as well as other OSIA responsibilities, such as training and equipping U.S. inspection and escort teams.

The combined FY 97 arms control budget for the three military services—the Army, Air Force, and Navy—to plan, prepare for, and implement arms control treaties and agreements totals approximately $144 million. The conduct of DoD research, development, technology and equipment (RDT&E) programs in support of compliance, verification and monitoring requirements is estimated at approximately $26 million in the DoD FY 97 budget. The general goal of this RDT&E effort is to provide effective and timely technical support and equipment for on-site and aerial inspections to verify arms control treaties and to assist U.S. government arms control implementation and compliance. In addition to these DoD costs, the other government agencies involved in arms control activities have costs related to OSI. These generally are included in their broader budgets and are not broken out into discrete OSI expenses. For example, the total budget of the U.S. Arms Control and Disarmament Agency for FY 97 is only $41.5 million, with no specific breakouts for the amount spent in the negotiation or implementation of OSI regimes.

Whether the overall direct and indirect financial costs of OSI inspections are too high will ultimately be a policy judgment, based partly on public and congressional appraisal of benefits of OSI and comparisons to other defense spending. Discussion will also focus on what other activities must be given up at the margin to fund such inspections. Currently, however, it does not appear that costs for OSI are, or are likely to be in the foreseeable future, so formidable that they will become the main driver of future U.S. positions on verification regimes, even in periods of relatively tight budgets.

Loss of Confidential Information

Openness is considered to be an inherently stabilizing element. But, while

Figure 12.2
DoD Arms Control Budget: FY 97

Treaty	Amount
CFE	17.021
CW	77.830
INF	23.024
Open Skies	14.118
NTT (CTBT& TTBT)	30.617
START I	63.529
START II	14.381
BW	2.400
Other	13.217
Verification Technology	26.199
	282.336

RDT&E	52.985
O&M	211.018
Procurement	18.333
	282.336
Air Force	56.324
Army	37.255
Navy	50.242
DNA	26.199
OSIA	112.316
	282.336

Source: **Office of Arms Control Compliance and Implementation, U.S. Department of Defense, Washington, D.C.**

OSI can help overcome secrecy and foster trends to transparency, it also can potentially result in the loss of classified national security or confidential business information. The degree to which such loss might occur due to specific inspection regimes is difficult to assess in advance. But most planners assume that routine arms control inspections, particularly of military facilities, that involve highly intrusive OSIs will almost certainly result in the loss of at least some sensitive information about U.S. military programs, procedures, and practices. Likewise, arms control inspections that involve intrusive, internal access to industrial facilities, such as CWC inspections or visits with right of special access under the Strategic Arms Reduction Treaty, could well result in the loss of classified business or other proprietary information about commercial production processes and technology. Such information could give potential adversaries a better understanding of U.S. forces, help them develop future countermeasures, reveal evidence of military or commercial RDT&E directions, or result in the loss of information on manufacturing processes, trade secrets, and technologies. Inspectors also might be able to identify base or plant workers and personnel for later targeting by intelligence agencies.

Virtually all inspections entail some risk. Indeed, the arms control agreements specifically require the sides to furnish detailed information about military assets and production activities that results in military information gains by all parties.

To this is added the additional information losses inherent to on-site inspections. The degree of risk of these additional loss is related to the relative intrusiveness of the inspections and to the amount and quality of prior preparation undertaken by the facility. All arms control agreements permit facilities to take reasonable actions, such as the shrouding of equipment and the removal or covering of key documents, to reduce the loss of sensitive information on activities not related to the inspection. They also contain provisions designed to protect the confidentiality of the information obtained during inspections. In the case of international inspectorates, such as those for the International Atomic Energy Agency and the CWC, provisions for protecting the confidentiality of inspections are given particular emphasis. In addition, the U.S. military services and the national military establishments of other countries devote considerable planning to protecting military assets and information under their control during arms control inspections. The U.S. DoD also has a special program—the Defense Treaty Inspection Readiness Program (DTIRP)—specifically designed to assist both military and industrial facilities to identify and protect sensitive information during OSIs.

Legal Issues

Finally, in striking a balance among the benefits, risks, and costs of different types of OSI, constitutional and other legal issues cannot be overlooked. In the United States, in particular, some scholars have raised serious legal questions about the constitutionality of highly intrusive OSI activities, particularly those involving warrantless searches to support suspect site or challenge inspections aimed at detecting suspected cheating.

Potentially highly intrusive on-site inspections, notably START visits with right of special access, CWC challenge inspections, and possibly future Biological Weapons Convention inspections, could impose an unprecedented degree of intrusiveness on private industry, thus raising important legal concerns in countries with strong constitutional or legal provisions protecting privacy. In the United States, for example, several constitutional provisions apply. The Fourth Amendment contains the right to be secure against unreasonable searches and seizures, while the Fifth Amendment prohibits the government from taking private property without due process, including just compensation.

As of this writing, no serious legal or constitutional challenges to the implementation of any of the arms control inspection regimes entered into by the United States have arisen in the courts. However, the potential for such challenges exists, particularly in connection with the entry into force of the CWC or the implementation of other highly intrusive arms control inspection rights, should these become targeted against recalcitrant private companies.

As one legal scholar has pointed out, the question of "who is being searched" is fundamental in connection with Fourth Amendment right against unlawful searches and seizures.[4] The great bulk of on-site inspections occurs at military facilities owned and operated by the U.S. government, and the question of the legality of warrantless suspect-site or challenge inspections does not arise in these cases because the federal government has no Fourth Amendment rights. The situation of a government defense contractor is somewhat more complicated, but many defense contracts already contain language implicitly or explicitly providing consent to various kinds of government inspection. OSIs can be easily added to these provisions, with separate inspection contracts negotiated to cover areas of special interest. In the interests of doing U.S. defense-related business, contractors have a strong incentive to agree to such contracts, while the U.S. government can adjust its pricing mechanism to cover the additional costs.

The situation becomes much more difficult in the case of a private firm that has no ongoing relationship with the government and which may object for various reasons to a highly intrusive challenge inspection. To enable the government to carry out its international legal obligations under a treaty, supplemental legislation sometimes is required, such as that to implement the CWC in the United States, to ensure compliance. In case of legal challenge to these laws, the courts would have to decide whether the required inspections could legally be carried out without warrants.

The unprecedented degree of intrusiveness imposed on the chemical industry, in particular, by the CWC has been justified on basis that the U.S. chemical industry is already a "heavily regulated industry" subject to government licensing and thus has a lessened expectancy of privacy. After thorough review of existing reporting requirements, the U.S. government has determined that the nature and scope of the information required from industry under the CWC is not already available by way of other regulatory mechanisms. To preclude any conflict with the Constitution, the U.S. Congress therefore prepared legislation to ensure compliance by the U.S. chemical industry both with the new data and inspection requirements. Such regulation is based on the consideration that CWC is essential to U.S. national security and that Congress therefore must take steps to prevent the pursuit of protection of constitutional rights from interfering with enforcement of the convention except for clear transgressions of the Fourth Amendment.[5]

The Fifth Amendment to the Constitution prohibits the government from taking private property without due process, including just compensation. Such issues conceivably could arise if a company incurs serious losses due to inspections. Such losses could occur, for example, if a company must shut down or seriously reduce production during an inspection or if sensitive proprietary information is compromised during an inspection, resulting in a loss of a company's competitive edge in its industry. Owners of private facilities subject to inspection conceivably could raise claims for compensation against the U.S. government in such cases, but it is unlikely that a court would block an inspection on the basis of a claim simply against threatened damage. Fifth Amendment protection against self-incrimination also could come into consideration in connection with CWC or other future inspections that involve personal interviews or file searches that would require acknowledgment of legal violations of other U.S. laws, for example, of environmental laws or export control legislation. In assessing the constitutionality of intrusive OSIs of private industry, the courts could be expected to give considerable, but not necessarily overriding, weight to the importance of such inspections in fulfilling the government's commitment to arms control and national security. The intrusiveness of the inspections, the availability of alternative means to monitor compliance, the invasion of privacy suffered by the parties inspected, and the threat to those parties' interests posed by the inspections would all be factors in such a consideration.

On balance, it is clear that OSIs make a substantial contribution to national security by enhancing verification, complicating the process of cheating, assisting confidence building, and offering a further mechanism for confirming the political and military intentions of possible adversaries. At the same time, care must be taken not to assign unrealistic expectations to such inspections. They do not provide an infallible mechanism for determining compliance with arms control agreements and they have political, financial, and legal costs that must be carefully considered both in evaluating current regimes and assessing future OSI proposals.

NOTES

1. This can be mitigated somewhat by imposing restrictions on the use of sensitive information necessary to carry out inspections. In the case of Iraq, for example, sensitive satellite photographs obtained from the United States can be used only to brief the Office of the Executive Chairman and chief inspectors of UNSCOM. They cannot be retained by UNSCOM staff for independent analysis or reference purposes. See Tim Trevan, "Ongoing Monitoring and Verification in Iraq," *Arms Control Today* (May 1994): p.4.

2. Ibid. p. 4.

3. Ibid. pp. 5-10.

4. David A. Koplow, "The Law of On-Site Inspection: Arms Control Verification and the Fourth Amendment," in *Arms Control Verification and the New Role of On-Site Inspection*, ed. Lewis Dunn and Amy Gordon (Lexington, MA: Lexington Books, 1990) pp. 207-229.

5. E. A. Tanzman and B. Kellman, "Legal Implications of the Multilateral Chemical Weapons Convention: Integrating International Security with the Constitution," *New York University Journal of International Law and Politics*: 22, no. 3, (1990) p. 475.

Appendix I

Implementation and Compliance Bodies for the Major Arms Control Agreements Cited in the Text

ANTI-BALLISTIC MISSILE (ABM) TREATY

Standing Consultative Commission (SCC): The SCC was established in December 1972 during the first negotiating session of second talks on Strategic Arms Limitations (SALT II) by a Memorandum of Understanding (MOU) between the U.S. and U.S.S.R. under the terms of the Anti-Ballistic Missile (ABM) Treaty. Its purpose is to promote the objectives and implementation of that treaty and consider questions of compliance, possible changes in the strategic situation that could have a bearing on provisions of the treaty, and proposals for amendments.

Initially the United states and the Soviet Union—the two ABM Treaty partners—were the only SCC participants. However, with dissolution of the U.S.S.R., the United States indicated its willingness to accept as treaty parties any of the new independent states of the former Soviet Union. Participants currently include Belarus, Russia, Kazakstan, Ukraine, and the United States. The SCC's operational procedures, which were developed by the two original parties, have been multilateralized to cover the new participants. In accordance with the original MOU, the SCC meets no less than twice a year in Geneva. By the end of 1995, it had held over fifty sessions.

TREATY BETWEEN THE U.S.A. AND U.S.S.R. ON THE ELIMINA-TION OF THEIR INTERMEDIATE-RANGE AND SHORTER-RANGE BALLISTIC MISSILES (INF TREATY)

Special Verification Commission (SVC): The SVC, established by Article XIII of the INF Treaty to promote the objectives and implementation of provisions of that treaty, first convened on June 6, 1988. Its operating procedures were developed by the two original signatories—the U.S. and U.S.S.R.—in a Memorandum of Understanding (MOU) signed December 20, 1988. Since the break-up of the Soviet Union, a number of the successor states have participated in the SVC, and multilateralization of its internal operating procedures is under discussion.

Twelve former Soviet republics have become successor states to the INF Treaty. Six of these—Russia, Ukraine, Belarus, Kazakstan, Turkmenistan, and Uzbekistan—have inspectable facilities covered by INF Treaty on their soil. The first four of these have become active participants in the work of the commission. Turkmenistan and Uzbekistan each have only one INF inspectable facility on their territory and, with the consent of all parties, do not attend meetings of commission or participate in INF inspections. The SVC meets in Geneva. As of the end of 1996, it had met a total of nineteen times.

STRATEGIC ARMS CONTROL TREATY (START I)

Joint Compliance and Inspection Commission (JCIC): The JCIC was established by START I and held its first meeting in fall 1991. Its purpose is to promote the objectives and implementation of the treaty's provisions. Specifically, it helps to resolve compliance questions, agree on any additional provisions needed to improve the viability and effectiveness of treaty, clarify ambiguities discovered in treaty provisions during implementation, and determine how to deal with any new kind of strategic offensive arm (SOA) that might be declared by either party. Following the dissolution of the Soviet Union, the four nuclear successor states—Russia, Belarus, Kazakstan, and Ukraine— became parties to the START Agreement. All are represented on the JCIC.

JCIC operating procedures permit equal participation by all four nuclear successor states, and each Party is entitled to participate in conclusion of any agreement reached in that body. However, to free the parties from the burden of participating in all sessions, certain agreements may be concluded in the JCIC without all parties actually signing them. If at least two parties, including the United States, sign an agreement, the agreement will be sent to the nonsigning parties for their review. Each nonsigning party provides its response in one of three ways: (1) a diplomatic note of acceptance within thirty days; (2) its objection to the agreement within thirty days, in which case it must attend the next session of the JCIC to resolve its concerns; or (3) consent by inaction or silence within thirty days. The only exception to this third rule is if one of the signing parties declares an agreement to be one in which the "consent of silence" rule shall not apply. The intent of these rules is to ensure clear and positive assent by a party when the agreement in question has practical consequences or imposes serious obligations on that party. The JCIC normally meets in Geneva. Through the end of 1996, it had held fourteen sessions.

STRATEGIC ARMS CONTROL TREATY II (START II)

Bilateral Implementation Commission (BIC): Article IV (Paragraph 2) of the START II Treaty establishes the BIC to resolve questions relating to compliance with treaty obligations and to agree on any additional provisions needed to improve the "viability and effectiveness" of the treaty. START II is a bilateral U.S.-Russian agreement and the BIC accordingly is also a bilateral body. However, because START II depends, with a few exceptions, on the START I Treaty for definitions, counting rules, and verification and implementation provisions, the work being done in the JCIC on implementation of START I will be directly relevant to implementation of START II. The BIC will convene, probably in Geneva, once START II enters into force.

TREATY ON CONVENTIONAL FORCES IN EUROPE (CFE TREATY)

Joint Consultative Group (JCG): The JCG was established by the CFE Treaty in November 1990 to promote the objectives of the CFE, implement its provisions, and resolve disagreements among states parties, in accordance with Article XVI of the treaty and its Protocol on the JCG. Specifically, state parties use the JCG to:

- address questions of treaty compliance;
- seek to resolve ambiguities and differences of interpretation arising out of treaty implementation;
- consider measures to enhance the viability and effectiveness of the Treaty;
- update the lists contained in the treaty's Protocol on Existing Types of Conventional Armaments and Equipment;
- resolve technical questions and seek common practices in treaty implementation;
- work out or revise the rules of procedure, working methods, and scale of distribution of costs of the JCG and inspections;
- adopt appropriate measures to ensure that information resulting from data exchanges are used solely for treaty purposes;
- consider any matter that a state party proposes for examination by a review conference;
- consider matters of dispute arising out of implementation of the treaty, propose amendments, and agree on improvements to it.

All thirty CFE states parties are entitled to representation on the JCG. Decisions are made by consensus, which the CFE Treaty defines to mean the absence of any objection by any representative to the CFE Treaty.

The JCG has dealt with such questions as the limits on conventional armaments and equipment in the flank zones of Europe; the distribution of costs for JCG participants, including how certain of the new independent states are to pay for reduction and conversion activities; and development of additional reduction and conversion procedures to supplement treaty provisions. Toward the end of the forty-two month equipment reduction period, it established an Implementation Working Group (IWG) to resolve outstanding implementation issues, such as destruction of equipment east of the Urals. A special IWG also developed the provisions for adapting the CFE Treaty to the changing European political landscape that were adopted in December 1996.

The CFE Treaty calls for the JCG to meet in regular sessions twice a year in Vienna, each session lasting four weeks, unless otherwise agreed. However, the JCG has been in virtually continuous session since its founding. Proceedings are confidential unless otherwise agreed, but statements by the chairman and by delegations made in plenary session, as well as final agreements, are unclassified.

THE ORGANIZATION FOR SECURITY AND COOPERATION IN EUROPE (OSCE)

OSCE Forum for Security Cooperation (FSC): The major security- and confidence-building organizations also have bodies to deal with implementation and compliance issues. The FSC was created in 1992 at the Helsinki Summit of the Conference on Security and Cooperation in Europe and its tasks were expanded in 1993 and 1994. All fifty-two members of the OSCE are members of the FSC, although Yugoslav participation was suspended during the Bosnian War. The FSC's mandate includes negotiating arms control, disarmament, and confidence- and security-building measures; enhancing regular consultation and intensified cooperation among participating nations on security matters; reducing the risk of conflict; implementing confidence- and security-building measures (CSBMs); and preparing seminars on matters of interest.

The FSC structure consists of working groups, which report to the plenary on their activities. The plenary then deliberates and adopts recommendations by consensus. Its work has focused on such matters as completion of a global military information exchange, implementing Vienna Document 1994 and other agreements, and the development of a framework for future arms control. It also has focused on improving the OSCE communications network, on nonproliferation issues and on military cooperation and contacts. It meets in Vienna.

OPEN SKIES TREATY

Open Skies Consultative Commission (OSCC): The OSCC was established by Article X of the Treaty on Open Skies in March 1992 to promote the objectives and facilitate implementation of that agreement. All twenty-seven states party to the treaty are entitled to participate in the OSCC, the chairmanship of which rotates among the member states for every session. The OSCC considers questions relating to compliance with the treaty, seeks to resolve ambiguities and differences of interpretation emerging during treaty implementation, considers and decides on applications for accession to the treaty, agrees on technical administrative procedures following accession, reviews distribution of active quotas annually, and proposes amendments to the treaty.

Any member state has the right to raise and place on the OSCC agency any issue related to the treaty. In addition, the OSCC may consider requests from bodies of the Organization for Security and Cooperation in Europe authorized to deal with conflict prevention and crisis management regarding the conduct of extraordinary observation flights. The OSCC operates through informal working groups which report to the plenary; the latter deliberates and decides by consensus. Through 1996, the OSCC has adopted twenty-two technical issues decisions, complementary and integral to the Open Skies Treaty. It meets in Vienna.

DAYTON ACCORDS

Balkan Arms Control Joint Consultative Commission (JCC) and Sub-Regional Consultative Commission (SRCC): The General Framework Agreement for Peace in Bosnia and Herzegovina (Dayton Accords) included a section of arms control. The arms control agreements subsequently negotiated created two separate bodies to oversee their implementation. The JCC created under the Agreement on Confidence- and Security-Building Measures (Article II Agreement) concluded in Vienna in January 1996 includes Bosnia and Herzegovina and its two entities the Federation of Bosnia and Herzegovina and the Republika Serbska. It meets either in Vienna or in Sarajevo or Pale. The Agreement on Subregional Arms Control (Article IV Agreement), signed in Florence, Italy, in June 1996, established the SRCC which includes in addition to the Bosnian parties, Croatia and the Federal Republic of Yugoslavia. It meets in Vienna.

Both implementing groups have met approximately monthly since their inception. They have focused on arms control inspections and reductions. The OSCE participated in both bodies, and the Contract Group of guarantor countries (the U.S., U.K., France, Germany, and Russia) provides special support to them.

Source: U.S. Arms Control and Disarmament Agency, *Threat Control Through Arms Control: Annual Report to Congress* (Washington, D.C.: ACDA, 1995 and 1996), with modifications by the author

Appendix II

Basics of the Treaties and Agreements Cited in the Text, Listed Chronologically by Date of Signature

PROTOCOL FOR THE PROHIBITION OF THE USE IN WAR OF ASPHYXIATING, POISONOUS OR OTHER GASES, AND BACTERIOLOGICAL METHODS OF WARFARE (THE GENEVA PROTOCOL)

Restates the prohibition of the 1919 Versailles and 1922 Washington treaties against the use of poisonous gases and adds a ban on bacteriological warfare. Signed June 17, 1925; entered into force February 8, 1928.

THE ANTARCTIC TREATY

Internationalizes and demilitarizes the Antarctic Continent and provides for its cooperative exploration and future use. Signed December 1, 1959; entered into force June 23, 1961.

MEMORANDUM OF UNDERSTANDING BETWEEN THE U.S.A. AND U.S.S.R. REGARDING THE ESTABLISHMENT OF A DIRECT COMMUNICATIONS LINK ("HOT LINE" AGREEMENT)

Ensures quick and reliable communications between the heads of governments of the two nuclear superpowers. Signed and entered into force June 20, 1963. Subsequent related agreements established two satellite communications circuits, with multiple terminals in each country (September 30, 1971), added a facsimile transmission capability (July 17, 1984), and upgraded facsimile capabilities (June 24, 1988).

TREATY BANNING NUCLEAR WEAPONS TESTS IN THE ATMOSPHERE, IN OUTER SPACE, AND UNDER WATER (LIMITED TEST BAN TREATY)

Parties to the treaty agree not to conduct nuclear weapons tests, or any other nuclear explosion, in the atmosphere, beyond atmospheric limits including outer space, or under water. Signed August 5, 1963; entered into force October 10, 1963.

TREATY ON THE NON-PROLIFERATION OF NUCLEAR WEAPONS (NON-PROLIFERATION TREATY)

Designed to prevent the spread of nuclear weapons, while promoting the peaceful uses of nuclear energy. Signed July 1, 1970; Extended indefinitely May 11, 1995.

AGREEMENT ON MEASURES TO REDUCE THE RISK OF OUTBREAK OF NUCLEAR WAR BETWEEN THE UNITED STATES OF AMERICA AND THE UNION OF SOVIET SOCIALIST REPUBLICS ("ACCIDENT MEASURES" AGREEMENT)

Requires cooperation to reduce the risk that an accidental or unauthorized action might trigger nuclear disaster. Signed and entered into force on September 30, 1971.

CONVENTION ON THE PROHIBITION OF THE DEVELOPMENT, PRODUCTION, AND STOCKPILING OF BACTERIOLOGICAL (BIOLOGICAL) AND TOXIN WEAPONS AND ON THEIR DESTRUCTION (BIOLOGICAL WEAPONS CONVENTION)

Establishes an agreement by the parties to the convention not to develop, produce, stockpile, or acquire biological agents or toxins "of types and in quantities that have no justification for prophylactic, protective, and other peaceful purposes," as well as related weapons and means of delivery. Signed April 10, 1972; entered into force March 26, 1975.

INTERIM AGREEMENT BETWEEN THE U.S.A. AND U.S.S.R. ON CERTAIN MEASURES WITH RESPECT TO THE LIMITATION OF STRATEGIC OFFENSIVE ARMS (SALT I INTERIM AGREEMENT)

Froze existing aggregate levels of U.S. and U.S.S.R. strategic nuclear missile launchers and submarines until an agreement on more comprehensive measures could be reached. Signed May 26, 1972; entered into force October 3, 1972. Expired October 3, 1977.

TREATY BETWEEN THE U.S.A. AND U.S.S.R. ON THE LIMITATION OF ANTI-BALLISTIC MISSILE SYSTEMS (ABM TREATY)

Provides that the two parties may each have only two ABM system deployment areas, so restricted and so located that they could not provide a nationwide ABM defense or become the basis for one. Signed May 26, 1972; entered into force October 3, 1972.

A subsequent protocol limiting each party to a single ABM system deployment area was signed July 3, 1974, and entered into force May 24, 1976.

A Memorandum of Understanding on Succession to the ABM Treaty and four related agreements were signed September 26, 1997 to resolve questions of succession to the treaty by states of the former Soviet Union and clarify the demarcation between anti-ballistic missile (ABM) systems, which are limited by the treaty, and theater missile defense (TMD) systems, which are not limited by the treaty.

TREATY BETWEEN THE U.S.A. AND U.S.S.R. ON THE LIMITATION OF UNDERGROUND NUCLEAR WEAPONS TESTS (THRESHOLD TEST BAN TREATY)

Prohibits underground nuclear weapons tests of more than 150 kilotons. Signed July 3, 1974; entered into force December 11, 1990, after changes in the verification structure.
A subsequent Protocol providing for additional verification provisions was signed on June 1, 1990 and entered into force on December 11, 1990.

CONCLUDING DOCUMENT OF THE CONFERENCE ON SECURITY AND COOPERATION IN EUROPE (CSCE) (HELSINKI FINAL ACT)

Establishes an agreement among the United States, Soviet Union, and thirty-three other nations to provide notification of major military maneuvers involving more than 25,000 troops, and other confidence-building measures. Signed and entered into force August 1, 1975.

TREATY BETWEEN THE U.S.A. AND U.S.S.R. ON UNDERGROUND NUCLEAR EXPLOSIONS FOR PEACEFUL PURPOSES (PNE TREATY)

Governs all underground nuclear explosions carried out at locations outside U.S. and Soviet weapon test sites specified under the Threshold Test Ban Treaty and limits any individual nuclear explosion to 150 kilotons. Signed May 28, 1976; entered into force December 11, 1990, after changes in the verification structure.

A subsequent protocol providing for additional verification provisions was signed June 1, 1990 and entered into force December 11, 1990.

TREATY BETWEEN THE U.S.A. AND U.S.S.R. ON THE LIMITATION OF STRATEGIC OFFENSIVE ARMS (SALT II TREATY)

Replaces the SALT I Interim Agreement (which expired in October 1977) with an agreement lasting through 1985, having broader scope and more detailed constraints on U.S. and Soviet strategic offensive arms. Signed June 18, 1979; but never ratified.

DOCUMENT OF THE STOCKHOLM CONFERENCE ON CONFIDENCE-AND SECURITY-BUILDING MEASURES AND DISARMAMENT IN EUROPE (STOCKHOLM DOCUMENT)

Contains a set of six concrete and mutually complementary confidence- and security-building measures, including mandatory ground or aerial inspection of military activities that improve upon those contained in the Helsinki Final Act. Adopted September 19, 1986; entered into force January 1, 1987.

AGREEMENT BETWEEN THE U.S.A. AND U.S.S.R. ON THE ESTABLISHMENT OF NUCLEAR RISK REDUCTION CENTERS

Establishes a Nuclear Risk Reduction Center in each nation's capital as well as a special facsimile communications between the centers to reduce the risk of nuclear war. Signed and entered into force September 15, 1987.

TREATY BETWEEN THE U.S.A. AND U.S.S.R. ON THE ELIMINATION OF THEIR INTERMEDIATE-RANGE AND SHORTER-RANGE MISSILES (INF TREATY)

Establishes an agreement between the United States and Soviet Union to eliminate and ban all ground-launched ballistic and cruise missiles with a range capability between 300 and 3,400 miles (500 and 5,500 kilometers). Signed December 8, 1987; entered into force June 1, 1988.

AGREED STATEMENT BETWEEN THE GOVERNMENT OF THE UNITED STATES AND THE UNION OF SOVIET SOCIALIST REPUBLICS

Establishes rules concerning the application of inspection procedures at the U.S. continuous monitoring inspection site at Votkinsk, Russia. Signed and entered into force December 8, 1988.

A second statement establishes rules concerning application of inspection procedures at the Soviet continuous monitoring inspection site at Magna, Utah. Signed and entered into force June 9, 1989.

WYOMING MEMORANDUM OF UNDERSTANDING

Provides for a two-phased chemical weapons data exchange and verification experiment between the U.S.A. and U.S.S.R. Signed and entered into force September 23, 1989.

MEMORANDUM OF AGREEMENT BETWEEN THE GOVERNMENTS OF THE U.S.A. AND U.S.S.R. REGARDING THE IMPLEMENTATION OF THE VERIFICATION PROVISIONS OF THE TREATY ON THE ELIMINATION OF THEIR INTERMEDIATE-RANGE AND SHORTER-RANGE MISSILES

Contains implementation arrangements, lists of inspection equipment, and procedures for its use. Signed and entered into force December 21, 1989.

A series of subsequent amendments:

Contains a technical description of the system for measuring the length and diameter of the second stage of the SS-25 missile and procedures for its use. Signed and entered into force April 4, 1991.

Permits INF inspectors to use dosimeters during inspections for personal health monitoring. Signed and entered into force April 4, 1991.

Establishes principles and procedures for settlement of INF expenses related to the conduct of inspections, and establishes procedures for updating diplomatic clearance numbers and flight routes for INF aircraft. Signed and entered into force December 11, 1991.

U.S.–U.S.S.R. CHEMICAL WEAPONS DESTRUCTION AGREEMENT

Calls for the destruction of the vast bulk of the U.S. and Soviet declared chemical weapons stockpiles, with on-site inspection to determine that destruction has taken place. Signed June 1, 1990; has not yet entered into force.

TREATY ON CONVENTIONAL ARMED FORCES IN EUROPE (CFE TREATY)

Reduces and sets ceilings from the Atlantic to the Urals on key armaments essential for conducting surprise attack and initiating large-scale offensive weapons. Signed by the thirty-four NATO and Warsaw Pact states on November 19, 1990; applied provisionally July 17, 1992. Entered into force November 8, 1992.

Several related documents take account of subsequent international events:

The *Tashkent Agreement* apportions the CFE Treaty military obligations and entitlements among the successor states of the Soviet Union within the treaty's area of application: Russia, Ukraine, Belarus, Armenia, Azerbaijan, Georgia, Moldova, and Kazakstan. Signed and entered into force on May 15, 1992.

The *Final Document of the* Extraordinary Conference *of the States Parties to the Treaty on Conventional Armed Force (Oslo Final Document)* enables implementation of the agreement in the new international situation. It notes the May 15, 1992, agreement in Tashkent among the states successor of the U.S.S.R. on the principles and procedures for implementing the CFE Treaty. Signed and entered into force June 5, 1992.

The *Concluding Act of the Negotiations on* Personnel *Strength of Conventional Armed Forces in Europe (CFE 1A)* contains CFE member states declarations of national limits on the personnel strength of their conventional forces in the Atlantic to Urals region. Signed July 10, 1992; entered into force July 17, 1992.

VIENNA DOCUMENTS (1990, 1992 AND 1994) OF THE NEGOTIATIONS ON CONFIDENCE- AND SECURITY- BUILDING MEASURES CONVENED IN ACCORDANCE WITH THE RELEVANT PROVISIONS OF THE CONCLUDING DOCUMENT OF THE VIENNA MEETING OF THE CONFERENCE ON SECURITY AND COOPERATION IN EUROPE

Document 1990 incorporates the Stockholm Document of 1986. Adds measures related to transparency about military forces and activities, improved communications and contacts, and verification. Adopted November 17, 1990; entered into force January 1, 1991.

Document 1992 incorporates the Vienna Document 1990. Adds further measures related to transparency regarding military forces and activities and constraints on military activities. Expands the zone of application for confidence- and security-building measures (CSBMs) to include the territory of the U.S.S.R. successor states that were beyond the traditional zone in Europe, that is, all of Kazakhstan, Kyrgyzstan, Tajikistan, Turkmenistan, and Uzbekistan. Adopted March 4, 1992; entered into force May 1, 1992.

Document 1994 incorporates the Vienna Document 1992 and adds provisions for defense planning and strengthens several existing CSBMs, allowing member states to monitor each other's military force structure, and activities. Entered into force January 1, 1995.

TREATY BETWEEN THE U.S.A. AND U.S.S.R. ON THE REDUCTION AND LIMITATION OF STRATEGIC OFFENSIVE ARMS (START I)

Establishes significantly reduced limits for intercontinental ballistic missiles and their associated launchers and warheads; submarine launched ballistic missile launchers and warheads; and heavy bombers and their armaments, including long-range nuclear air-launched cruise missiles. Overall deployed strategic missiles will be reduced by 30 to 40 percent, with a reduction of as much as 50 percent in the most threatening systems, a total of over 9000 warheads. Signed July 31, 1991; entered into force December 5, 1994.

A subsequent protocol (Lisbon START Protocol), constituting an amendment to, and integral part of, the START Treaty, provides for Belarus, Kazakhstan, Russia, and Ukraine to succeed to the Soviet Union's obligations under the treaty. In the protocol, Belarus,

Kazakstan, and Ukraine acceded to the Nuclear Nonproliferation Treaty and, in accompanying letters, committed themselves to eliminate all nuclear weapons from their territory within seven years. This was accomplished when Belarus completed removal of all nuclear warheads from its territory on November 27, 1996. Lisbon Protocol signed May 23, 1992; ratified by the U.S. Senate October 1, 1992.

TREATY ON OPEN SKIES

Commits twenty-seven member nations in Eurasia and North America to open their airspace on a reciprocal basis, permitting the overflights of their territory by unarmed observation aircraft in order to strengthen confidence and transparency with respect to their military activities. Signed and applied provisionally March 24, 1992; ratified by the United States November 2, 1993; has not yet entered into force.

CONVENTION ON THE PROHIBITION OF THE DEVELOPMENT, PRODUCTION, STOCKPILING, AND USE OF CHEMICAL WEAPONS AND ON THEIR DESTRUCTION (CHEMICAL WEAPONS CONVENTION)

Establishes a global ban on the production, acquisition, stockpiling, transfer, and use of chemical weapons. Drafted by the U.N. Conference on Disarmament; forwarded to the United Nations on September 7, 1992; endorsed by consensus, with 145 sponsors, on November 30, 1992; entered into force on April 29, 1997, without U.S. ratification. Subsequently ratified by the U.S. Senate.

JOINT TRILATERAL STATEMENT ON BIOLOGICAL WEAPONS

Statement on agreed activities between the governments of the United States, United Kingdom, and the Russian Federation to address concerns with regard to Russian compliance with the 1972 Biological Weapons Convention. Signed September 14, 1992.

TREATY BETWEEN THE U.S.A. AND THE RUSSIAN FEDERATION ON FURTHER REDUCTION AND LIMITATION OF STRATEGIC ARMS (START II)

Calls for the signatories further to reduce strategic offensive arms by eliminating all intercontinental ballistic missiles (ICBMs) with multiple independently targeted re-entry vehicles (including all "heavy" ICBMs) and reducing the overall total of warheads for each side to between 3,000 and 3,500. Signed January 3, 1993; ratified by the U.S. Senate January 2, 1996. Will enter into force following ratification by Russia.

GENERAL FRAMEWORK AGREEMENT FOR PEACE IN BOSNIA AND HERZEGOVINA (DAYTON ACCORDS)

Seeks to bring about peace and long-term stability to the region through a three step approach: (1) a confidence-building agreement among the parties of Bosnia and Herzegovina; (2) an arms reduction agreement among the parties of Bosnia and Herzegovina, Croatia and the Federal Republic of Yugoslavia; and (3) a regional arms control regime including states neighboring the former Yugoslavia. Initialed in Dayton, Ohio, on November 21, 1995 and signed in Paris on December 14, 1995.

Subsequent agreements include:

The *Agreement on Confidence- and* Security-Building *Measures in Bosnia and Herzegovina* signed in Vienna on January 21, 1996, adding new measures to support the military cease fire agreement and providing for inspections of military forces and monitoring of weapons manufacturing capabilities.

The *Agreement on* Sub-*Regional* Arms *Control* signed in Florence, Italy on June 14, 1996, establishing ceilings on weapons requiring reductions by all parties to be completed by November 1997.

THE COMPREHENSIVE TEST BAN TREATY (CTBT)

Bans all nuclear weapons test explosions and all other nuclear explosions. Adopted by the United Nations General Assembly on September 10, 1996; opened for signature and signed by the United States on September 24, 1996. Will enter into force when forty-four states that were members of the U.N. Conference on Disarmament as of June 18, 1996 and have nuclear research or power reactors deposit their instruments of ratification; but no earlier than September 24, 1998. As of fall 1997, three of the forty-four necessary states (India, Pakistan and North Korea) have not signed the CTBT.

FISSILE MATERIAL CUTOFF TREATY (FMCT)

Proposes a ban on the production of fissile materials for use in nuclear explosives or outside of international safeguards. Negotiating mandate and establishment of Ad Hoc Committee agreed in Conference on Disarmament in March 1995; however beginning of negotiations has been linked to beginning of movement on other nuclear issues.

CONVENTION ON THE USE, STOCKPILING, PRODUCTION AND TRANSFER OF ANTI-PERSONNEL MINES AND ON THEIR DESTRUCTION (OTTAWA TREATY)

Obligates each state-party to eliminate anti-personnel landmines and to destroy their stockpiles and all such landmines in mined areas. Signed in Ottawa on December 4, 1997 and could enter into force in mid-to-late 1998. Treaty lacks extensive implementation, verification and compliance provisions and was not signed by several major powers, including the United States, Russia and China as well as a number of states in regions of tension, such as the Middle East and South Asia.

Source: United States Arms Control and Disarmament Agency, *Threat Control Through Arms Control: Annual Report to Congress* (Washington, D.C.: ACDA, 1995 and 1996), with modifications by the author

Selected Bibliography

Books

Altmann, Jurgen, and Joseph Rotblat, eds. *Verification of Arms Reductions: Nuclear, Conventional and Chemical*. Berlin: Springer-Verlag, 1989.

Arms Control Association. *Arms Control and National Security: An Introduction*. Washington, D.C.: Arms Control Association, 1989.

Arnett, Eric H. *Implementing the Comprehensive Test Ban: New Aspects of Definition, Organization and Verification*. New York: Oxford University Press for Stockholm International Peace Research Institute, 1994.

Arnett, Eric H., ed. *New Technologies for Security and Arms Control: Threats and Promise*. Washington, D.C.: American Association for the Advancement of Science, 1989.

Aronowitz, Dennis S. *Legal Aspects of Arms Control Verification in the United States*. Columbia Arms Control Verification Study; Dobbs Ferry, NY: Oceana Publications, 1965.

Bailey, Kathleen. *Strengthening Nuclear Non-Proliferation*. Boulder, CO: Westview Press, 1993.

———. *The UN Inspections in Iraq: Lessons for On-Site Verification*. Boulder, CO: Westview Press, 1995.

Barnaby, Frank, ed. *A Handbook of Verification Procedures*. New York: St. Martin's Press, 1990.

Berkowitz, Bruce D. *Calculated Risks: A Century of Arms Control, Why It Has Failed, and How It Can Be Made to Work*. New York: Simon and Schuster, 1987.

Boutilier, James A., ed. *Arms Control in the North Pacific: The Role for Confidence Building and Verification*. Ottawa, Canada: Non-Proliferation, Arms Control and Disarmament Division, Department of Foreign Affairs and International Trade, 1994.

Boutros-Ghali, Boutros. *New Dimensions of Arms Regulation and Disarmament in the Post-Cold War Era*. New York: U.N. Department of Political Affairs, 1993.

Brown, James, ed. *New Horizons and Challenges in Arms Control and Verification*. Amsterdam: VU University Press, 1994.

Bunn, Matthew. *Foundation for the Future*. Washington, D.C.: Arms Control Association, 1990.

Burrows, William. *Deep Black: Space Espionage and National Security*. New York: Random House, 1986.

Calogero, Francesco, Marvin L. Goldberger, and Sergei P. Kapitza, eds. *Verification: Monitoring Disarmament*. Boulder, CO: Westview Press, 1991.

Carter, April. *Success and Failure in Arms Control Negotiations*. Oxford: Oxford University Press, 1989.

Dahlitz, Julie, ed. *Avoidance and Settlement of Arms Control Disputes*. New York: United Nations Publications, 1994.

Dando, Malcolm. *Biological Warfare in the 21st Century: Biotechnology and the Proliferation of Biological Weapons*. New York: Brassey's, 1994.

Dorn, A. Walter. *The Case for a United Nations Verification Agency: Disarmament under Effective International Control*. Ottawa, Canada: Canadian Institute for International Peace and Security, 1990.

Dunn, Lewis A., and Amy E. Gordon, eds. *Arms Control Verification and the New Role of On-Site Inspection*. Lexington, MA: Lexington Books, 1990.

Feldman, Shai, ed. *Confidence Building and Verification: Prospects in the Middle East*. Boulder, CO: Westview Press, 1994.

Fischer, D., and P. Szasz. *Safeguarding the Atom: A Critical Appraisal*. London: Taylor and Francis, 1985.

Gardner, Gary T. *Nuclear Non-Proliferation: A Primer*. Boulder, CO: Lynne Reimer Publications, 1994.

Garwin, Richard L. *Richard Garwin on Arms Control*. Lanham, MD: University Press of America, 1989.

Haass, Richard. *Beyond the INF Treaty*. Cambridge, MA: Center for Science and International Affairs, 1988.

Hampson, Fen Osler, Harald von Riekhoff, and John Roper, eds. *The Allies and Arms Control*. Baltimore, MD: Johns Hopkins University Press, 1992.

Harahan, Joseph P. *On-Site Inspections under the INF Treaty*. Washington, D.C.: U.S. Government Printing Office, 1993.

Harahan, Joseph P., and John C. Kuhn III. *On-Site Inspection under the CFE Treaty*. Washington, D.C.: U.S. On-Site Inspection Agency, U.S. Department of Defense, 1996.

Holloway, David. *The Soviet Union and the Arms Race*. New Haven, CT: Yale University Press, 1983.

Hume, Cameron R. *The United Nations, Iran and Iraq: How Peacemaking Changed*. Bloomington, IN: Indiana University Press, 1994.

Kelly, Peter. *Safeguards in Europe*. Vienna: International Atomic Energy Agency, 1985.

Kirk, E. J., ed. *Technology, Security and Arms Control for the 1990s*. Washington, D.C.: Program on Science, Arms Control and National Security, American Association for the Advancement of Science, 1988.

Kokeyev, Mikhail, and Andrei Androsov. *Verification: The Soviet Stance—Its Past, Present and Future*. Geneva: United Nations Institute for Disarmament Research, 1990.

Kokoski, Richard, and Sergey Koulik, eds. *Verification of Conventional Arms Control in Europe: Technological Constraints and Opportunities.* Boulder, CO: Westview Press, 1990.

Krass, Alan. *Verification—How Much Is Enough?* London: Stockholm International Peace Research Institute; Taylor and Francis, 1985.

Krepon, Michael. *Arms Control Verification and Compliance.* New York: Foreign Policy Association, 1984.

———. *The Politics of Arms Control Ratification.* New York: St. Martin's Press, 1991.

———. *The Politics of Verification.* 2d Ed. Washington, D.C.: The Henry L. Stimson Center, 1991.

Krepon, Michael, and Mary Amberger, eds. *Verification and Compliance: A Problem Solving Approach.* London: Macmillan, 1988.

Krepon, Michael, and Amy E. Smithson, ed. *Open Skies, Arms Control and Cooperative Security.* New York: St. Martin's Press, 1992.

Krepon, Michael, P.D. Zimmerman, L.S. Spector and M. Umberger eds. *Commercial Observation Satellites and International Security.* New York: St. Martin's Press 1990.

Mataija, S., and L. C. Bourquet, eds. *Proliferation and International Security: Converging Roles of Verification, Confidence Building and Peacekeeping.* Toronto: Center for International and Strategic Studies, York University, 1993.

Morel, Benoit, and Kyle Olson, eds. *Shadows and Substance: The Chemical Weapons Convention.* Boulder, CO: Westview Press, 1993.

Morris, Ellis. *The Verification Issue in United Nations Disarmament Negotiations.* New York: United Nations Institute for Disarmament Research, 1987.

Mutimer, David, ed. *Control But Verify: Verification and the New Non-Proliferation Agenda.* Toronto: Center for International and Strategic Studies, Yale University, 1994.

Panofsky, Wolfgang Kurt Heremann. *Arms Control and SALT II.* Seattle, WA: University of Washington Press, 1979.

Platt, Alan, ed. *Arms Control and Confidence Building in the Middle East.* Washington, D.C.: U.S. Institute of Peace, 1992

Poole, J. B., and R. Guthrie, eds. *Verification 1995: Arms Control, Peacekeeping and the Environment.* Boulder, CO: Verification Technology Information Center and Westview Press, 1995.

Potter, William C., ed. *Verification and Arms Control.* Lexington, MA: Lexington Books, 1985.

Richelson, Jeffrey. *America's Secret Eyes in Space: The U.S. Keyhole Satellite Program.* Toronto: Harper and Row, 1990.

Roberts, Brad, ed. *Ratifying the Chemical Weapons Convention.* Washington, D.C.: Center for Strategic and International Studies, 1994.

Rowell, William, F. *Arms Control Verification: A Guide to Policy Issues for the 1980s.* Cambridge, MA: Ballinger, 1986.

Rueckert, George. *Global Double Zero: The INF Treaty from Its Origins to Implementation.* Westport, CT: Greenwood Press, 1993.

Scheinman, Larry. *The International Atomic Energy Agency and World Nuclear Order.* Washington, D.C.: Resources for the Future, 1987.

Schrag, Philip. *Listening for the Bomb: A Study in Nuclear Arms Control Verification Policy.* Boulder, CO: Westview Press, 1989.

Scribner, Richard A., Theodore J. Ralston, and William D. Mertz. *The Verification Challenge: Problems and Promise of Strategic Nuclear Arms Control Verification.* Boston: Birkhauser, 1985.

Scrivener, David, and Michael Sheehan. *Bibliography of Arms Control Verification.* Brookfield, VT: Gower Publishing Co., 1990.

Sharp, Jane, "Conventional Arms Control in Europe: Problems and Prospects." In *SIPRI Yearbook 1988.* Oxford University Press, pp. 315-337.

SIPRI Yearbooks: *World Armaments and Disarmament.* Stockholm: International Institute for Peace Research, (Annual).

Slack, M., and H. Chestnut, eds. *Open Skies: Operational, Legal and Political Aspects.* Toronto: York University Centre for International and Strategic Studies, 1990.

Spiers, Edward. *Chemical and Biological Weapons: A Study of Proliferation.* New York: St. Martin's Press, 1995.

Talbot, Strobe. *Deadly Gambits: The Reagan Administration and the Stalemate in Nuclear Arms Control.* New York: Alfred A. Knopf, 1984.

Timerbayev, Roland. *Problems of Verification.* Moscow: General Editorial Board for Foreign Publications, Nauka, 1984.

Tower, John G., James Brown, and William K. Cheek, eds. *Verification: The Key to Arms Control in the 1990s.* Washington, D.C.: Brassey's, 1992.

Trapp, Rolf. *Verification under the Chemical Weapons Convention: On-Site Inspection in Chemical Industry Facilities.* New York: Oxford University Press for SIPRI, 1993.

Tsipis, Kosta, David W. Hafemeister, and Penny Janeway, eds. *Arms Control Verification: The Technologies that Made It Possible.* Washington, D.C.: Pergamon-Brassey's, 1986.

Wander, W., E .J. Kirk, and E. H. Arnett, eds. *Science and Security: Technology and Arms Control for the 1990s.* Washington, D.C.: Program on Science, Arms Control and National Security, American Association for the Advancement of Science, 1989.

Articles, Chapters, and Speeches

Adelman, Kenneth. "Verification in an Age of Mobile Missiles." *Department of State Bulletin 87* (September 1987): 27.

Batsanov, Sergei. "Practical Aspects Concerning the Implementation of the Convention Prohibiting Chemical Weapons." *Disarmament.* XVI, no. 3 (1993): 123–140.

Biden, Joseph R., Jr., and John B. Ritch, III. "The Treaty Power: Upholding a Constitutional Partnership." *University of Pennsylvania Law Review* (May 1989): 1529–1557.

Blix, Hans. "Verification of Nuclear Non-Proliferation: the Lessons of Iraq." *The Washington Quarterly* (Autumn 1992): 57–65.

Chauvistre, Eric. "The Future of Nuclear Inspections." *Arms Control* (August 1993): 23–64.

Colby, William. "The Intelligence Process." In *Arms Control Verification: The Technologies that Make It Possible,* ed. Kosta Tsipis, Dave Hafemeister, and Penny Janeway. Washington, D.C.: Pergamon-Brassey's, 1986.

"CTB Treaty Executive Summary." *Arms Control Today* (August 1996): 17-18.

Culpepper, Michael. "Audits and Examinations: Keeping the Other Guy Honest." *On-Site Insights* (February 1996): 10-11.

Downey, Tim. "Cooperative Threat Reduction: Agency Plays Important Role." *On-Site Insights* (July 1996): pp. 1, 4-6.

Dunn, Lewis. "Arms Control Verification: Living with Uncertainty." *International Security* (Spring 1990): 14, 4.

Earl, Ralph. "Verification Issues from the Point of View of the Negotiator." In *Arms Control Verification: The Technologies that Make It Possible*, ed. Kosta Tsipis, Dave Hafemeister, and Penny Janeway. Washington, D.C.: Pergamon-Brassey's, 1986.

Ekeus, Rolf and Ann B. Florini. "The Opening Skies: Third-Party Imaging Satellites and US Security." *International Security* (Fall 1988): 91–123.

Goldman, Ira. "NPT Verification and Enforcement: Problems and Prospects." In *New Horizons and Challenges in Arms Control and Verification*, ed. James Brown. Amsterdam: VU University Press, 1994.

Harahan, Joseph. "Comparative history of Arms Control from World War I, World War II, and the Cold War." *Militaire Spectator*, no. 7 (July 1994): 285-294.

———. "Great Britain's Joint Arms Control Implementation Group—JACIG." *On-Site Insights* (August 1996): 8-10.

———. "New Director Inherits Agency with a Brief History, But a Proud One." *On-Site Insights* (August 1995): 6-8.

———. "The Belarus Republic Agency for Control and Inspection." *On-Site Insights* (September 1995): 8-9.

———. "The Kazakstan Center for Monitoring Arms Reductions and Supporting Inspection Activities." *On-Site Insights* (June 1996): 6-7.

———. "The Russian Federation's Nuclear Risk Reduction Center." *On-Site Insights* (November/December 1995): 12-13.

———. "Verification Center of the Armed Forces of Ukraine." *On-Site Insights* (February 1996): pp. 4,28.

Hirschfeld, Thomas J. "The Toughest Verification Challenge: Conventional Forces in Europe." *Arms Control Today* (March 1989): 16–21.

Holum, John. *Remarks to the Congressional Research Service Seminar on the Future of Arms Control*. Washington, D.C.: U.S. Arms Control and Disarmament Agency, Office of Public Affairs, January 9, 1997.

Hooper, Richard. "Strengthening IAEA Safeguards in an Era of Nuclear Cooperation." *Arms Control Today* (November 1995): 14-18.

Hough, Jeffrey F. "Soviet Arms Control Policy in Perspective." *Brookings Review* (Winter 1988): 39–45.

Hyland, William G. "Soviet Theater Forces and Arms Control Policy." *Survival* 23, no. 5 (September/October 1981): 194–199.

Ifft, Edward. "The Use of On-Site Inspections in the Avoidance and Settlement of Arms Control Disputes." In *Avoidance and Settlement of Arms Control Disputes*, ed. Julie Dahlitz. New York: United Nations, 1994.

Jones, David. "Redefining Security, Expanding Arms Control." *Arms Control Today* (October 1990): 3–7.

Jones, Christopher. "The Soviet View of INF." *Arms Control Today* vol 12, no. 3 (March 1982): 4–8.

Keeny, Spurgeon, M., Jr. "The On-Site Inspection Legacy." *Arms Control Today* no. 9 (November 1988): 18.

Koplow, David. "The Law of On-Site Inspection: Arms Control Verification and the Fourth Amendment." In *Arms Control Verification and the New Role of On-Site Inspection*, ed. Lewis Dunn and Amy Gordon. Lexington, MA: Lexington Books, 1990.

Krass, Allen S.   "The Politics of Verification." *World Policy Journal* 2 no.4 (Fall 1985): 731–752.

Krepon, Michael. "The Politics of Treaty Verification and Compliance." In *Arms Control Verification: The Technologies that Make It Possible*, ed. Kosta Tsipis, Dave Hafemeister, and Penny Janeway. Washington, D.C.: Pergamon-Brassey's, 1986.

Lacey, Edward. "A United States Perspective on Bilateral Verification." *Disarmament* 14, no. 2 (1991).

————. "Arms Control and Antarctica: On-Site Inspections on the Frozen Continent." In *New Horizons and Challenges in Arms Control and Verification*, ed. James Brown. Amsterdam: VU University Press, 1994.

McFate, Patricia Bliss, and Sidney N. Graybeal. "The Price for Effective Verification in an Era of Expanding Arms Control." *Annals of the American Academy of Political and Social Science* (November 1988): 73.

Monohan, Bill. "Giving the Non-Proliferation Treaty Teeth: Strengthening the Special Inspection Procedures of the International Atomic Energy Agency." *Virginia Journal of International Law* (Fall 1993): 161–196.

Morocco, John D. "Verification Raises Cost, Technology Concerns." *Aviation Week and Space Technology* 133, no. 6 (August 1990): 44.

Mendelsohn, Jack. "INF Verification: A Guide for the Perplexed." *Arms Control Today* (September 1987): 25–29.

Myer, Stephen M. "Verification and Risk in Arms Control." *International Security* (Spring 1984): 111–126.

Nolan, Janne E. "The Politics of On-Site Verification." *Brookings Review* (Fall 1988): 15–22.

Pearson, Graham S. "Forging an Effective Biological Weapons Regime." *Arms Control Today* (June 1994): 14–17.

Pell, Claiburne, "The Post-Cold War Era: Has Arms Control a Significant Future?" *The Brown Journal of World Affairs* (Spring 1994): 30–40.

Rueckert, George. "Managing On-Site Inspections: Initial Experience and Future Challenges." In *Verification: The Key to Arms Control in the 1990s*, ed. John Tower, James Brown, and William Cheek. Washington, D.C.: Brassey's, 1992.

Seaborg, Glenn T. and Benjamin S. Loeb. "Approaching a Comprehensive Test Ban: A United States Historical Perspective." *Disarmament* 165, no. 3, 1993: 35–56.

Simes, Dimitri. "Are the Soviets Interested in Arms Control?" *Washington Quarterly* 8, no. 2 (Spring 1985): 147–157.

Smithson, Amy E. "Implementing the Chemical Weapons Convention." *Survival* (Spring 1994): 80–95.

Stovall, Don O. "A Participant's View of On-Site Inspections." *Parameters: US Army War College Quarterly* (June 1989): 2–17.

————. "The Stockholm Accord: On-Site Inspections in Eastern and Western Europe." In *Arms Control Verification and the New Role of On-Site Inspection*, ed. Lewis Dunn and Amy Gordon. Lexington, MA: Lexington Books, 1990.

Sutherland, R. G. "The Chemical Weapons Convention: the Problems of Implementation." *Peace Research* (February 1994): 7–12.

Tanzman, Edward and Barry Kellman. "Legal Implications of the Multilateral Chemical Weapons Convention: Integrating International Security with the Constitution." *New York University Journal of International Law and Politics*, vol. 22, no. 3 (1990): 475–518.

Trevan, Tim, "UNSCOM Faces Entirely New Verification Challenges in Iraq." *Arms Control Today* (April 1993): 11–15.

———. "Ongoing Monitoring and Verification in Iraq." *Arms Control Today* (May 1994): 11–15.

Tucker, Jonathan. "Dilemmas of a Dual-Use Technology: Toxins in Medicine and Warfare." *Political and Life Sciences* (February 1994): 51–62.

———. "Lessons of Iraq's Biological Weapons Programme." *Arms Control: Contemporary Security Policy* (December 1993): 229–271.

———. "Monitoring and Verification in a Noncooperative Environment: Lessons from the U.N. Experience in Iraq." *Nonproliferation Review* (Spring-Summer 1996): 1–9.

Ziffero, Maurizio. "Iraq and UN Security Council Resolution 687: The Role of the IAEA and Lessons to be Learned." In *New Horizons and Challenges in Arms Control and Verification*, ed. James Brown. Amsterdam: VU University Press, 1994.

Papers and Monographs

Banner, Allen V. *Overhead Imaging for Verification and Peacekeeping*. Ottawa: three studies prepared for the Arms Control and Disarmament Division, External Affairs and International Trade Canada, 1991.

Bibliography on Arms Control. Third Update. Ottawa, Canada: Department of International Affairs and Foreign Trade, Non-Proliferation, Arms Control and Disarmament Division, October 1994.

Bunn, George, and Roland M. Timerbaev. *Nuclear Verification under the NPT: What Should It Cover—How Far Should It Go?* Southampton, U.K.: Mountbatten Center for International Studies; Program for Promoting Nuclear Non-Proliferation, April 1994.

Carnegie Panel on US Security and the future of Arms Control. *Challenges for U.S. National Security: The Soviet Approach to Arms Control Verification, Problems and Prospects, Conclusions*. Washington, D.C.: Carnegie Endowment for International Peace, 1983.

Corduneaunu, Nicolae. *Main Lessons Learned from the Implementation of the CFE Treaty and the CFE 1-A Final Act*. Paper presented at U.S. Defense Nuclear Agency, Fifth International Conference on Controlling Arms, Norfolk, Virginia, June 1996.

Graybeal, Sidney, and Patricia McFate. *Verification to the Year 2000*. Ottawa, Canada: Arms Control and Disarmament Division, External Affairs and International Trade, 1991.

Hamburg, Eric. *Arms Control Verification and the U.S. Constitution: A Working Paper for the Center for International Security and Arms Control*. Stanford, CA: Stanford University Press, 1989.

Kellman, Barry, and Edward Tanzman. *Implementing the Chemical Weapons Convention: Legal Issues*. Washington D.C.: Lawyers Alliance for World Security and the Committee for National Security, July 1994.

Krazter, Myron B. *International Nuclear Safeguards: Promise and Performance*. Occasional Paper Series. Washington D.C.: The Atlantic Council, April 1994.

Lindsey, George. and Alex Morrison. *Verifying Limitations on Military Manpower*. Ottawa, Canada: Arms Control and Disarmament Division, External Affairs and International Trade, 1991.

Mataija, S., and J. Marshall Beier, eds. *Multilateral Verification and the Post-Gulf War Environment: Learning from the UNSCOM Experience*. Symposium Proceedings. Toronto: Center for International and Strategic Studies, York University, Toronto, Canada, 1992.

McFate, Patricia Bliss, et al. *The Converging Roles of Arms Control Verification, Confidence Building Measures and Peace Operations: Opportunity for Harmonization and Synergies*. Ottawa, Canada: Non-Proliferation, Arms Control and Disarmament Division, Department of Foreign Affairs and International Trade, 1994.

Moore, James. *Conventional Arms Control and Disarmament in Europe: A Model of Verification System Effectiveness*. Ottawa, Canada: Arms Control and Disarmament Division, External Affairs and International Trade, 1990.

Nedimoglu, Necil. *Lessons Learned from Coordinating Conventional Arms Control Implementation and Verification*. Paper presented at Defense Nuclear Agency, Fourth International Conference on Controlling Arms, Philadelphia, Pennsylvania, June 1995.

Rauf, Tarig, ed. *Strengthening IAEA Safeguards and Regional Non-Proliferation Strategies*. Aurora Paper 23. Ottawa, Canada: Canadian Center for Global Security, 1994.

Schiefer, H. B. and J. F. Keeley, eds. *International Atomic Energy Agency Safeguards as a Model for Verification of a Chemical Weapons Convention*. Arms Control Verification Occasional Paper no. 3. Ottawa, Canada: Arms Control and Disarmament Division, External Affairs and International Trade, 1989.

Shearer, Richard L. Jr. *On-Site Inspection for Arms Control: Breaking the Verification Barrier*. Washington, D.C.: National Defense University, 1988.

Thompson, David B. *The Strategic Arms Reduction Treaty and Its Verification*. Los Alamos, NM: Center for National Security Studies, Los Alamos National Laboratory, 1992.

Woolf, Amy. *On-Site Inspections in Arms Control: Verifying Compliance with INF and START*. Washington, D.C.: Congressional Research Service, November 1, 1989.

U.S. Government Publications

Congressional Research Service. *Verifying Arms Control Agreements: The Soviet View*. Washington, D.C.: U.S. Government Printing Office, 1987.

United Nations. *United Nations Focus: UNSCOM*. U.N. Information Pamphlet on the United Nations Special Commission. New York: U.N. Secretariat. No date.

U.S. Arms Control and Disarmament Agency. *Chemical Weapons Convention Update for Industry*. Washington D.C.: ACDA Public Affairs, June 1994.

———. *Arms Control and Disarmament Agreements: Texts and Histories of the Negotiations*. Sixth Edition. Washington, D.C.: ACDA Public Affairs, 1990.

————. "Tripartite Report to the Committee on Disarmament: Comprehensive Test Ban. July 30, 1980. *Documents on Disarmament*. Washington, D.C.: ACDA, 1980: 317-320.

————. *Threat Control Through Arms Control: Annual Report to Congress*. Washington, D.C., ACDA, Annual Report 1992-present.

————. *Understanding the INF Treaty*. Washington, D.C.: ADCA Public Affairs, 1988.

U.S. Congress, Office of Technology Assessment. *Seismic Verification of Nuclear Testing Treaties*. OTA-ISC-361, Washington, D.C.: U.S. Government Printing Office, May 1988.

————. *The Chemical Weapons Convention: Effects on the U.S. Chemical Industry*. Washington, D.C.: U.S. Government Printing Office, 1994.

————. *Verification Technologies for Monitoring Compliance with the START Treaty*. Washington, D.C: U.S. Government Printing Office, 1990.

U.S. Department of State. "Article by Article Analysis of the Treaty Text." In *Treaty with the Union of Soviet Socialist Republics on the Reduction and Limitation of Strategic Offensive Arms, Treaty Document 102-20*. Washington, D.C.: U.S. Government Printing Office, 1991.

————. *Report to Congress on Soviet Noncompliance with Arms Control Agreements*. Washington, D.C.: U.S. Department of State. Annual Report, 1988-1991.

U.S. House of Representatives, Committee on Foreign Relations. *Report, Together with Additional Views, on the CFE Treaty*. Executive Report 102-22. Washington, D.C.: U.S. Government Printing Office, November 1991.

————. *Verifying Arms Control Agreements: The Soviet View*. Report Prepared for the Subcommittee on Arms Control, International Security and Science. Washington, D.C.: U.S. Government Printing Office, 1987.

Index

About the Author

GEORGE L. RUECKERT has more than 27 years experience on national security and arms control issues as a Foreign Service Officer with the U.S. Department of State. Upon implementation of the INF Treaty, he served as the first Principal Deputy Director of the newly established U.S. On-Site Inspection Agency. After retiring from the government, Dr. Rueckert was a senior manager and program director for DynMeridian, a major arms control issues contractor.

ISBN 0-275-96047-1

90000>

EAN

9 780275 960476

HARDCOVER BAR CODE